SOUND Theory
SOUND PRACTICE

AFI Film Readers
a series edited by
Edward Branigan and Charles Wolfe

Psychoanalysis and Cinema
E. Ann Kaplan, editor

Fabrications: Costume and the Female Body
Jane Gaines and Charlotte Herzog, editors

The American Film Institute
P.O. Box 27999
2021 North Western Avenue
Los Angeles, California 90027

SOUND THEORY
SOUND PRACTICE

EDITED BY

RICK ALTMAN

ROUTLEDGE

New York • London

Published in 1992 by

Routledge
An imprint of Routledge, Chapman and Hall, Inc.
29 West 35 Street
New York, NY 10001

Published in Great Britain by

Routledge
11 New Fetter Lane
London EC4P 4EE

Library of Congress Cataloging in Publication Data

Sound theory/sound practice / editor, Rick Altman.
     p. cm.—(AFI film readers)
  Includes bibliographical references.
  ISBN 0-415-90456-0 (HB) : —ISBN 0-415-90457-9 (PB)
  1. Sound motion pictures. 2. Motion pictures—History.
I. Altman, Rick, 1945– . II. Series.
PN1995.7.S69 1992
791.43—dc20   91-46026
                                         CIP

British Library Cataloguing in Publication Data

Sound Theory/Sound Practice
  I. Altman, Rick
  791.43

  ISBN 0-415-90456-0 (HB)
  ISBN 0-415-90457-9 (PB)

Contents

General Introduction:
Cinema as Event

Rick Altman

A dozen years ago, I edited an issue of *Yale French Studies* entitled *Cinema/Sound*. Featuring essays on the role of the sound track in film theory, history, and analysis, *Cinema/Sound* served as a catalyst for further work on film sound. Though *Cinema/Sound* is now out of print, many of the individual articles have gone on to influence scholars in the United States and around the world. The introduction and almost half of the articles have been reprinted, with several translated into a number of languages, including Russian.

As influential as *Cinema/Sound* may have been, a decade's distance reveals the limitations of the articles that it contains. With few exceptions, these articles treat cinema as a series of self-contained texts, divorced from material existence and the three-dimensional world. Heavily marked by the project of semiotics, most of the articles aim at describing the properties of sound, the relationship between image and sound, or the functioning of sound in a particular textual situation. Treatment of the audience is limited to the experience of film-viewing; contemporary culture is alluded to only when it constitutes a film's specific subject matter; sound technology is treated as if it were used only for films. Published in 1980, *Cinema/Sound* clearly bears the stamp of its text-oriented era.

In retrospect, the cost of *Cinema/Sound*'s text-based strategies becomes clear. Though the volume was conceived as a rehabilitation of the sound track, in all its diversity, *Cinema/Sound* actually stresses only a very narrow range of sound-oriented concerns. The sounds of silent films are hardly mentioned; sound technology is almost entirely neglected; no attention is paid to non-narrative, non-feature, or non-western films. More important still, sound itself is most often treated as if it were an ideal conveyor of linguistic or musical information, received by an ahistorical audience in a generic viewing situation, with no particular moviegoing purpose. While it sensitized film scholars to the importance of the sound track, *Cinema/Sound* masked certain very real problems of the period's film scholarship.

For the present volume, I propose a different model, a new way of thinking about cinema in general and the sound track in particular. Building on recent theoretical developments, this new approach radically extends the range of critical discourse appropriate to film studies, while offering a new coherence among the various types of scholarship currently devoted to cinema.

For decades, film has been regularly defined as a text, an autonomous aesthetic entity most closely related to other autonomous aesthetic entities. During this period, film theory stressed relationships internal to individual films or characteristic of cinema as a whole. Film history typically sorted films according to textual similarity and assessed the evolution of the resultant generic or thematic categories. Film analysis was built on the tacit assumption that differing audiences nevertheless shared the same basic film-viewing experience, regardless of differences in gender, class, or viewing situation. In recent years, this text-oriented model has begun to waver in the face of discursive approaches, feminist theory, cultural studies, and other critical methods sensitive to a broader notion of what film is and how it affects human activities. Considered as a text, each film appears as a self-contained, centered structure, with all related concerns revolving around the text like so many planets.

In opposition to the notion of film as text, I have found it helpful to conceive of *cinema as event*. Viewed as a macro-event, cinema is still

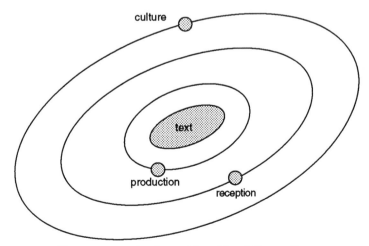

The text-centered universe of traditional film studies.

seen as centered on the individual film, but according to a new type of geometry. Floating in a gravity-free world like doughnut-shaped spaceships, cinema events offer no clean-cut or stable separation between inside and outside or top and bottom.

In this three-dimensional Moebius strip world, the textual center is no longer the focal point of a series of concentric rings. Instead, like the pinhole at the center of an hourglass, it serves as a point of interchange between two "V" shapes, one representing the work of production, the other figuring the process of reception. Beginning as a subset of culture at large, one "V" progressively narrows as the work of film production runs its course, first broadly, with diverse ideas and scripts, sets and rushes, technicians and rewrites, until eventually the work of production has been resolved into a single narrow product: the text. The process of reception then broadens out again, eventually reaching the point where it

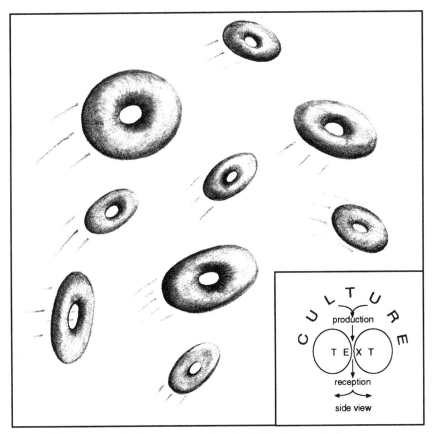

The geometry of cinema events: Doughnut holes in gravity-free space.

is indistinguishable from the culture in general. In a gravity-free world, however, this hourglass system is entirely reversible. Just as production flows through the text toward reception, so reception regularly influences production.

Each "V" opens out onto an infinite cultural space, containing other cinema events, that eventually bends back around toward the opposite "V". In other words, this Moebius vessel fails to distinguish between inside and outside, though it does have two distinct domains of interchange: the narrow textual isthmus connecting the two "V"s, and the indeterminate peripheral culture which offers any number of avenues of interchange between the open ends of the two "V"s.

Because this new type of geometry does not allow for clear distinctions between inside and outside, between top and bottom, the event that is cinema cannot be identified as privileging one particular aspect of the system. Instead, the cinema event is constituted by a continuing interchange, neither beginning nor ending at any specific point. No fixed trajectory characterizes this interchange, nor is it possible to predict which aspect of the system will influence which other aspect.

Seen as a macro-event, cinema is conveniently characterized by an even dozen attributes: multiplicity, three-dimensionality, materiality, heterogeneity, intersection, performance, multi-discursivity, instability, mediation, choice, diffusion, and interchange. In the paragraphs that follow, while treating in greater detail these various aspects of cinema as event, I will show how the study of film sound in particular is affected by this new approach to the phenomenon that we call cinema.

Multiplicity

By concentrating on cinema's major product, the individual film, traditional approaches to cinema have sought to bring a semblance of unity to a complex phenomenon. Ignoring differences among release prints (both planned and accidental), critics have fastened on the film itself as cinema's common factor. If we consider for a moment the lengthy process of conception-investment-production-distribution-exhibition-reception, we recognize that the completed film constitutes the only step in the progression representing apparent unity. Until completion, the film is characterized by the multiplicity of its conceptors; after distribution, the film is characterized by the multiplicity of its receptors.

By stressing the single moment of apparent unity between two periods of multiplicity, critics have effectively neutralized much of cinema's complexity. In doing so, they have systematically concentrated on the uniformity of the image (itself compromised by the difference between film and television formats), thus neglecting such essential variations in the sound track as 1) three decades of live, unstandardized accompaniment of "silent" films, 2) simultaneous release of silent and sound versions during the late twenties and early thirties, and 3) parallel distribution of magnetic and optical track versions during the fifties and sixties, as well as mono, stereo, and surround versions in the seventies and eighties.

Three-Dimensionality

Symbolic of the attempt to base the definition of cinema on the coherence of the individual film is the care with which film theaters have concentrated attention on a two-dimensional screen. As in Plato's cave, movie theaters hold our bodies in a fixed position in relation to the screen; complemented by carefully arranged lighting, this reduced mobility serves to convince us that film-viewing is limited to the experience of the two-dimensional rectangle before us. Even before 1910, newly built theaters were often engineered to include a ground-floor projection room, thus avoiding a keystoned image and the resultant recognition that the image is the product of a three-dimensional projection system (rather than an automatically produced replica of the seemingly two-dimensional celluloid original).

While the prestige of the image may be enhanced by this emphasis on two-dimensionality, sound is poorly served indeed, for sound cannot exist in a two-dimensional context. Though conventional speaker placement attempts to identify sound sources with the two-dimensional area of the screen, sound occurs only in the three-dimensional volume of the theater at large. Because sound is always recorded in a particular three-dimensional space, and played back in another, we are able to sense the spatial cues that give film sound its personalized spatial signature.

Materiality

Rather than conceiving of cinema as a unified chain of film images, we might instead stress cinema's material existence. Though the material history of painting and sculpture provides ample models for this type of approach (due to the material nature of their medium), note that the publishing history of literature and music offers little encouragement in this direction (since their medium has usually been judged, wrongly, not to be material). Lyric poetry may well have been written for oral delivery to a specific group on a set occasion, but critics have for centuries treated poems as texts made up of words alone. However dependent the novel may have been on developments in the printing industry, critical discourse has systematically abstracted the novel's aesthetic existence from its materiality, overtly privileging the former over the latter while actively neglecting reception conditions. When critics read the filmic text ideally, as music scholars typically read the musical score or literary scholars regularly interpret the literary text, they break all ties with the text's material conditions of existence.

Conceived as a series of events, cinema reveals rather than dissimulates its material existence. From the complexity of its financing and production to the diversity of its exhibition, cinema must be considered in terms of the material resources that it engages. From the standpoint of sound, this shift is of capital importance, for it removes cinema from the customary, purely visual definition. As a material product, cinema quickly reveals the location and nature of its sound track(s), the technology used to produce them, the apparatus necessary for reproduction, and the physical relationship between loudspeakers, spectators, and their physical surroundings. Such an approach encourages us to move past the imaginary space of the screen to the spaces and sounds with which cinema must compete—the kids in the front rows, the air conditioner hum, the lobby cash register, the competing sound track in the adjacent multiplex theater, passing traffic, and a hundred other sounds that are not part of the text as such, but constitute an important component of cinema's social materiality.

Heterogeneity

For many years the film image/text has been the source of a fundamental paralysis in cinema studies. Ostensibly analyzing *the* film, cinema critics have been at pains both to homogenize the lived experience of film-viewing and to avoid undermining that homogeneity. Rather than recognize the legitimate existence of multiple versions of a film, based on diverse social and industrial needs (censorship, standardized length, colorization, foreign-language dubbing, etc.), critics have regularly made a fetish of locating the "original" version. Instead of attending to the variety of exhibition spaces where a given film is projected, or to the diversity of audiences present, or to the various social contexts in which the film is seen, critics typically mold a film's reception to fit a single mode, apparently "neutral" in nature, but typically covertly reflecting each critic's particular reception stance. Text-based criticism often finds a place for decisions and personnel deemed to have contributed to producing the image, but it has rarely known what to do with the non-filmic components of film exhibition: live acts sharing a film program, commercial tie-ins, ticketing policies, seating practices, theater acoustics, intermission activities, popcorn availability, sales of residual products (sheet music, records, videotapes, T-shirts, etc.), and many more.

Recognition of the heterogeneous nature of the cinema experience not only opens the field to consideration of a broad spectrum of objects, processes, and activities, but has an especially direct impact on the study of sound. As soon as we move away from film as a single, homogeneous phenomenon, we become aware of the heterogeneous chain of objects and spaces which serve as a vehicle for sound. What kind of sound head is installed? On what sort of projector? What type of amplifier is used? With what speaker system? Where are the speakers located? How are they aimed? What are the characteristics of the house acoustics? Do they change according to audience size? Can they be modified? Throughout the history of cinema, exhibitors have paid close attention to these problems, but their concerns have rarely been shared by the scholarly community. Without attention to these matters it is not possible to explain why theater seats evolved from hardback uprights to plush armchairs, why theater architecture and outfitting changed radically shortly after the conversion to sound, or why Tomlinson Holman and Lucasfilm felt the need to develop the THX theater sound system.

Intersection

Just as Foucault proposes replacing history by an archaeology in which the individual strands making up any single event are teased out and separately followed up, we can usefully conceive of cinema events as the intersection of many separate lines of endeavor, throughout the production, reception, and cultural spheres. In the past, little attention has been paid to a film's technical credits; the laborers have systematically been passed over in favor of the architect and contractor. Conception has been preferred to execution, to the point where critics have apparently convinced themselves that film technicians do no more conceiving or take no more initiative than ditchdiggers. Belied at every point by the intellectual quality of cinema's technical journals, the assumption that technicians execute rather than conceive has led critics to neglect the collaborative nature of film production.

Yet the cinema experience results from the intersection of more than just production personnel. For any given film exhibition to take place, the activity of many groups and individuals is required, from cinema architects and screen manufacturers to film distributors and projectionists. Conceived as an intersection, each viewing event involves *lines* of activity, intersecting during the event but beginning beforehand and continuing afterwards. The theater is not there by chance; it was conceived by a firm experienced in designing concert halls or multipurpose recreation centers (the difference between two such firms going a long way to explain the disparity in the acoustical dimension of two cinema events). The musical accompaniment does not happen in an instant separated from time; on the contrary, it is the result (in sound as well as silent film) of an entire industry with evolving ties to other music industries and cultural precedents. To understand the event is to understand the complexity of this contribution.

Even the spectator must not be conceived as present by chance. While recent theories of subject formation typically posit a single, specific explanation of spectator presence or desire (often psychoanalytic in nature), they rarely attempt to take into account the multiplicity of motives that bring diverse audience members to the theater. While it would be absurd to treat all viewers as separate individuals, sharing no common interests or cultural positions, the notion of the cinema event as intersection has the definite virtue of emphasizing the trajectory bringing each spectator to the theater. And not just to the theater, but away from the theater as well. For an understanding of cinema depends just as much on a knowledge of the activities that cinema engenders or promotes as it does on the desires that bring the audience in. The vogue of the theme song, for example, especially strong in the late twenties and early fifties, cannot be explained by reference to textual evidence alone (although theme songs certainly do have textual ramifications); to understand this phenomenon we need to investigate at least three intersecting lines: the purchase of music companies by Hollywood studios, the growth of a hit-parade approach to radio programming, and the tendency of spectators to perpetuate their experience of a particular film by purchasing sheet music in the twenties or a record in the fifties (the difference between the two revealing the disparity between the active nature of singing around the piano and the passivity of listening to a record).

Performance

Textual approaches to cinema are based on the notion of an unvarying text, thus negating the scandal of variety, neutralizing cinema's need for a spatio-temporally specific projection, and effacing cinema's heritage as a performing art. While standardized presentation has long been the dream of cinema producers, it has never been fully realized in practice. One of the reasons for this is that exhibitors have every reason to employ presentational differences as a prime method of product differentiation. This strategy was especially salient throughout the silent period, when differences in accompaniment (piano, organ, orchestra, lecturer, voices behind the screen, effects, etc.) served as an important method of individualization, along with the other films, acts, and music on the program, not to mention the ushers' costumes, the theatrical décor, giveaway programs, and what have you. However much producers would like to think of film as an ideal image, automatically conveyed to the ultimate ideal consumer, we all know that the film must pass through the hands of a projectionist, whose performance is constantly open to criticism. While current theaters tend toward what we might call the zero degree of performance (standard-ized spaces, automatic projection, a program limited to the feature film), even the drab multiplex theater usually constructs the marquee or the lobby as a performance space, featuring still photos, cut-out stand-up characters, and other presentational devices.

Instead of considering the elaborate showmanship and diverse accompa-niments of the silent era as an anomaly, or the presentation acts of the thirties as an outmoded practice, we need to recognize that film is always the product of performance (more or less self-conscious, more or less complex, more or less commodified). Basing their conception of cinema on a consistent attempt to dissimulate cinema's performance orientation, critics have regularly neglected important aspects of earlier film exhibition. Silent films are interpreted without reference to their musical accompani-ment; feature films are treated independently of the full program of music, shorts, and newsreels that originally accompanied them; the conversion-to-sound practice of switching the sound from one speaker to another (music to the pit speaker, dialogue to the screen speaker) is consistently forgotten; the difference between projection practices in Latin America and New York is entirely bypassed; the problematic location of surround speakers receives no commentary; the reverberation differences between television sets with speakers on the front or on the side are elided. Cinema will recover some of its richness when we learn to remember that for most of its history it was a performance-oriented medium—less spectacularly so than vaudeville, perhaps, but performance-oriented nevertheless.

Multi-Discursivity

After the story-oriented sixties and early seventies, the "discovery" of cinema's discursive nature was one of the most important theoretical processes of the late seventies and eighties. Following Metz and others, recent critics have been quick to recognize the discursive investment of cinematic texts. Typically conceived as addressed by a cinema industry to an undifferentiated audience, films are considered as employing discur-sivity to construct subjectivity, to propagate ideology, or to create a situation of hegemony. As compared to the cinema-as-text approach, this recognition of discursivity clearly constitutes an improvement. However, the current notion of discursivity, typically collapsed into the singular, fails to capture the complexity of cinema's existence as event. Who addresses the audience in cinema? Is it the culture? the industry? the writers? the director? the actors? the exhibitor? Certainly no single answer is appropriate here, nor will the same answer be appropriate for different films, or even for the "same" film exhibited in divergent ways in differing places.

On the contrary, the complexity of the cinema experience derives from cinema's extraordinary ability to serve as the intersection of a variety of discourses, framed by diverse groups and addressed to populations varying from single individuals to the entire culture. Sharing the same space and time, these discourses commonly hide one another, with a given film-viewing thus successively revealing little bits of each individual discourse. A film does not carry a single message, unified, unilinear, and univocal. Instead, it is more like a *scarred palimpsest*, at various points revealing diverse discursive layers, each one recorded at a different point in time.

This recognition of the text's layered, potentially contradictory nature offers a new opportunity for attention to sound's discursive contributions. Much ink has flowed recently over the development of narrative images during the nineteen hundreds and the early teens; perhaps it is time now to recognize that the contemporary rejection of short, coherent musical forms (primarily the lapidary popular song) contributes heavily to the development of a unified narrative editing style. In many filmmaking styles, differing types of sound make contradictory discursive appeals. Throughout the thirties, in Europe as well as the United States, films merged rough regional or lower-class speech with the newly popularized, mellifluous radio accents. Hollywood regularly contrasts hyper-intelligible dialogue lacking any spatial markers with point-of-audition sound carrying appropriate volume and reverberation shifts. Television sound often transfers into its narrative programs the volume differentials that typically exist between commercials and public service announcements (or other strictly informative messages), thus splitting the program itself between informer and advertiser of its own information. In a world where sound is commonly taken as an unproblematic extension of the image, within a comfortably unified text, the concept of multi-discursivity is bound to enfranchise sound, concentrating attention on its ability to carry its own independent discourses.

Instability

In spite of cinema's historical connections to theater and the performing arts in general, critics have preferred to emphasize cinema's debt to the novel. Treating a film as the heir apparent to novelistic prose has made it easy for critics to construct cinema as a minimally material object that easily maintains its identity from decade to decade. But film is not made of language, nor is it printed with movable type. Cinema will never have its Gutenberg, because its very existence depends on its multi-discursive performance orientation. Standardization of print made the novel appear to escape from its material grounding; eventually, standardization of theaters, projection, seating, advertisement, and so forth could possibly reduce cinema's debt to the material differences of performance. For the time being, however, differing discursive investments maintain cinema's material dimension and its performance base. Because of this aspect of the cinema event, what we refer to as "the film" is fundamentally unstable in nature.

It's not just that we almost never see and hear a film as it was originally seen and heard; in fact, we would be hard put to identify what the phrase "originally seen and heard" actually means, since there never was a single original. For silent film music, do we mean Manhattan's Rialto, with its standing orchestra and staff of arrangers, or Thomas Brown's Iowa City Nickeldom, with the first Wurlitzer unit orchestra west of the Mississippi? Is it the proper Eastern style, eschewing rag and comic effects, or is it the broader Western approach, with its syncopated rhythms and aural jokes? Is it the downtown theater with a four-man orchestra, or the rural weekends-only theater with a young girl practicing her recital pieces at the piano? However similar the image in all these cases, the cinema events involved are anything but stable. Surprisingly, the conversion to sound changed little of this. Just because the sound track happens to be inscribed down the side of the film, there is no guarantee of standardized performance. Add to this equation the radical changes in dynamic and frequency response between a first-run theater and a portable television, and the instability of the cinema event (and thus of the cinema text) becomes all too clear.

Mediation

As long as cinema scholars were laboring to establish cinema as an autonomous art and cinema studies as an independent intellectual domain, there was good cause, rhetorically speaking, to play down cinema's debt to other media. Consequently, there has been a regrettable undertheorizing of the relationship between cinema and the extraordinary variety of media to which it is related. Because the cinema event includes the spectator and, by extension, the spectator's experience of other media, we must conclude that one measure of a film's success derives from spectator evaluations based on a set of preestablished notions about what constitutes reality, acceptable ending points, moral behavior, entertainment, and so forth. In other words, the values and standards associated with cinema cannot be described independently of the models through which they are mediated.

The mediation factor is especially important in the case of sound, because sound technology has changed so often over the past century.

Whereas the film image has undergone little more than successive tinkerings (along with the more important developments in color and image shape), film sound has been revolutionized many times, each time in connection with contemporary developments affecting other entertainment and communication industries besides cinema. Once we recognize the mediated nature of the cinema event, film appears caught up in a complex web of potential models. Besides vaudeville and melodrama, the late nineteenth-century concert hall provided a model for silent film's handling of music and effects. In the early and mid-twenties, radio served as a regular model for cinema sound, while later on in the decade the phonographic record provided an ineluctable model for a film sound technology which is based, after all, on phonographic records. (For an overview of mediation in the U.S. film industry during this period, see the introduction to Section Two, "Historical Speculations.") If musicals in the fifties were constantly criticized for slavishly imitating Broadway plays, it is partly because Hollywood was actually emulating the original cast albums of the resurgent long-playing record industry. For years, critics have discussed cinema's tendency to imitate its own previous successes, yet the intertextual motif within film is far more prevalent on the image side; sound, on the other hand, regularly finds its models outside the film medium, whence the necessity to expand the definitional limits of the cinema event.

Choice

Just as the mediation factor expands our notion of the cinema event, so does the phenomenon of choice, whether operative on the production side or the reception side. When a financier chooses to back a show, where is the money *not* going? When a sound man selects a microphone, what types is he implicitly rejecting? When an exhibitor purchases a sound-filtering screen, what were his choices? When a spectator chooses to spend an hour's wage on a film, what were the alternatives? The road not taken is just as much a part of the cinema event as cinema itself. Would the exact "same" movie really be the same in 1915, 1940, 1965, and 1990? No, because its rivals would respectively be vaudeville, radio, television, and video, or perhaps barbershop singing, Bing Crosby ten-inch 78-rpm records, Top 40 seven-inch 45s, or music videos (among others), with each bringing out a different aspect of the film.

Now, while this example is simplified in the extreme, it does serve to highlight the importance of cinema as part of a differential system, in the strong sense of Saussure's semiotics: there are no positive terms, only differences. The same logic applies, then, to the spectator's choices about whether to spend money on the cinema or on baseball, fast food, a new tie, or a Saturday night special. To be sure, we can hardly analyze all spectator choice patterns, even for a single showing of a single film; we must, however, find some place for these choices in our theories about how cinema works and what it means.

Diffusion

What does cinema facilitate? What are its residual effects? What kind of afterlife does the cinema event have? Sheet music and sing-alongs or Smurf glasses and trips to Disneyworld? For too long, assuming that cinema constitutes a world of its own, we have turned a blind eye to cinema's impact on the urban landscape or living room design, and a deaf ear to its influence on music preferences and dialogue delivery styles. In the concluding chapter of my book on *The American Film Musical* (Altman 1987), I labeled this aspect of cinema its "operational" component. Especially strong in the musical, which achieved diffusion throughout the culture in the form of various operational strategies, cinema's operational aspect leads in a number of largely unexpected directions. As we can see from any Hollywood pressbook of the twenties through the fifties, diffusion of the cinema event hardly took place by accident.

Indeed, some of Hollywood's most successful strategies involve attempts to capitalize on cinema's ability to be diffused throughout the culture. When Erno Rapée wrote his first two hit theme songs in the late twenties ("Diane" and "Charmaine"), he was simply carrying out his role as music director and intermittent composer. Soon, however, every studio was looking for the shot in the arm that could be provided by a hit song. When the major studios snapped up all available music publishing houses, the circle was closed; now the publishers could provide publicity for the films, and vice versa. It is through strategies such as this that the culture is marked by the diffusion of cinema's residual effects.

Interchange

It is tempting to assume that all cinema events take place in a predictable downward direction through the center of the cinema event hourglass: production distills multiple inputs into a single text, which is in turn received by an expanding set of spectators. Indeed, this is the way that cinema has traditionally been studied. However, this approach neglects the cinema event's gravity-free Moebius strip nature. The production-text-reception continuum appears to be the "inside" of cinema, with everything else on the outside, yet the unexpected construction of the cinema event suggests that "outside" and "inside" are so continuous as to be indistinguishable. We are accustomed to analyzing the interchanges that take place through the intermediary of the text; we must now become more attuned to the interchanges between the production-text-reception system and the culture(s) at large.

While this interchange is too large a topic to cover in any detail here, we easily note the important role that sound is destined to play in this area. Sound's ability to diffuse the cinema event throughout the culture is matched by sound's equal capacity to infuse cinema with elements of the culture's soundscape. Through the mediation of the culture's other sound technologies—live and recorded music, radio, television, and many others—film sound is in a constant state of interchange with the culture at large. Standards of intelligibility developed for the telephone invaded Hollywood by the early thirties; Hollywood frequency response and dynamic range set expectations for the radio and record industries; film music now fills our living rooms and shopping malls. Radio-enforced standardization of speech around a middle-class, non-regional model has had an enormous impact on the social ramifications of speech patterns, while cinema has given increased meaning to the smallest sound events of everyday life. Today, political writers learn their trade from cinema scriptwriters; the politicians try to deliver their one-liners with the panache of movie comedians; and now television and cinema have begun to edit dialogue in imitation of political sound bites. Everywhere we turn, we find sound providing a perpetual and highly charged interchange between cinema and its culture(s).

Cinema as event, replacing cinema as text: this will be the watchword of the nineties, as we shall see in many of the essays that make up this collection.

1

The Material Heterogeneity of Recorded Sound

Rick Altman

When we understood cinema as a text, we borrowed our terminology and our methodology from previously established textual domains. An understanding of cinema as event requires new terms and models for a new type of multi-dimensional analysis. It seems especially appropriate to begin this retooling process with the development of a new vocabulary for sound analysis, for sound itself is particularly event-oriented itself. Whereas image analysis has given us many terms and techniques fully consonant with a textual approach to cinema, sound's heterogeneity has much to offer to an event-oriented aesthetic. In order to reap sound's harvest, however, we must take a new approach to sound, replacing the idealist models offered by musical analysis with increased sensitivity to sound's three-dimensional materiality.

Current approaches to film sound systematically borrow a musical model. The most influential introductory film textbook of the last decade defines the acoustic properties of sound as *loudness, pitch,* and *timbre.*[1] This definition is based on the apparent assumption that all film sounds have the nature of musical notes, that is, they are single phenomena, produced instantaneously, emitted from a point source, and perceived in an immediate and direct fashion. With a definition like this one, we can explain many aspects of film sound, such as contrasts or confluences in volume, frequency, and tone.

In fact, since the terminology is borrowed from the realm of music, we find that with these terms we can handle almost any of the types of analysis typically practiced on a musical score. We note Hitchcock's suspenseful diminuendo from a loud slam to muffled scratching, the harmony of Orson Welles' bass and Joseph Cotten's tenor, the melodic gifts of Cary Grant and Katharine Hepburn, the awkward timbre of Zasu Pitts and Jerry Lewis, or the varied instrumentation of the "Symphony of Sounds" with which Rouben Mamoulian opens *Love Me Tonight*. It we could notate all film sounds according to the musical criteria of loudness, pitch, and timbre, then these three criteria would suffice for the analysis of film sound.

Yet this is precisely what we cannot do. While all film sounds have loudness, pitch, and timbre, not a single sound in cinema can be adequately described with this musical terminology. In fact, not even musical sounds can be fully described with musical terminology. More appropriate for describing musical scores than individual performances, musical terminology pays little attention to the details of any particular performance, concentrating instead on the common factors joining all performances of the same score. If I attend three concerts of Mozart's "Little Night Music," one in a well-upholstered salon, another in a large concert hall, and a third in a city park, I am in one sense hearing the "same" music three times, that is, music that is represented by a single, identical score. Yet how different are the sounds that reach my ears during the three concerts!

Musical notation assumes that each sound is single, discrete, uniform, and unidimensional. Stressing the formal concerns of music's internal, self-referential aspect, musical notation diverts attention from sound's discursive dimensions, concealing the fact that sound is in reality multiple, complex, heterogeneous, and three-dimensional. As a concept, middle C exists independently of space and time, in the abstract notion of a sound of approximately 262 cycles per second. As a reality, however, no two versions of middle C are identical, because of the different temporal and spatial circumstances in which they originate and are heard. The middle C located on the first line below the G clef may be only a concept, but the sound that we hear with our ears—whether on the street or in a movie theater—is a heterogeneous event that carries its own temporal and spatial dimensions and constitutes a full-fledged narrative. When we listen to recorded sound we are therefore always listening to a particular account of a specific event.

In order to respect the discursive complexity that is characteristic of all sound events, we can no longer continue to depend on a fundamentally conceptual terminology that remains insensitive to sound's phenomenality. Instead we must have a terminology capable both of respecting sound's heterogeneous nature and of figuring the narrative component built into the very process of recording and reproducing sound. This article proposes such a terminology, based on a schematic but systematic review of the physical phenomenon that we call sound.

Sound Events: The Production of Sound

What is sound? What happens when a sound is made? While this is hardly a technical treatise, it will nevertheless be useful to recall the manner in which sounds are produced. Three elements are required for the production of any sound. First, there must be *vibration*, such as that of the vocal cords or a violin string. Second, the vibration must take place in a *medium* whose molecules can be set in motion, such as air, water, or a railroad rail (sound cannot be transmitted through a vacuum). Third, the transmitting medium must absorb and transmit the original vibrations in the form of *changes in pressure*. When a violin string is plucked or bowed, the molecules of the surrounding medium are compressed, with the pressure passed on from one molecule to the next. When the string reaches the end of its travel, maximum *compression* is achieved. As the string starts back, the molecules rush back to fill up the void left by the departing string. When the string reaches the end of its travel in the opposite direction, maximum *rarefaction* occurs. In order to create a specific, recognizable note this process must be repeated in rapid succession hundreds or even thousands of times a second. For example, the G string on a violin causes the surrounding air to go through 196 *compression/ rarefaction cycles* per second, commonly expressed as a frequency of 196 cps or 196 Hz. In other words, what we call the musical note G below middle C is in fact a series of rapid changes in pressure.

Even taking the three-dimensional nature of sound events into account, however, this description vastly oversimplifies the situation. Whereas an electronic tone generator is capable of producing pure tones, all musical instruments produce notes that combine a *fundamental* frequency (such as the violin's 196 Hz G string) with a series of partials: *harmonics* (tones whose frequency is a whole number multiple of the fundamental) and *overtones* (tones whose frequency is related to the fundamental according to a more complex formula). Depending on the instrument and the way it is played, the combination of harmonics and overtones can vary tremendously. When played in such a way as to emphasize the upper harmonics, for example, the violin sounds harsh and strident, while a mellow tone results from stressing instead the lower harmonics. If the oboe, trumpet, flute, and cello sound so recognizably different, it is primarily because they produce radically different combinations of partials.

While few people are trained to hear harmonics and overtones, most listeners will rapidly recognize their absence, as when music is played through the telephone or over an old record player with limited frequency response. While the loss of these partials reduces our pleasure in listening to music, it may have an even more radical effect on other sounds. Spoken language becomes far more difficult to understand, voices and familiar sound effects may become harder to differentiate, even our ability to judge the distance and direction of a sound source may be impaired. In other words, the composite nature of sounds is hardly limited to music.

In fact, most of the events that we think of as a single sound are not singular at all. The musical model of tone generators and violin strings is extremely misleading. If a violin note could be produced by a violin string alone, then Stradivarius would never have become a household name. Every violin note is a complex event combining the vibrations of a string, a wooden case, and the air trapped inside that case. Each of these three contributes to the overall tone of the note played.

For what we call a sound is typically made up not only of multiple frequencies, but actually has multiple different fundamentals produced over a period of time. Think of the following familiar sounds: a refrigerator, snoring, a lawnmower, the wind, a squeaky door. We think of each as a single sound, but none is actually single in the way that an A-440 produced by a tuning fork is unitary. Each of these sounds constitutes an event taking place in time, involving multiple separate sounds organized in a familiar, recognizable fashion. Given the importance of rhythmic and melodic elements for our recognition of each of these sounds, it would be more appropriate to compare them to musical phrases than to individual notes.

Yet even individual notes have a temporal dimension. Returning for a moment to our violin string, consider the difference between plucking and bowing the string. In one case the sound starts suddenly, reaching its full volume extremely rapidly; in the other case the violinist seems to be sneaking up on the note, teasing the molecules into moving rather than suddenly shoving them. Whether violent or peaceful, this initiation of the sound event is termed the *attack*. It is followed by the *sustain*. How long is the note hold? How long does it stay at full volume? Finally, the sound fades away. This stage is called the *decay*, implying not only a temporal measure but also a qualitative one. Compare, for example, the decay of a plucked string that is simply allowed to spend its own energy and the decay of a plucked string instantaneously dampened by a finger.

As parts of the *sound envelope*, the stages of attack, sustain, and decay apply equally to any sound event. Contrast, for example, the smooth attack of Orson Welles' opening voice-over in *The Magnificent Ambersons* to the sharp attack of Georgie Minafer's dialogue. How essential to the *soundscape* of *The Wizard of Oz* is the gulf separating Margaret Hamilton's staccato attack and nearly instantaneous decay from Judy Garland's ability to ease in and out of speech! Anyone who has ever tried to edit dialogue will understand just how important the elements of the sound envelope are for the establishment of auditory realism. Even when the initial or final words of a sentence are perfectly comprehensible, they create an uneasy feeling whenever part of their attack or decay has been cut off in the editing process.

The production of sound is thus a material event, taking place in space and time, and involving the disruption of surrounding matter. This doesn't mean that we have to be molecular physicists or sound engineers to understand sound, but it does suggest a very precise basis for our description of sound events. It is no longer sufficient to analyze a musical score or a written text to understand the effects of a particular performance event. Recognizing the extent to which sound sets matter in motion—albeit invisibly—we readily see the importance of developing a vocabulary and a methodology appropriate to the complex materiality of sound. Instead of describing just a sound's loudness, pitch, and timbre, we stress the extent to which every sound event includes multiple sounds, each with its particular fundamental and array of partials, each with its characteristic sound envelope, each possessing its own rhythm within the sound event's overall temporal range.

The Sound Narrative: The Story of a Sound Event

In order to understand sound as it is produced, we need to recognize the material heterogeneity of sound events. Sound production is only part of the story, however, for sound, like the proverbial tree falling in the forest, must be heard in order to take on its narrative and social significance. By offering itself up to be heard, every sound event loses its autonomy, surrendering the power and meaning of its own structure to the various contexts in which it might be heard, to the varying narratives that it might construct. Beginning as the vibration that induces molecular movement, sound is not actualized until it reaches the ear of the hearer, which translates molecular movement into the sensation of sound. Just as the sound event necessarily introduces a temporal dimension into the production of every sound, so the process of perception always guarantees sound's spatial nature.

When we speak of language, we implicitly agree to disregard certain aspects of linguistic discourse as somehow sub-linguistic. Fred Astaire and Ginger Rogers may make something of the difference between ee-ther and eye-ther, but no normal user of the English language shows such a concern. Regional accents and personal idiosyncrasies produce recognizable differences, but these are not taken to be differences in language. Whether it's ee-ther or eye-ther, it's still the English word "either." Our understanding of sound works in a very similar fashion. We know that our neighbor's lawn mower sounds very different when it's mowing on the near or the far side of the house (and *vive la différence!*), yet that difference does not change our nomenclature. Whether the sound comes from the near side or the far side of the neighbor's house, it is still the sound of the neighbor's lawn mower. The sounds are different, but the *name* of the sounds is not (Metz). Systematically, the name of a sound refers to the production of sound and not to its consumption, to the object making the sound rather than the person perceiving it.

Yet the hearing process necessarily involves important variables that often outweigh the sound itself in importance. It doesn't take children long to learn that the word "Boo!" does not by itself produce surprise. When a child jumps out from behind a chair at the other end of the room and shouts "Boo!" the reaction is likely to be mild indeed. When my ten-year-old suddenly emerges from beneath my desk, on the other hand, she can be assured of a good return on her "Boo!", however quietly it may be spoken. To be sure, the sharp attack of the letter "b" contributes to the effect. (If perchance you are not convinced of this, try to scare someone with the pastoral attack of a "Moo!") Still more important, though, is the proximity effect obtained by a good surprise. The effect is dissipated if the booer holds her hand in front of her mouth or looks away from the booee. The reason for this is very simple: the surprise is created largely by the sudden arrival of a zone of sound pressure on the ear. Anything that diminishes the sharpness of this experience (standing too far away, whispering instead of shouting, facing away from the booee, or uttering the "Boo!" before emerging from the hiding place) spoils the effect. Having learned to distinguish between various versions of the "same" sound, our ears tell us how to react not on the basis of the sound event alone, but also according to our perceived relation to that sound event.

How does a sound event contribute to hearing? And what are we actually perceiving when we hear? In the previous section, I explained the molecular basis for sound's characteristic compression/rarefaction cycle. Vibration creates pressure, which is communicated through a medium. At the other end of sound's path, the human ear collects that pressure and transforms its mechanical energy into electrical impulses that the brain understands as sound. Sensitive to frequency (pitch), amplitude (loudness), and many other factors, the human ear is a marvelously sensitive organ capable of very minute distinctions. The ear hears not only a sound's fundamental frequencies, but its harmonics and overtones as well, thus facilitating the distinction between male and female voices or French horns and saxophones. Through the ear's ability to sense not only pressure but the rate of changes in pressure as well, we are able to measure even minute differences in the sound envelope, and thus to distinguish between individual voice patterns.

The ear must do far more than this, however, for until now I have assumed that sound arrives directly to the ear, in a single pencil of pressure. This is precisely not the case. Imagine an actress standing in the center of a stage in a large auditorium, 150 feet wide and 200 feet deep. Since sound travels at about 1130 feet per second at 70 degrees Fahrenheit, the actress's voice takes approximately one-eighth of a second to reach a member of the audience sitting three-quarters of the way back in the orchestra.

But what happens to the sound that goes straight to the spectator on the edge of the auditorium? Certainly it doesn't die there; it must eventually reach the ears of other audience members as well. Radiating out like a cone from the actress's mouth, the sound pressure soon films up the entire auditorium, bouncing off the walls, the floor, and the ceiling, and bending around audience members, chairs, and posts until it is finally completely absorbed.[2] The notion that sound travels in a straight line from sound event to hearing ear is thus radically incomplete. In addition to *direct sound*, there is also a great deal of *reflected sound* or *reverberation*, produced by the sound that reaches the hearing ear only after bouncing off one or more surfaces. In a large room, the delay between the arrival of direct sound and the arrival of the last reflections can be quite long. When the full effect of three-dimensional reverberation is considered, delays of multiple seconds may easily be encountered.

Contrary to popular assumptions, even apparently instantaneous sounds thus have a considerable temporal dimension. Our notation systems for sound reinforce a received notion that separately produced sounds are also perceived separately. As they are printed, Hamlet's words "To be or not to be" provide a blueprint for sounds that are clearly separate and sequential. As they are perceived, however, the direct sound of one word is often heard before the reflected sound of the previous word ceases. Musical notation systematically distinguishes between *melody* (sequential sounds) and *harmony* (simultaneous sounds). Yet the sounds notated as sequential are heard as overlapping, thus confounding the received distinction. The reflected sounds of the first beat of the measure continue to be heard as the direct sound of later beats reaches our ears.

Such a distinction might easily appear purely academic and theoretical. Our ears know, however, that this is not just a question of splitting hairs. Who has not been in a large auditorium, cafeteria, or gymnasium and had trouble making out the speaker's words. The master of ceremonies may be saying "The winning numbers are seventeen, forty-three, fourteen, and seventy-two," but what we actually hear is more like "The win—— num—— seven—— four—— four—— seven——." Because we know what to expect in this context, we easily complete the opening words, but strain as we might, there is no understanding the all-important numbers, for the reflected sound of the first part of each word is bouncing all around the cafeteria—off chairs, tables, floor, walls, and ceiling—long enough to obscure the direct sound of the second half of each number. We are all aware of the difficulty of understanding a telephone message with the competition of a nearby conversation; our ears know that speakers in large halls often provide their own competition.

The subsistence of reflected sound does more than block understanding, however. Our ears are marvelously tuned instruments, extraordinarily capable of making fine distinctions of which we remain largely unaware.

Imagine that there are two actors on our stage, one facing the audience, the other facing backstage. The lights are low; the audience cannot always be sure of seeing which actor's lips are moving. Yet we never have any doubt whatsoever about who is speaking. Our ears tell us.

The first actor, facing the audience, sends a strong ray of sound directly to each spectator (as well as an infinite number of rays that reach individual spectators as reflected rather than direct sound). The words pronounced by actor two, away from the audience, are prevented by the actor's own head from reaching spectators directly. In order to be heard at all, these sounds must rebound off the set or backdrop, thus taking up to three times as long to reach spectators. Fortunately, these spectators are also auditors. Their ears rapidly process this data and easily distinguish between the words that are being spoken directly to them and the words that have to bounce around the theater before arriving. This ability to measure the *ratio of direct to reflected sound* provides one of our most important capacities: the ability to distinguish between sounds that are being spoken to us and those that are meant for others. Imagine John Wayne walking down a line of new recruits standing at attention. The script might read "Johnson, straighten up. Jackson, button that top button. Jones, get that chin down. Altman, where'd you learn to tie a tie?" and so forth. The name at the beginning of each sentence, apparently spoken to gain each recruit's attention in turn, is actually quite redundant, for as Wayne moves down the line there is a change in the ratio of direct to reflected sound heard by each recruit. I need no course in acoustics to know when it's my turn, when I am the one being addressed.

In other words, the fact that a "single" sound reaches our ears over a period of time permits us to reconstitute certain facts about the circumstances surrounding the production of that sound. What our ears are doing is a form of narrative analysis. They are analyzing the narrative produced by sound pressure, in all of its complexity, in order to ascertain how, by whom, and under what conditions that sound pressure was produced. To be sure, some people have ears that are better trained in this process of narrative analysis than others, but we have *all* developed over the years a great deal of expertise in this area. We use the delay between visual information and the first arrival of direct sound to determine the distance of the sound source. The difference in the characteristics of sound arriving at our two ears permits us to locate the sound source laterally. The ratio of reflected to direct sound helps us to decide whether the speaker is facing us or not. Combined with other information, this ratio also helps us recognize the size of the room in which the words are spoken. By noting how long the reflected sound lasts, we refine our conclusions about the originating space.

In fact, we regularly draw still other conclusions from the other aspects of sound's itinerary. During the course of its picaresque journey from production to perception, sound not only takes many specific courses, it sets in motion a particular medium and is reflected off particular surfaces. Imagine the difference that would be made by staging the preceding example of two onstage actors in two different theaters, one a plush Broadway theater with a velvet backdrop and the other a high school gymnasium with a concrete wall at the back of the stage. Just like a tennis ball thrown toward the back of the stage, the actor's words will in one case be muffled by the backdrop while in the other case they will shoot off of it at nearly their original velocity and volume. While few people are aware of the theory underlying such differences, our ears are surprisingly attentive to them. They seem to know that certain surfaces reflect different frequencies better than others, that some surfaces absorb more sound and dampen specific frequencies more than others, that some environments will continue to reflect sound almost indefinitely, while others will restrict reflected sound to a minimum. In this way, even before we look out the window, our ears tell us that it has snowed during the night. They help us distinguish between the recording of a junior high concert made in the gymnasium and the next day's recording of the "same" concert made in an upholstered, acoustically treated auditorium. They help us to get the "feel" of every room we enter, without ever touching any of the room's surfaces.

The fact that we come equipped with two functioning ears each makes still more information available to us. Because all sounds that are not exactly equidistant from both ears arrive at our ears one after the other, and under slightly different conditions, our ears are able to localize sound laterally as well as in terms of distance. Especially when aided by a radar-like rotation of the head, our own personal sonar gives us varied information about our soundscape.

Our ears are so good at decoding sound that it would be a shame to deprive our terminology of our ears' expertise. Without entering the specialized worlds of acoustics, audio engineering, and otology, we must nevertheless find ways of respecting not only sound's material heterogeneity, but also the cleverness of our ears in analyzing the auditory narratives that it constitutes. Constantly delayed, dampened, reinforced, overlapped and recombined, sound provides us with much of the information we need to understand its origins and its itineraries—but the existing terminology clearly does not.

The Sound Record: Recording the Story of a Sound Event

Every sound initiates an event. Every hearing concretizes the story of that event. Or rather, it concretizes a particular story among the many that could be told about that event. When the baseball broke the window, I was outside, more than a little worried; I heard the sound of the break directly, with little reflected sound, since there are no walls and ceiling outdoors to keep the reverberation going. My father was sitting in his favorite chair, right next to the broken window; he was subjected not only to the direct sound of the impact but also to a roomful of reflected sound. My mother was ironing in the back room; she thought something had broken, but the muffled reflected sound that reached her didn't specify whether it was a window, a vase, a car headlight, or something else still. Doing her homework in the second floor back bedroom, my sister hardly knew anything had happened. At least until she heard my father bellow.

All four of us heard the "same" sound, yet all four of us heard a "different" sound. Or, to put it in a more useful fashion, each of us heard a different narrative of the same event. Sound's existence as both event and narrative immensely complicates—and enriches—our understanding. Usually discussed as the most transparent of classical narratives, sound is in fact a *Rashomon* phenomenon, existing only in the separate stories of various perceivers of the original event. Potentially important apropos of any sound and its perception, this fact takes on special significance in all media that make use of recorded sound. For what the record contains is not the sound event as such but a record of a particular hearing, a specific version of the story of the sound event. Every recording is thus signed, as it were, with the mark of the particular circumstances in which it was heard. A recording of the shattering window made next to my father's easy chair will be signed in a different way from a recording of the "same" event made next to my sister's desk. Every recording carries the elements of this *spatial signature*, carried in the audible signs of each hearing's particularities. Even when those signs are contradictory or have been tampered with, even when they seem not to match the visual data provided with the sound record, they still carry information that is narrative and spatial in nature.

The situation is immensely complicated by the fact that sound records never convey exactly the same information that a given auditor would experience. Far from arresting and innocently capturing a particular narrative, the recording process simply extends and complicates that narrative. Just as the upholstery of a particular soundscape has an impact on the sound narrative, so the way in which sound is collected and entered into memory becomes part and parcel of the overall sound phenomenon.

Even in the simplest of sound collection systems, decisions regarding the location of the microphone carry enormous importance, especially when the sound is to accompany a related image. Should sound collection take place in the same room as the sound to be recorded? At what distance? Under what acoustic conditions? Or should sound collection be in a remote location, thus reducing volume, dampening certain frequencies, and increasing the ratio of reflected to direct sound? This approach will certainly convince auditors that they are not located in the same sound space as the speaker. In fact, if the reverb level is high enough and the image slightly out of focus, the sound may even appear to have been collected in a time frame different from its production.

The process of editing further complicates the question of microphone location. Should the microphone location be changed every time the camera is moved and the shot changes? Or should sound logic remain entirely independent of image logic? To what extent is consistency of sound collection needed? Must sound collection decisions be subordinated to narrative concerns? Under what conditions may the volume and spatial characteristics of synchronized sound be modified during the editing process? Are there special volume and reverberation requirements for sound effects recorded separately from dialogue? All these and many other questions are implied by the simple necessity of choosing a microphone location.

Since the very beginnings of sound cinema, filmmakers have been convinced that intelligibility is one of the most important requisites of recording speech. Indeed, nowhere else are the stakes of microphone location so clear. Imagine that we are recording a sentence spoken by a woman to the man she is facing. While she is speaking a child walks silently past, catching the woman's attention and causing her to turn away from her interlocutor. Now, in order to maximize the intelligibility of the woman's words we might legitimately decide to "pan" the microphone with her, so that she is always talking directly into the mike, maximizing direct sound and thus intelligibility. Note, however, that this decision robs the sound track of its spatial characteristics. Instead of telling us that the woman turned away from her initial position, the sound track implies that she continued to face in the same direction.

If, instead, we choose to retain the initial microphone position throughout, the sound track will exhibit a faithful spatial signature, but it will almost certainly reduce our ability to understand the final parts of the woman's sentence. We will realize that the woman has turned her head while talking, but, like the man to whom she speaks, we may miss some of her words. Recording choices, as we easily see from this example, govern our perception of particular sound events. Far from simply recording a specific story of a specific sound event, the sound engineer actually has the power to create, deform, or reformulate that event. In the example just illustrated, the sound engineer must choose to allow either deformation of the dialogue or mistaken perception on the part of the auditor.

Nor is microphone location the only variable available to the sound engineer. The microphone itself makes many choices regarding the type, amount, and source of sound that will be collected. It is perhaps useful, in an image-oriented world, to think of the microphone as a "sound-camera," a collection device for sound that shares many of the characteristics of familiar image-collection devices. Just as cameras may have wide-angle or telephoto lenses, changing the angle of image collection and thus the apparent distance of the object filmed, so microphones vary from omnidirectional to narrowly focused, thus changing both the angle of sound collection and the apparent distance of the sound source. In addition, the change in the ratio of direct to reflected sound that accompanies a change in microphone may also affect perception of room size and other characteristics.

Microphones also vary in their sensitivity to specific sound frequencies. The familiar carbon microphone in our telephones has an extremely limited frequency response. Sound heard over the telephone thus always sounds dull and lifeless. Close-miking with a telephone mike (or stripping the sound of appropriate frequencies in postproduction) thus gives the impression that all sounds presented are being heard through a telephone. Since no microphone is equally sensitive to all frequencies, the choice of a microphone fairly assures that some sounds will be boosted, while others will be dampened.

Many other microphone characteristics may come into play as well. It is often assumed that every microphone produces a faithful sound record. Actually, *no* microphone produces an entirely faithful sound record. Not only does every microphone have its own particular *directional characteristics* (omnidirectional, bidirectional, cardioid, shotgun and so on), but every microphone also has its own particular frequency response, sound configuration, and power requirements. In addition, many microphones produce unwanted sounds of various types (hum, pop, hiss, buzz, crackle and so on) in a wide variety of situations (loud sound signal, wind pressure, close sound source, vibration and so on).

Recorded sound thus always carries some record of the recording process, superimposed on the sound event itself. Added to the story of sound production we always find the traces of sound recording as well, including information on the location, type, orientation, and movement of the sound collection devices, not to mention the many variables intervening between collection and recording of sound (amplification, filtering, equalization, noise reduction, and so forth). Indeed, the recording system itself provides one of the most important determinants of sound characteristics; as such it not only provides a record of sound, it also participates in the overall sound narrative. Think for example of the differing frequency responses of 78 rpm records and digital compact disks. It is so difficult to compare musical performances recorded on these two radically different technologies that the masterworks of Toscanini and Furtwangler seem diminished without the wonders of digital remastering (which is none other than an attempt to restore the frequencies to which pre-war disk recording was not sensitive).

To record is thus to recall to mind, as the dictionary would have it, but like most mnemonic devices, sound recordings must heighten some aspects of the original phenomenon at the expense of others. So-called recordings are thus always representations, interpretations, partial narratives that must nevertheless serve as our only access to the sounds of the past.

Sound Reproduction: Playing the Record of the Story of a Sound Event

But how can we gain access to those sounds? A recording, as we all know, is not a sound. Without some sort of playback device, a recording can only sit silently on the shelf. And as long as it sits on the shelf, it has only one space: the space of the recording of the original sound event. My record of Oistrakh and Rostropovich playing the Brahms Double Concerto with George Szell and the Cleveland Philharmonic Orchestra was recorded in Severance Hall. Once I put the record on my stereo and set the needle down, however, the Concerto becomes very Double indeed. Not only do I hear the fabulous acoustics of the Cleveland Orchestra's home concert hall, but at the same time I have to put up with the less than ideal acoustics of my own living room. Every sound I hear is thus double, marked both by the specific circumstances of recording *and* by the particularities of the reproduction situation.

The late twenties were a time of particularly intense reflection on this problem. Throughout the twenties, movie theaters had grown increasingly large and ornate. While the desire to accommodate growing numbers of higher class patrons was an important factor in the rise of the picture palace, theater acoustics played a part as well. Silent films depended heavily on music chosen from familiar nineteenth-century sources. Now, the nineteenth century had little use for chamber music or small baroque organs, preferring instead large orchestras and enormous choirs, along with the long-lasting reverberations and high indirect-to-direct sound ratios characteristic of spacious concert halls or churches. The music that silent cinema inherited from late romantic composers was thus expected to sound as if it were being played in large, enclosed spaces. Ornate picture palaces, with their multiple levels, private boxes, rows of fluted columns, and endless plaster moldings, were thus a perfect environment for the sounds of silent cinema.

When synchronized dialogue came to cinema, however, a new set of requirements was rapidly imposed. The words had to be comprehensible; to that end the amount and duration of reflected sound had to be kept extremely low. Studios thus rushed to create acoustically treated sets, open-ended studios, and other devices designed to limit reverberation and maximize intelligibility. The biggest stumbling block of all turned out, however, to have nothing to do with film production. It was film exhibition that caused all the problems. Built to maximize reverberation, those drafty barns called picture palaces made it nearly impossible to understand the spoken word. When played over the loudspeakers of a huge, hard-surfaced Roxy with three second decay time, even intimate scenes recorded to give the impression of small, private spaces sounded as if they were set in cavernous public halls. Carefully recorded speech turned into the same auditory mush that had become the trademark of romantic church organs and mighty theater Wurlitzers alike. Only careful redesign and costly acoustic treatment were able to solve this problem.

Even with the practical problem solved, however, the theoretical difficulty remains. Which acoustics am I listening to? The Hollywood sound stage or the Rialto? Severance Hall or my living room? For that matter, which sound am I listening to? The original sound event or its loudspeaker reproduction? In order to understand sound—cinema sound in particular— we must recognize both the narrative and the represented nature of sound as it reaches our ears in the movie theater. The sound system plays the record of the story of an event. At every point in that chain, new variables enter, new elements of uncertainty. Sound heads, amplifiers, leads, loudspeakers, and theater acoustics all force new auditory data on the audience, just as the recording process itself had earlier introduced an implicit viewpoint.

Hearing Events: Hearing the Record of the Story of a Sound Event

Just as sound events remain only hypothetical sound sources until they are actualized by a hearer, so the playing of a sound record takes on meaning only in the presence of an audience. Yet the process of hearing a recording differs significantly from listening to a live sound event. This should come as no surprise to anyone who has contemplated the difference between a photograph and the scene that it represents. When we look directly at a scene we gain a sense of depth from our binocular vision, by rotating our head, or by moving to the left or right. If we want to know what's underneath a chair we have but to lean down. In order to get a clearer view of a specific object, we need only adjust the focus of our eyes. Yet all of this is to no avail when we view a photograph. No amount of rotating, moving, leaning, or adjusting will deliver information that the photograph lacks. We may have two eyes, but we might as well all be Cyclops when it comes to sensing distance in a photograph, for here the concept of distance is encoded through size, masking, and detail rather than sensed by the parallax implicit in binocular vision. Without requiring any special education, we have all learned to use our eyes radically differently when we view three-dimensional space and when we view a two-dimensional representation of that space.

A similar situation obtains with the sound representations that we call recordings. When attempting to locate a crying child we normally call heavily on our binaural hearing system to provide cues regarding lateral location. When we listen to a recording of a crying child, no such localization is possible. However much we might rotate our heads or change positions, we remain unable to make use of the directional information that was present when the sound was produced, but which is no longer available in the recording (unless it is in stereo, and even then the location of microphones and speakers plays just as important a role as the location of the original sound source). For listening to the sound pouring out of a loudspeaker is like hearing a lawn mower through an open window: wherever the lawn mower may actually be, it always appears to be located on the side of the house where the open window is.

When we listen for a crying child, we are marvelously effective at cutting out extraneous sounds and concentrating on the cries that we recognize as those of our own child. Dubbed the *cocktail party effect* by Colin Cherry, the process of selective auditory attention is far more difficult when we are listening to recorded material. Whereas live sound provides an extraordinary number of variables, each permitting and promoting selective attention, recorded sound folds most of those variables into a single, undifferentiated source. In a live situation, we easily differentiate among the various sound sources surrounding us, but with recorded sound no such clear distinctions are possible.

Live sound situations reveal the actual relationship between the sound producer and perceiver, while recordings suggest only an apparent relationship. If I sit in an auditorium and listen with my eyes closed to a series of speeches, I remain constantly aware of the speakers' location. I know what direction they are facing, how loud they are speaking, and what tones of voice they are using. When I listen to a recording of the same meeting, I can no longer locate the speakers. Nor can I be sure of their original body positions, volume, or tones. Depending on the type, location, and movement of the microphone(s) used in the recording process, the recorded sound substitutes an apparent sound event for the original phenomenon. Revealing its mandate to *represent* sound events rather than to *reproduce* them, recorded sound creates an illusion of presence while constituting a new version of the sound events that actually transpired.

What happens in the course of a hearing event is thus not the expected detective activity wherein the hearer searches the recorded sound track for clues permitting reconstitution of the original sound event. Instead, we follow the trail that has been laid for us all the way to an apparent sound event having all the aural guarantees of reality but only partial correspondence to the original sound event. Indeed, it is the partial nature of the relationship that makes hearing events so fascinating. If there were no connection between the apparent sound event and the original sound source, recorded sound would not have its extraordinary capacity for ideological impact. It is precisely because recorded sound seems to reproduce an original phenomenon that recordings attract and hold audiences so readily. Between the illusion of reproduction and the reality of representation lies the discursive power of recorded sound.

We hear recordings with the same ears we use for live sound. We reach conclusions about the evidence provided by recordings in the same way that we interrogate and evaluate live sound. We constitute apparent sound events just as we directly perceive live sound events. Yet recordings systematically fail to justify our confidence in them. Most listeners have learned to concentrate on the aspects of sound events that are most faithfully rendered by recordings and to pay little attention to the aspects introduced or transformed by the recording process. A proper theory of sound will accept no such selective deafness. It will pay special attention to those very points where confusion is possible, recognizing in such moments of imprecision, indecision, or incoherence the very place where sound seizes the opportunity to take an active role in the definition and exploitation of culture.

Sound Terminology: Talking about Hearing the Record of the Story of a Sound Event

Often called "distortions," on the theory that sound recording is a science of reproduction rather than an art of representation, the variables introduced by sound's material heterogeneity, along with the system constituted to record (that is, represent) it, lie at the very heart of film sound. Though they may constitute distortions for the sound engineer, the marks of the sound narrative and the recording process that appear as part of any sound record constitute the very text of the sound analyst, the fundamental signs of the sound semiotician, the basic facts of the sound historian.

Central to the interpretation of film sound is the fact that multiple moments and operations must be carried simultaneously by the same final sound track. The characteristics of sound production, sound recording, sound reproduction, and audience perception are all superimposed in a single experience. When we hear any particular film sound, how do we know to whom to attribute it? Which part of the sound chain has produced, selected, highlighted, or masked it? Does a decrease in the ratio of direct to indirect sound mean that the character has turned away, an obstacle has been introduced, the microphone has been moved, the sound engineer has fiddled with the dials, or the spectator has shifted her position?

To study film sound is to take seriously the multiplicity of possible determinants of any given audience perception. As a complex representation of a complex sound event, cinema sound offers sound designers infinite possibilities for creation and obfuscation. As such, it also offers theoreticians and critics of cinema sound fascinating opportunities to recognize and analyze the techniques, conventions, codes, and ideological investments of the sound chain. This work is only beginning. It will move more quickly if we adopt a vocabulary that reflects the material, heterogeneous nature of sound presented here.

Theoretical Perspectives

Introduction: Four and a Half Film Fallacies

Rick Altman

Logically, every theory of cinema should address the problem of film sound. Practically speaking, such has hardly been the case. On the contrary, a surprising number of theoreticians blithely draw conclusions about the nature of cinema simply by extrapolating from the apparent properties of the moving image. If this were just a question of oversight, the problem would be rapidly corrected. In fact, the theoreticians who overlook sound usually do so quite self-consciously, proposing what they consider strong arguments in favor of an image-based notion of cinema. Indeed, some of these arguments have reached the level of truisms, uninterrogated assumptions on which the entire field is based. In the pages that follow, I propose to reopen the cases of these arguments, cross-examining the very assumptions that have guided cinema theory over the years.

The Historical Fallacy

The late twenties' worldwide conversion to synchronized sound was received by many film-makers as an affront (Clair, Eisenstein, and Pudovkin, among others). Intent on exacting satisfaction, they found a clever method of disenfranchising the offending sound track. Cinema was cinema before the sound track was added, they said, so sound cannot be a fundamental component of the cinematic experience. Historically, sound is an add-on, an afterthought, and thus of secondary importance.

Ironically, it is precisely because of insufficient historical knowledge and reflection that these avengers err. As a purely historical argument, the notion of sound-as-afterthought cannot stand careful scrutiny. Apparently convinced that "silent" film had always conformed to the mid-twenties model of standardized organ or orchestral accompaniment, sound's critics

35

set up an all-or-nothing opposition that has been perpetuated by genera-tions of critics. On one side an ethereal cinema of silence, punctuated only by carefully chosen music; on the other side, the talkies, with their incessant, anti-poetic dialogue. Too heavily dependent on the practice of the twenties, this is an unacceptable assessment of the first thirty years of cinema history.

Here, for example, is a pop quiz that is not likely to be passed by sound's detractors. In what year did the following editorial appear? "In our opinion the singing and talking moving picture is bound sooner or later to become a permanent feature of the moving picture theater." 1926? 1927? 1928? Wrong by a wide margin. This 1910 *Moving Picture World* editorial came at the height of sound film's expansion. Cameraphone, Chronophone, Cinephone and dozens of other competing systems were not only invented in this period; during the end of the century's first decade they were installed in hundreds of theaters across Europe and from coast to coast in the United States. Their competition came, by the way, not from silent films, with or without musical accompaniment, but from road shows with extremely sophisticated and carefully synchronized effects (a technique originated by Lyman Howe), and from the many "wheels" (vaudevillelike circuits) of human-voice-behind-the-screen companies, with colorful names like Humanovo, Actologue, Humanophone, Humano-scope, Natural Voice Talking Pictures, Ta-Mo-Pic, and Dram-o-tone. In short, the world did not wait until *Don Juan* and *The Jazz Singer* to discover the entertainment (and financial) value of synchronized sound. From a purely historical point of view, the notion that sound is a Johnny-come-lately add-on to a thirty-year-old silent medium simply will not stand.

Even if the historical information had been correct, however, the claims of sound's early critics would still have been fallacious. Though their appeal is apparently to history, these unconditional lovers of "silent" cinema actually close themselves off from history, refusing to recognize that the identity and form of the media are in no sense fixed. Why do we identify the human appendix as vestigial? Because we recognize that it is possible for evolution to redefine the structure and even the nature of the human body. How can we tell when one system has given way to another? This we can do only by analyzing the functioning of the system. The fact that one element appeared before or after another carries no weight in this evaluation. At stake here is the very ability to take into account historical change in theoretical arguments. It is regularly assumed that a single term (like cinema) covers a single object. If our theories are to become sufficiently sensitive to historical concerns, we must abandon that assump-tion, recognizing instead that historical development regularly occurs within an apparently single object, thus often hiding under a single name two or more historically distinct objects. In other words, even if silent film were the object that sound's detractors claim, the sound-as-afterthought argument would still not hold up. Cinema changes, and the action of sound is one of the prime reasons for that change.

The Ontological Fallacy

Though they continue to influence cinema studies, historical fallacy arguments were especially popular among the filmmakers of the late twenties and early thirties. Later in the thirties, a new argument appeared in the writings of such influential critics as Rudolf Arnheim and Bela Balazs. Eschewing historical arguments, they make the formal case that the image without sound still constitutes cinema, while sound without an image is no longer cinema. Clearly assuming that cinema is a firm, unchanging category, immune to history, these critics present their arguments as logical and permanent. Indeed, so strong is the apparent appeal of this ontological claim that it regularly reappears in the writings of current theoreticians.

Two primary considerations undermine the ontological argument. The first is a practical concern relating to the way in which ontological critics use their claims. Like the historical case, the ontological argument seeks to disenfranchise sound, to prove that sound has (or should have) little effect on overall film structure. Even if we were to accept the notion that film is a fundamentally image-oriented medium, this conclusion begs the larger question of the relationship between ontology and structure. May we affirm with confidence that an object's structure can be predicted from its nature? The answer to this question depends on the way in which we construe the term "nature." If nature is defined through structure, that is, if all claims about the nature of a class of objects are derived from analysis of the structures characteristic of the objects, then we can treat nature as predictive of structure. But this is precisely what sound's ontological critics do not do. On the contrary, they base their claims about cinema on a single surface aspect rather than on a careful inspection of the structure of actual films and the system that produces them. Indeed, the acerbic vocabulary and prescriptive exhortations of these critics suggests that they are more interested in influencing the structure of future films than they are in analyzing the structure of existing ones.

What about the truth value of ontological critics' claims? The problem with these apparently rock solid claims, I would suggest, is that they are actually built on sand. Presented as absolute and unchanging, appeals to the nature of cinema appear to be independent of history. In spite of appearances, however, the evidence actually offered is all historically specific. To say that a particular configuration would not be recognized as cinema, while another would, is to affirm that *in the present conditions* these conclusions would be reached. Present conditions, though, have to do with the way in which a given configuration has been used, and not with some transhistoric category. The ontological argument, it turns out, is only falsely ontological.

Even in the absence of a properly ontological argument, however, the historical claim would remain: cinema has indeed been exploited as a visual medium, to the point where audiences identify the medium with the image rather than the sound. To the extent that it represents a carefully documented historical argument, this position has a certain amount of merit (however unontological it may be). Even when the ontological argument is reduced to its historical evidence, however, hesitations must still remain. For the historical circumstances assumed by ontological critics have not always obtained. During the many periods when cinema was heavily marked by its relation to the music industry, for example, music accompanied by a blank screen has regularly been recognized as cinema: the long overtures to the early Vitaphone sound-on-disk features, the introduction of a film's theme song before the images or its continuation after the post-credits (as in *Nashville*), and the use of a totally black screen in recent music videos. These examples hardly prove that cinema is regularly taken as a sound-based medium, but they do suggest the *historical* possibilities of cinema as an audio-visual medium, in which sound-oriented proclivities regularly confront image-based tendencies, thus producing a varied history belying claims of a solely image-oriented ontology.

Since first pointing out the ontological fallacy in *Cinema/Sound*, I have become aware of an even more problematic appeal to ontology in the study of sound. Surprisingly, this dependency on ontological arguments comes not from the enemies of sound, but from its greatest defenders. In their celebrated book on *Composing for the Films*, Theodor Adorno and Hanns Eisler attribute to hearing a privileged relation to pre-individualistic collective times; music thus has a pre-capitalistic nature, being more direct and more closely connected to the unconscious. While their other arguments are by and large well attuned to historical differences, this approach to hearing and sound edges dangerously close to an ontological claim, apparently capable of predicting sound's nature in any given situation, but actually able only to locate sound's action in certain past situations.

A similar danger lurks in the work of Mary Ann Doane, Kaja Silverman, Michel Chion, Claudia Gorbman, and other critics who have leaned heavily on the psychoanalytic theories of Guy Rosolato and Didier Anzieu, who characterize the voice as archaic, based on the notion that we hear the soothing voice of the mother from the womb long before we are able to see. It is not surprising that such a transhistoric proposal, apparently predictive of sound's role in any situation whatsoever, should lead to such conclusions as Doane's claim that "the aural illusion of position constructed by the very approximation of sound perspective and by techniques which spatialize the voice and endow it with 'presence' *guarantees* the singularity and stability of a point of audition, *thus* holding at bay the potential trauma of dispersal, dismemberment, difference" (Doane 1980b, 171; my emphasis). Yet we know from actual listening that very few films construct an approximation of sound perspective. Can it then be said that "the subordination of the voice to the screen as the site of the spectacle's unfolding makes vision and hearing work together in manufacturing the 'hallucination' of a fully sensory world"? (Doane 1980b, 171) The problem here is that an apparently ontological claim about the role of sound has been allowed to take precedence over actual analysis of sound's functioning. (In my article "Sound Space," later in this volume, I suggest a different approach to the same question, based not on an assumption of unity and concordance, but on a perceived conflict between sound scale and image scale.) While it would be unreasonable to cut short speculation on the sources of sound's attraction, it is essential that such speculation not be taken as a prescription, as a binding assumption about the way sound must work in all cases. If we are fully to restore a sense of sound's role in creating our sense of the body, we must depend on historically grounded claims and on close analyses of particular films rather than on ontological speculations that presume to cover all possible practices.

The Reproductive Fallacy

In spite of the fact that, as a storage medium, sound recording lags behind the image by tens of thousands of years, recorded sound has from its very beginnings held a great fascination for critics. Whereas the image, however carefully rendered, clearly reduces a three-dimensional original to two dimensions, sound appears to reproduce the original faithfully, in its full three-dimensionality. By no means limited to early admirers of the newfangled technology, this position was until recently held by a majority of sound critics (many of whose pronouncements are quoted at the beginning of Jim Lastra's article, below). By and large, critics remain convinced that sound is literally *reproduced* by a high quality recording and playback system, in spite of Alan Williams' demonstration of the contrary in his *Cinema/Sound* article ("Is Sound Recording Like a Language?").

Sound, it is worth recalling, cannot be construed independently of the volume of air (or other medium) in which it is heard. Typically, we notate sound (through writing or musical notation) as if sounds were ideal entities. But volume, frequency, and timbre cannot exist independently of several material factors which preclude reproduction as such. To be sure, in some sense a G# is a G#, whether it is played at home or on stage, but that does not make the two sounds identical. By restricting our description of sounds to familiar musical terminology, we have bamboozled ourselves into believing that sound itself is restricted to those characteristics. Does the G# have a slow attack? a long decay? an echo? reverberation? Does it bounce around like a superball in a hollow cavity? Or does it rapidly lose its force, like a beanbag hitting a pillow? If all we want to know about a sound is that it was a G#, then all G#s are the same, but if we care about the material differences between two sounds, and the spatial configurations that cause them, then we must recognize that no recording can possibly reproduce an original sound.

Recordings do not reproduce sound, they represent sound. According to the choice of recording location, microphone type, recording system, postproduction manipulation, storage medium, playback arrangement, and playback locations, each recording proposes an interpretation of the original sound. To be sure, one of the common strategies involved in this process is an attempt to convince the audience that they are listening not to a representation but to a reproduction. We must not, however, be taken in by advertisements for "high fidelity" sound. The notion of "fidelity" is not a measure of success in reproduction, but a way of assessing a recording's adherence to a set of evolving conventions, like the parallel standards established for such culturally important qualities as "realism," "morality," or "beauty." The concept of fidelity is thus a strange hybrid of engineers' aspirations and ideology, serving to mask recording's representational nature.

Considered as a reproduction, recording seems to fall under the aegis of technology and engineering. Construed as a representation, however, sound inherits the double mantle of art. Simultaneously capable of misrepresentation and of artistically using all the possibilities of representation, sound thus recovers some of the fascination lost to its reputation as handmaiden of the image. Indeed, it is recording's very ability to manipulate sound that makes it so amply worthy of our interest.

The Nominalist Fallacy

In order to show that recording cannot possibly reproduce the original sound, critics (Williams, Levin, Altman) have regularly made the following points: (1) sound exists as pressure within a volume; (2) it is impossible to collect all the sound of a particular performance, since it disperses differently into the various parts of the theater or other surrounding space; (3) even at a live performance, different spectators hear different sounds, depending on where they are seated and which way they and the performers are turned; (4) sound systems always enforce a particular set of values in selecting microphone type and location, frequency response, volume levels, and many other recording and playback characteristics; (5) playback involves the same set of differences and choices involved in recording.

Within this apparently coherent argument lurks a potential danger. Stressing the material nature of sound in order to counter fundamentally idealist assumptions, this approach fragments sound to the point where the emission of a single sound apparently gives rise to the perception of a multiplicity of different sounds. By concentrating on the differences between the sound as heard in the orchestra and the "same" sound as heard from the balcony, this argument has rendered the important service of sensitizing critics to the materiality, complexity, and context-based nature of sound. At the same time, however, these defenses against the reproductive fallacy have failed to address the problem of the communicative language used by auditors having heard the "same" sound to overcome the fact that they actually perceived physically different sounds.

This is an old problem, closely identified with the weaning of philosophy from theology in the latter part of the Middle Ages. When I pick up two different rocks and call them "rocks," what is the status of the name that I attribute to them? Is the name itself real? Or is the name just a convenient label? To put it another way, is the shared category to be understood as actually existing, or are the objects themselves the only things that exist? Is there such a thing as the category "rock," or are there only objects, on which for the sake of convenience we confer names (such as "rock") which have no existence independent of the objects they represent? The traditional position, usually identified with Plato and Augustine, is termed "realism," because it takes the general category as real; the radical position, championed by William of Ockham and generally thought to have been instrumental in paving the way for Renaissance individualism, is known as "nominalism," because it considers that the general category is just a convenient name. Especially concerned to recognize individual difference (and thus the value of the created world), the nominalists accused the realists of subordinating the entirety of creation to a set of preexisting universals.

This is precisely where we stand today with regard to sound. As Jim Lastra demonstrates so well in his article, below, the critics of the reproductive fallacy have edged dangerously close to an ultra-nominalism in which differing auditor perceptions make a single original sound appear like so many different rocks with no common identity save their common name. The very names used to identify sounds are suspect, disrespectful of sound's material heterogeneity. Yet we do discuss the film as we file out of the theater. In spite of the fact that we have literally, really heard different sounds, we still manage to find a common ground on which to base our conversation.

At this point in time, the study of sound shares the position of reception studies. I once witnessed an interchange that says a great deal about the project of reception studies. After demonstrating that neither the author nor the text can possibly determine readings, that each reader may read the text in differing ways, Tony Bennett opened the floor to questions. Said Paul Hernadi: "This is all well and good, but if what you say is true, how did I understand what you just said?" Taking an ultra-nominalist stance (which, by the way, he has toned down since), Bennett laid such heavy emphasis on our freedom of interpretation from textual constraints that he jeopardized the very notion of understanding. Even today, reception studies need to concentrate more fully on the bridges, the terms, the categories, the reading formations that permit a Paul Hernadi to understand a Tony Bennett.

A similar situation holds in sound studies. While not abandoning for a moment the notion that every auditor of the "same" performance actually hears different sounds, we need actively to interrogate the cultural phenomena that permit us to compose sentences, frame ideas, and ultimately communicate about the sounds which are heard. A decade or two ago, it would no doubt have been politically essential to defend at all costs the free play of the signifier; today it seems far more important to remember with Saussure that signification can occur only through the repression of the signifier and to call for increased sensitivity to the many strategies adopted by various cultures to assure the repression of sound's differences in favor of language's communicative value.

Indexicality: Half a Fallacy Working on the Other Half

Inherited from photography, one of the most deeply ingrained notions about cinema is that it depends primarily on recording. Unlike painting or writing, it is commonly supposed, cinema uses motion picture photography and sound recording to fix and retain in memory a physical image of the pro-filmic scene. Whereas representational painting is based largely on iconic resemblances, and writing is built around symbolic relationships (according to the terminology of Charles Sanders Peirce), cinema is thought to depend especially strongly on indexical connections, that is, those revealing a particularly close existential relationship between the represented item and its representation (such as that which exists when light rays bouncing off an object expose motion picture film, or when sound waves either drive the stylus of a disk recorder or, once transformed into light, expose the sound track portion of the film). This close connection of course creates an iconic relationship between the pro-filmic object or sound and its filmic representation (that is, the object and its representation have the same shape), but critics and theoreticians have consistently stressed the indexical ties over the iconic resemblance. In particular, André Bazin's realist criticism has been especially influential in popularizing an indexical approach to cinema. For Bazin, cinema is like a mold that takes each scene's impression; cinema thus works like a death mask or the Shroud of Turin, recording as it were by sacred contact.

During the early history of photography, photographs could be produced only through indexical relationships. As photography matured, however, photographers discovered various methods of "correcting" nature, typically adding painted-in iconic details to the photograph's indexical base. From the very start, however, such techniques were roundly condemned. Offering ontological arguments about photography's nature, critics insisted that certain types of retouching constituted a highly undesirable form of "cheating." The moralistic tone of this argument carried over intact to motion picture. In spite of early cinema's non-indexical display of color, "silent" cinema's iconic and symbolic approach to sound, or the late twenties' creation of the falsely indexical playback system, critics and theorists continued to stress the ability of the motion picture camera, like that of its still picture cousin, to take snapshots of reality. As cinema developed, to be sure, the scenes recorded by the camera began to depend on an increasing amount of manipulation (through set design, costuming, makeup, and so forth), and the final film image was increasingly constructed from a combination of separate images (through mattes, background projections, and other processes). For all this prestidigitation, however, the basic assumption was never jeopardized: cinema is primarily an indexical medium, directly dependent on the photographic recording of each pro-filmic scene (or scene fragment).

Throughout the history of cinema, the image has by and large corresponded to this indexical, recording-oriented definition (with the exception of special cases like scratch-animation, computer graphics, or electronically generated images). Cinema sound, on the other hand, has rarely been the result of straightforward indexical recording. Long before the cinema industry converted to sound, the market for telephonic communication, phonograph records, public address systems, and radio entertainment had led engineers to investigate the possibilities of "enhancing" sound in order to achieve greater volume, presence, or intelligibility, while reducing unwanted characteristics. At first, engineers concentrated on the recording process itself, laboring to increase the indexical fidelity of the sound recording apparatus. Soon, however, sound's capacity for post-recording transformation became apparent. Why *record* the reverberation associated with sounds produced in a large hard-walled room if you can simply process the reverb in later? Throughout the thirties, parallel developments in electronics and film sound led to the creation of myriad devices designed to produce final-release sound differing radically from the sound originally recorded on the set.

Little by little, the indexical nature of film sound became compromised by the ability of acoustic networks and electronic circuits to alter or simulate sound. Once the sole province of high-end sound production facilities (such as those found in New York, Hollywood, and a few other important centers around the world), the electronic revolution has now made it possible to produce all the music and effects for a film sound track without recording a single cricket or musical instrument. For a decade, film sound has been heavily influenced by digital systems like MIDI and the Synclavier. Even the most inexpensive films feature sound tracks that are no longer primarily recorded. In cinema, television, and disk production, sound has definitely surpassed the era of indexicality.

Today, the customary electronic manipulation and construction of sound has begun to serve as a model for the image. Though the film image currently depends primarily on a chemical (and thus indexical) technology, the electronic nature of the television image provides a different model, whose influence is increasingly felt in the cinema world. In order to create Mickey Mouse, Walt Disney had to do more than just make thousands of drawings; he had to record them with the same (indexical) motion picture process used for live actors. Today's animators work in an entirely different fashion. While most still depend in part on drawing, they make heavy use of electronics and its ability to produce iconic relationships without depending on the indexicality of recording. A similar shift has taken place in color technology. Whether two- or three-strip, whether additive or subtractive, traditional color processes systematically depended on indexical relationships: the color was fixed by the existential contact of the object with the film. Today, films are colorized by an electronic process that owes nothing to recording. It is only a matter of time before the plunging prices of all electronic processes turn colorization from a postproduction technique into a production device.

In short, the recording medium that cinema once was has now been massively transformed and risks ultimate obsolescence. However accurate it may once have been to understand cinema as recording its object by sacred contact, we must recognize that three-quarters of a century of electronics has radically desacralized cinema, substituting circuitry for direct contact, constructed iconicity for recorded indexicality, and the infinite imagined possibilities of the keyboard for the restricted immediacy of recording reality. Not so very long ago, treating cinema as *écriture* was a radical move; the technology itself is now turning this metaphor into a reality. Once, cinema was recorded with a camera; now, it is increasingly written with a keyboard.

So far, it is only half a fallacy to treat cinema as a recording medium. By the end of the century, however, cinema will be well on its way toward full digitalization. The end of the indexical era looms large. Perhaps it is time to revise our theories and our vocabulary to take this transformation into account. More experienced in this domain than the image, sound must lead the way.

2

Sound Space

Rick Altman

"The real can never be represented; representation alone can be represented. For in order to be represented, the real must be known, and knowledge is always already a form of representation." From this claim, which I made in an earlier article on the role of technology in the history of representation (1984), we can deduce several essential principles for the writing of cinema history. In particular, we readily conclude that the "reality" which each new technology sets out to represent is in large part defined by preexistent representational systems. In order for its new mode of representing to achieve acceptance, photography had to conform not to reality as such, but to the visual version of this reality imposed by a certain style of painting and engraving. In the same manner, the early years of sound cinema were marked by a heavy debt to contemporary arbiters of sound representation: radio, theater, phonography, and public address.

Such a theory is hardly devoid of problems, however. While it helps us to understand how a nascent technology leans on preexisting forms, it remains all too static, offering little insight into the processes whereby a new form of representation is liberated from its models, eventually offering to subsequent technologies its own representational norm. A constant source of debate during the Hollywood thirties, the problem of sound space provides a particularly clear test case, a unique occasion where a change in representational norms is carefully discussed, documented, and even quantified by contemporary technicians.

The single most important question occupying Hollywood sound technicians during the late twenties and early thirties was this: what relationship should obtain between image scale and sound scale? Disarmingly simple, this question in fact implies a complex series of related problems. What type of microphone should be used? Where should it be placed? May it be moved during a take? Is it appropriate to make multiple image and/or sound takes simultaneously? What sound take should be paired with what image? What volume level should be used? Is it appropriate to mix multiple takes? Under what circumstances must reverberation be added? And many others. Indeed, as the most perceptive of sound technicians recognized from the start, the question of sound scale foregrounds to an unexpected extent problems of audience identification, of spectator pleasure, and of subject placement.

Concentrating on the broad range of problems implied by the question of sound scale, this essay will be divided into three parts. First, I will trace through its various stages the industry's desire for a match between image scale and sound scale. Second, I will attempt to reach some general conclusions about the standard sound practices which evolved in Hollywood during the thirties. Third, I will consider the ramifications of the representational system thus constituted for the placement of the hearing and seeing subject.

The Dream: Correlating Sound and Image

The question of sound scale, as contemplated by Hollywood technicians of the early sound years, must be seen as part of a longer chain of attempts to assure sound localization. Roughly stated, the three main approaches involve:

1. manipulation at the place of exhibition, largely through speaker placement and switching mechanisms (1927–31);
2. manipulation during production, especially of microphone choice and placement, along with control of sound levels during editing (1929–present);
3. development of multi-channel technology, eventually including stereophonic localization capability (1930–present).

While the latter approach falls largely outside the scope of this study, some information on the first stage will provide appropriate background for the second stage, on which the remainder of this article will concentrate.

That early attempts to localize cinema sound should have concentrated on the movie house itself is hardly surprising. After all, for a quarter of a century movie theater owners had been designing the sound accompaniment to silent pictures. Even before *The Jazz Singer*, Lee DeForest was insisting that loudspeakers be located in the orchestra pit "to simulate a fifty-piece orchestra" (DeForest, 72). As soon as the spoken word became a staple of sound cinema, a second horn was added to the standard orchestra pit speaker, this one above the screen and facing out, whereas the orchestra horn typically aimed straight up (Rainey, Wilcox, Peck, Hopkins 1930a and 1930b). The presence of two speakers, each destined to reproduce a different type of sound, of course required a switching mechanism. The projectionist, who needed to know the sound track like an orchestra conductor, would simply switch the sound output to the appropriate speaker each time there was a change from music to dialogue or back. This of course assumes sound tracks where music and dialogue are not mixed, a requirement assured by the difficulty of mixing separate tracks before late 1930, by which time the separate speaker arrangement had largely disappeared.

But if sound could be localized either on screen or in the orchestra pit, then it could also, at least theoretically, be reproduced at different spots on the screen, depending on where the person speaking is portrayed. Never to my knowledge realized, this project, reported by J. C. Kroesen in July, 1928, demonstrates the extent to which early technicians assumed the necessity of tying sound to the image. "The screen," said Kroesen, "should be divided and so arranged that sound will be reproduced only at or as near the point of action as possible" (Kroesen, 8). Pity the poor projectionist trying desperately to operate the switching mechanism!

Nor was lateral placement the only possibility afforded by careful speaker location. In an October, 1930, discussion, the Society of Motion Picture Engineers reviewed the possibilities afforded by the recently introduced multiple sound track technology. Realistic offstage effects can be produced, a Mr. Ross pointed out, "by employing separate sound film having a plurality of sound tracks, each related to a group of loudspeakers located at points from which the sounds are to be produced. . . ." In this manner, Ross suggested, depth localization as well as lateral placement may be assured. "Any sound," he said, "that one might wish to produce from points other than the immediate foreground depicted on the screen may be handled in this manner. Loudspeakers may be placed at remote portions of the stage or auditorium. There are decided advantages for this arrangement which are quite evident to anyone who has tried it."[1] Ross's protestations notwithstanding, Hollywood was not yet ready for the multiple-channel solution.

Exhibitors were quite ready, however, to dispense with the need for manual switching. Neither better instructions nor the short-lived introduction of automatic switching through control tracks could stem the tide. By 1931, the dream of sound localization through speaker placement was a dead letter. In his description of the Western Electric Reproducing System, Bell engineer S. K. Wolf clearly opposed the old-fashioned system ("when it was desired that reproduced music should simulate accompaniment by a theatre orchestra") to what he called "modern practice," which recognized the fact that "in most instances the sound is desired to come from the screen, and accordingly the horn or horns are placed behind it" (Wolf, 287).

Though the multiple-speaker approach to sound localization died an early death, driven to its grave like many other innovations by the economics of exhibition and by the growing complexity of Hollywood's sound tracks, the need to stress sound's spatial characteristics remained at the center of debate in the limited but influential world of sound technicians.[2] Whereas the proponents of localization through speaker placement and mechanical switching had clearly in mind a theatrical or silent cinema model, the most influential sound men of the period proposed a more familiar and seemingly uncontested model: that of nature itself. Like numerous other technicians of the period, Carl Dreher, chief sound engineer for RKO, stressed the importance of maintaining a "natural" proportionality between image and sound (Dreher 1929a, Dreher 1931, Miller). Dreher's appeal to nature, that is, to the apparently natural relationship that exists between the picture of a speaking person and the voice associated with it, no doubt overlooked the extent to which such correspondences differ from culture to culture and thus must be learned by individuals from other practitioners within their culture, yet it clearly identified the source and force of early arguments for some sort of sound/image match.

A second group of technician-theoreticians, headed by J. P. Maxfield, chief of Western Electric's west coast distribution wing, Electric Research Products Incorporated (ERPI), reinforced this appeal to nature by a parallel argument centering on the human body. Already in 1928, Lewis W. Physioc had insisted that viewers would not accept a lack of auditory perspective, because their eye/ear coordination would not allow them to (Physioc, 24–25). Supporting his own argument that sound scale must always match image scale, Maxfield insisted repeatedly that the eyes and ears of a person viewing a real scene in real life must maintain "a fixed relationship" to one another (Maxfield 1930a).

Reference to the human body as a strategy to circumvent history and culture reached its height in a short but powerful 1930 article by RCA sound technician John L. Cass. In order to maintain intelligibility of dialogue, Cass claimed, more and more studios were resorting to the use of multiple microphones, with a mixer choosing the best, that is, the most intelligible, sound. "The resultant blend of sound," asserted Cass, "may not be said to represent any given point of audition, but is the sound which would be heard by a man with five or six very long ears, said ears extending in various directions" (Cass, 325). In other words, the current practice resulted in the constitution of a monstrous spectator, of a being neither found in nature nor worthy of existence. Cass thus decried the way in which current image-editing practices forced the spectator to "jump from a distant position to an intermediate position, and from there to close-up positions on important business," while the practice of mixing multiple mikes made the sound "run throughout as though heard from the indefinite position described above" (325). Cass concluded: "Since it is customary among humans to attempt to maintain constant the distance between the eye and the ear, these organs should move together from one point to another in order to maintain our much mentioned illusion [of reality]" (325). Demonstrating nothing short of missionary zeal in his attempts to save the spectator from monstrosity, Cass failed to consider the possibility, to which we shall return later, that spectators do not remain from age to age the same, that even the body and its functions are culturally determined, and that spectators who live long enough with monstrosity learn to consider it not only beautiful, but even, eventually, normal.

Before the normality of a many-eared spectator could be contemplated, however, numerous other attempts at codifying methods for assuring an appropriate image/sound match would appear. The key figure here was again Maxfield, the most powerful voice within the Bell/Western Electric/ ERPI complex that dominated the Hollywood sound scene until the early thirties. In a series of articles which reiterated numerous times the same points, Maxfield hammered home the need to limit most takes to a single microphone (Maxfield 1929, 1930a, 1930b, 1931). Thus solving the problem posed by Cass, Maxfield showed how the use of a single mike, placed near the camera's line of sight, automatically coordinates sight and sound by providing a sound record of the characters' movements toward and away from the camera. Characters approaching the camera automatically approach the microphone as well, thus matching closer image scale to closer sound scale; conversely, the character who speaks from the background demonstrates distant characteristics in sound and image alike.

While the use of a single, stable microphone assures the matching of sound scale with image scale within a shot, a different set of guidelines was necessary in order to assure proper matching of succeeding shots. These guidelines, first proposed by Maxfield in 1931 (in the graphic, empirical style characteristic of Bell's scientific pretentions in the early thirties), and reiterated in 1938, indicate proper microphone placement in varying image situations (Maxfield 1931, Maxfield 1938). Throughout the decade, Maxfield had been a pioneer in isolating the aspects of sound which determine the spectator's perception and evaluation of specific sound phenomena. Demonstrating that volume alone is an insufficient marker of distance, Maxfield had earlier revealed the importance of reverberation (or more accurately, the ratio of reflected sound to direct sound) for determining perception of sound scale. In addition, Maxfield showed that the focusing capabilities of the listening binaural human subject, permitting humans selectively to cut out a certain percentage of reflected sound, have no parallel in the monaural sound collection system of cinema.

A monaural correction factor is thus built into all Maxfield's careful determinations.[3] Taken as a whole, Maxfield's enormously influential writings provided a complete program for matching sound scale to image scale, within and between shots.

The Reality: Mismatching Image Scale and Sound Scale

With Maxfield's influential articles reprinted in journals of all sorts throughout the thirties, referred to by one Bell author after another, and imitated throughout the industry, one might well assume that Hollywood practice followed Maxfield's strictures to the letter. A careful survey of the period's sound practices is far from bearing out such an assumption. Unfortunately, space does not permit full treatment of this important question. A few examples, along with a rough sketch of the period's general penchants, must suffice. As in every period, examples abound of atypical practices, but here I will stress instead what I take to be the accepted norm from the late twenties through the Second World War. An appropriate starting point might be Rouben Mamoulian's *Applause*, one of the few films of 1929 to be universally praised for its revolutionary approach to the sound track. My purpose here, however, is not to dwell on Mamoulian's many innovations, like the subjective use of sound levels in the opening parade scene, but to show that even *Applause* neglects the careful matching of sound scale to image scale.

The first stage scene in *Applause*, for example, exhibits a sound track of uniform volume and reverberation characteristics. The sound track's uniformity is hardly matched by the image track, however, which reveals a heavily edited theater scene, combining shots of varying scales and angles. The "Doctor in the house" routine which calls the scene to a close, for example, is clearly shot with a single microphone, while two cameras are churning out images of different scales. Once edited together, the two simultaneous camera takes produce a scene typical of the period. Perhaps it is fitting to remark here that the term editing, entirely appropriate for the images, is less so for the sound, since the sound take used is apparently continuous and uncut. In fact, it would be perfectly correct to say that the contemporary practice of using a single microphone system synchronized to two or three cameras fairly begged early editors to use a continuous sound track as the bench mark to which they edited the various images.[4]

For obvious economic and technical reasons, multiple-camera shooting remained the rule throughout the early sound period. Soon, however, an important change took place in the type of sound record associated with the multiple-camera arrangement. The condenser mikes used in the late twenties required extremely close placement in order to provide a distinct dialogue record (Hunt, 482). Often, the mike had to be so close to the

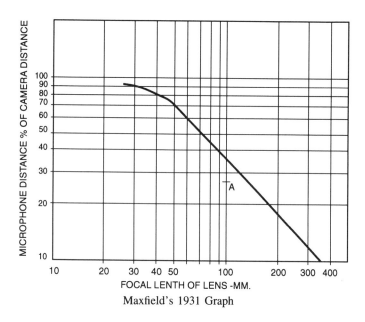

Maxfield's 1931 Graph

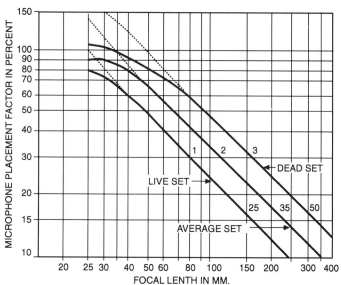

Relation between focal length of camera and microphone position, for achieving acoustic perspective.

Maxfield's 1938 Graph

speaker that it could not be kept out of the field in a medium shot, thus resulting in the common practice of handling action in medium shot, while flashing into close-up for the sound record (thereby avoiding revelation of the microphone, which would be visible in the medium shot of the same scene). During this period, where a series of dialogue locations were built into a single shot, preference was often given to a multiple-microphone setup, with a mixer choosing the clearest sound record. More intimate scenes easily accommodated the increasingly widespread choice of single-miking.

In the early thirties, however, new microphones became available; lighter, more compact, and requiring no amplification stage near the mike, these new units made the microphone boom far more practical (Altman 1985b, Altman 1986a). Whereas the twenties often used what Dreher dubbed "prop pick-ups" (Dreher 1929b), microphones which had to be hidden in a prop in order to get close enough to the speaker to achieve acceptable sound quality, the thirties adopted the mobile mike, suspended from a boom which could be moved silently about, always pausing at the appropriate point to capture a perfect rendition of lines which otherwise might have turned out garbled or fuzzy. Furthermore, the mobile boom made it relatively easy to stay out of the camera field while remaining at proper distance for sound recording.[5] In short, the combination of multiple-camera shooting and single-miking with a mobile boom made for an ideal combination, for two related reasons. First, the boom simplified the sound problems inherent in the multiple-camera arrangement, thus preserving an important economy factor (Hunt, 481–82). Second, the boom changed radically the character of the sound "in the can." With a single immobile mike, such as that championed at the turn of the decade by Maxfield, the spatial characteristics of the pro-filmic scene were already inscribed on the sound track. A character receding or turning away from the mike was recorded with a higher ratio of reflected to direct sound; similarly, the size of the room had its effect on volume, reverberation, and frequency characteristics. With the new system, however, the microphone is perpetually kept within approximately the same distance of the speaker, thus canceling out nearly all the factors which the earlier system retained.

Coupled with devices for adding reverberation, voice equalization, effort equalization, and so forth, in which the mid-thirties abound, this new approach assured Hollywood both the economic benefits and the requisite control associated with a system permitting the *construction* of a sound track rather than the direct *recording* of already constructed sounds. Parallel to the many image-treatment processes which permitted the Hollywood of the thirties to exercise control over the image while reducing the cost of its production, sound construction processes serve to enhance the ability of the boomed mike to provide a clean, clear, continuous sound record, oblivious to image scale but attuned to dialogue intelligibility, story continuity, and freedom of action.[6]

Perhaps most telling of all is the 1938 article in which Maxfield reiterated his strictures regarding microphone placement. Still insisting on a careful matching of image and sound scale, Maxfield again explained his chart providing proper microphone placement, but this time his instructions were interspersed with remarks reflecting years of experience watching technicians use his chart. These remarks reveal a fascinating tendency:

> It has been the author's experience, and that of some of the microphone men with whom they have discussed the problem, that unless some such guide is used there is a tendency to set the close-up takes correctly and to make the microphone positions for the long-shot and semi-long-shot takes decidedly too close. The use of the curve, of course, helps to keep the judgment of the operator calibrated. (Maxfield 1938, 672)

Now, Maxfield's original microphone distance chart was based on so-called empirical data, generated by the experience of the first three years of sound film. In 1931, Maxfield explained that his data came from his own records of "several pictures with which the writer was associated" (Maxfield 1931, 74). In the seven or eight years since Maxfield's data were first collected, however, something had evidently changed. Whereas the 1931 chart was derived from actual experience, producing the straight-line function presented in both charts, the 1938 article clearly admitted that the chart must be used to *control* and *rectify* the intuitions of technicians, who without such a guide would always tend to set microphones at a distance producing close-up sound quality.

In other words, the "gut reaction" of sound technicians has changed over the course of the decade. Their intuition in 1938 clearly reflected the changing practice of the thirties; having internalized a new standard, the technicians no longer sought to match sound scale to image scale through "correct" microphone placement, but instead sought to produce a continuous sound track of nearly level volume and unbroken close-up characteristics. Throughout the thirties it was for the clarity of their sound tracks that sound technicians had been praised and rewarded, rather than for their spatial realism.

What once appeared as monstrosity had now become the norm. In fact, Maxfield himself recognized the extent to which careful scale-matching had disappeared. "There are occasions," he admitted, "when it is necessary to use several cameras on the same scene simultaneously. Where acoustic perspective has no dramatic importance, a single close-up track can be used for all the picture takes, the sound being dubbed at slightly lower level for the long-shot scenes" (672). This capitulation by the champion of scale-matching coincides exactly with numerous contemporary remarks by top sound men. To quote but one, stereo pioneer W. H. Offenhauser stated categorically that "it is our practice . . . to record all our sound with the microphone placed close to the sound source" (Offenhauser, 146).

Why this striking change? Sound was not yet in its teens and already sound technicians had reversed their position about sound space, not only in theory but also in practice. It is no exaggeration to claim that this reversal represented a fundamental turnabout in human perception. We often give lip service to the notion that cinema teaches us to see and to hear, that the media determine our very notion of reality. Yet we are rarely privileged to isolate the moment when and the process whereby our perception changes.

During the early years of sound cinema, theoreticians regularly insisted that sound be treated according to the model provided by the human body. While these appeals to nature carry strong rhetorical value, they frequently disguise other, more important models. According to the theory elaborated by Maxfield and followed by many early sound men, the sound track must carry, independently from the image, all the information necessary to reconstruct the "real" space of the scene (that is, the one represented by the image). In this approach we easily recognize the technique of a representational system with a decade's experience in creating sound space. Maxfield and his colleagues may have stressed nature and the body, but their method owed more to radio technique than to the fixed distance between the eyes and the ears. For where had Hollywood found its sound technicians? By far the majority, like Carl Dreher, had come from the radio studios. The early years of sound cinema were thus heavily marked by the version of reality offered by other modes of representation—first silent cinema, then radio.

"The real can never be represented; representation alone can be represented." Up to now, this theory would appear confirmed: the audio technique of early sound cinema refers to other systems of representation. Not only silent cinema for the location of loud speakers and radio for sound perspective, but other models as well. Due to space limitations I will outline only one of these here: the acoustics of large public spaces (church, palace, concert hall), with their continuous reverberation and long decay time. In spite of the importance of limiting reverberation in order to assure dialogue intelligibility, Hollywood sound technicians regularly insisted on reproducing music with a high degree of reverb, corresponding to the large reverberant halls in which we are accustomed to hearing nineteenth-century "serious" music played.

Silent cinema, radio, the concert hall: can history be built on the simple notion that each new representational system derives its initial task from a previous system? Certainly not, for while such a theory helps us to understand the early logic of a new representational technology, it fails to explain eventual modifications in the representational use of that technology. In order to understand the alterations in Maxfield's claims from 1931 to 1938, we need to be able to explain how the construction of sound tracks changed over that period.

A few examples should help us to understand these changes. The opening scene from Paramount's 1939 *Union Pacific* provides a particularly representative case, directed as it is by one of the period's most conservative and exemplary directors, Cecil B. DeMille. This debate on the floor of the U.S. Senate exhibits a sound track of uniform volume and reverberation characteristics, with differences in sound level attributable to the senators' rhetoric or intensity rather than to any technical considerations. Yet this uniform sound track is matched to a heavily edited image track, revealing shots of radically differing scales. In particular, one camera movement stands out for its clear demonstration of the lack of concern for sound/image scale-matching: during one speech, the camera tracks constantly back, reducing the scale of the actor, while the senator's speech level remains unchanged, with neither volume nor reverb varying in the slightest. We note, therefore, that the choice of image to accompany any particular sound is in no case dependent on the spatial characteristics of the sound. Instead, the choice depends entirely on the *narrative* characteristics of the sound. The sound track remains uniform throughout, displaying medium close-up characteristics from beginning to end. The image changes scale repeatedly, however, matching the dramatic effect of the words uttered. The constant-level sound track thus serves to anchor a pasted-up, discontinuous image sequence which remains obedient to narrative concerns.

A second example comes from the same year's *Only Angels Have Wings*, made for Columbia by Howard Hawks, another filmmaker known for thematic rather than technical innovations, and who might thus be expected to reflect the industry's standard pre-war practice.[7] At the end of the opening sequence, Jean Arthur is invited by Noah Beery and a fellow pilot to have a drink. Their conversation is interrupted by the arrival of the restaurant owner. During the ensuing scene there is a cut-in to a medium close-up of the owner, without any accompanying change in sound level. In the exterior conversation that follows, we witness another cut which eloquently testifies to the period's presuppositions about the sound/image match. In the *Applause* and *Union Pacific* scenes, image cuts always occur between speeches or during pauses, like punctuation in a paragraph. While no change in sound level or characteristics is noticeable, the practice clearly sets up a rhythmic correspondence between sound and image, one which might just as well have been used to establish a scale match between sound and image.

In the exterior conversation from *Only Angels Have Wings*, however, the cut is made right smack in the middle of a phrase. Something different is going on here. Far from matching sound scale to image scale—the dream of technicians and theoreticians alike in the early thirties—Hawks uses the uniformity and continuity of the medium-close-up sound track to cover over a cut. Now, this technique obviously assumes a system in which no match between sound scale and image is sought. Whereas *Union Pacific*'s practice of making image cuts in the silences between phrases could have attenuated the effect of a change in sound level, the cut during a speech in *Only Angels Have Wings* would create a naked juxtaposition of the two levels if there were to be a match in scale, thus revealing the processes of image editing and sound mixing alike, thereby foregrounding an apparatus which Hollywood would rather hide. That cutting during dialogue has become routine by the late thirties reveals the extent to which the uniform sound track has become the rule, unmatched to and independent of the image.[8]

A second example from the same film further illustrates this fact. When Noah Beery flies off to his death in the following scene, numerous shots of the plane accompany a homogeneous, uniform-level sound track of the plane's engine noise. With one exception, the sound level remains the same, whether we see the plane in long shot or just the pilot in medium shot. As the camera closes in on the plane, no change in sound ties the sound track to the image scale. Only when an internal auditor is implied does the sound scale match the image, a situation which occurs when Cary Grant and Jean Arthur listen to the plane disappear down the far end of the runway, the fading of the motor sound replicating its growing distance from the listeners. (More on this special situation in my final section.)

That the practices illustrated by *Union Pacific* and *Only Angels Have Wings* represent the industry standard and continue through the forties is clearly demonstrated by the authoritative comments of one of Hollywood's most knowledgeable and influential sound men, John G. Frayne:

> To insure high intelligibility in a sound-stage pickup it is customary practice to place the microphone as close to the actor as possible, the distance usually being limited only by the camera angle of the scene. . . . no attempt is ordinarily made in practice to try to obtain the same acoustic as visual perspective of the scene. . . . "Panning" of the microphone by the "boom" man is an accepted technique in production recording and is omitted only if the physical location of the actors makes it impossible for the boom man to keep up with the action.

> Panning from one actor to another or following the movements of an actor tends to keep a constant relationship between microphone and speaker with respect both to distance and to orientation of the sound pressure axis. Thus a constant-frequency characteristic is preserved, and a change in tonal inflection of the actor as he moves around in the sound field is avoided. . . . (Frayne, 52–53)

No longer is there any question of matching sound scale to image scale, unless it is to show how any indication of sound scale can be avoided. We have moved a long way from the repeated demands for scale-matching during sound's early years.

Cinema's Bifurcated Subject: Seeing/Hearing

Why did early technicians' calls for scale-matching fall, as it were, on deaf ears? Or, rather, why is it that early thirties proponents of auditory perspective had by the end of the decade abandoned their dedication to the creation of sound/image proportionality? What factors determined the sound level practices which dominate Hollywood's studio years? Two related considerations come immediately to mind. A third is perhaps less obvious.

Whether expressed in terms of "story continuity" (Mueller), the "business of the play" (Dreher) or the creation of a persuasive illusion (DeForest, Cass, Maxfield, Dreher), the criterion of intelligibility of dialogue retained its primary importance throughout the period under study (Altman 1985b, Altman 1986a). For Harold B. Franklin, speaking in 1930 as head of Fox West Coast Theaters for exhibitors everywhere, sound cinema's greatest advantage was the "ability to present every word so clearly and distinctly that no one need strain to hear what is being said, at least when recording and reproducing is properly conducted. A whisper is clearly audible from the front row in the orchestra to the last row in the balcony" (Franklin, 302). Franklin thus echoed one of the creators of the medium, Lee DeForest, for whom "one of the great advantages of Phonofilm is that, in common with the 'Public Address' system, the voice of the screen image is far more distinct and clear in the far reaches of the house and gallery than would be the normal human voice of a speaker on the stage."[9] For DeForest, cinema was thus an improved megaphone, a mechanical aide for the hoarse actor and the carnival barker.

That the ideal of intelligibility might contradict the desire for a faithful matching of sound scale to image scale occurred to many early theoreticians of sound editing. While Bell's Maxfield tried to dodge the problem, however, by blithely asserting that proper scale-matching produces intelligibility (Maxfield 1931, 71), RCA's Dreher openly faced the problem, recognizing that there are two potentially contradictory requirements of good recording: "(1) intelligibility of dialog" and "(2) naturalness, or acoustic fidelity to the original rendition," within which category he included the need to retain the spatial characteristics of the original, and thus a sound/image match.[10] Influencing sound technology throughout the thirties (especially the development of the microphone boom, sound collector, and directional mikes), the ideal of intelligibility remained a central factor throughout the period. Indeed, as I have written elsewhere, this insistence on intelligibility at the expense of fidelity to the pro-filmic situation suggests that the referent of Hollywood sound is not the pro-filmic scene at all, but a narrative constructed as it were "behind" that scene, a narrative that authorizes and engenders the scene, and of which the scene itself is only one more signifier (Altman 1985b, Altman 1986a).

A second, related, consideration regards changing standards of reality during the early years of sound cinema. In the late twenties and early thirties, as we have seen, the reality standard constantly held up to the cinema sound track was daily life in the real world. For inventors and engineers like DeForest, Miller, and Dreher, sound cinema would succeed only if it was "natural;" other theoretically inclined technicians, like Physioc, Maxfield, and Cass, stressed instead the natural coordination of the eyes and ears within the overall system of the human body. In calling for a careful matching of sound scale to image scale, early theoreticians clearly assumed that sound cinema needed to match a reality code derived from daily life, where small-scale people—distant individuals—have small-scale voices, and close-up people have close-up voices. Competing with this daily life model, expressed in terms of scale-matching, there ran throughout the decade another model, this one expressed in terms of intelligibility.

We find here once again the familiar opposition of intelligibility to naturalness (or acoustic fidelity), but it was rewritten in terms of differing codes of reality. On the one side, daily life, on the other the medium that taught the audiences of the twenties and thirties to expect visual narrative to provide intelligible dialogue. I speak of course of the theater, that old enemy of "pure cinema," back to haunt the faithful once again. For if sound cinema continued to practice intelligibility in spite of repeated appeals for acoustic fidelity, it was because cinema continued to find in the theater a long-consecrated code of reality applicable to audiovisual narratives. Not even the naturalist theories of an Antoine could radically alter the theater's commitment to understandable dialogue, achieved through such devices as the stage whisper, playing toward the audience, and the declamatory style (which would be replaced only when sound cinema's superior ability to assure intelligibility led theater to borrow the cinema's technological means for amplifying dialogue[11]). To call for intelligibility in the language of the thirties' cinema technicians is thus to call for adherence to the theater as code of reality. With the theater of the period itself stressing textual comprehension more than ever,[12] it is hardly surprising that Hollywood felt the need to follow suit, abandoning the image/sound match in favor of intelligibility, the everyday life model in favor of a code of reality provided by the theater.

A third consideration involves nothing less than the subject placement implied by the dominant sound model adopted by Hollywood during the thirties. In order to elucidate this process, I must at this point expand on the model described earlier. At one point during the scenes I have described, an impression of auditory perspective is created by a change in volume and reverberation levels. In *Only Angels Have Wings*, when Noah Beery's plane disappears into the night at the end of the runway, the next shot, a two-shot of Cary Grant and Jean Arthur, is matched to the dwindling sound of an airplane motor in the distance. Situations like these, which have mistakenly caused some critics to see auditory perspective as a common aspect of thirties' sound tracks, are indeed common throughout the Hollywood studio years, but they must not be confused with the scale-matching discussed earlier.[13] In both these cases we are dealing with what might be called "point-of-audition" sound, a clumsy term whose only merit is to recall unfailingly the "point-of-view" shot.

Frequently used to establish spatial relationships among neighboring spaces which cannot be presented visually in a single master shot, point-of-audition sound is identified by its volume, reverb level, and other characteristics as representing sound as it would be heard from a point within the diegesis, normally by a specific character or characters. In other words, point-of-audition sound always carries signs of its own fictional audition. As such, point-of-audition sound always has the effect of luring the listener into the diegesis not at the point of enunciation of the sound, but at the point of its audition. Point-of-audition sound thus relates us to the narrative not as external auditors, identified with the camera and its position (such as would have been the case with Maxfield's acoustic perspective), nor as participant in the dialogue (the standard situation of the "intelligible" approach), but as internal auditor. When, in 1938, Maxfield alluded to the potential "dramatic importance" of auditory perspective, he was referring to those situations where the auditory perspective involved is that of a character. Whereas in 1931 he was wholly concerned with the perspective of the external auditor, by 1938 Maxfield—and Hollywood as a whole—showed increased interest in the internal auditor.[14]

We are asked not to hear, but to identify with someone who will hear for us. Instead of giving us the freedom to move about the film's space at will, this technique locates us in a very specific place—the body of the character who hears for us. Point-of-audition sound thus constitutes the perfect interpellation, for it inserts us into the narrative at the very intersection of two spaces which the image alone is incapable of linking, thus giving us the sensation of controlling the relationship between those spaces.

What is it then that is happening during those numerous moments, exemplified by the long legislative scene from *Union Pacific*, where no such identification is called for, where we find a sound track of uniform level with no spatial characteristics? First, something important is clearly *not* happening here: the auditor is at no point made aware of the sound track as sound track by the radical changes in volume which would have to accompany a careful sound/image match. This initial negative consideration has numerous ramifications, not the least of which is the dissimulation of the sound apparatus itself. The construction of a uniform-level sound track, eschewing any attempt at matching sound scale to image scale, thus takes its place alongside the thirties' numerous invisible image-editing devices within the overall strategy of hiding the apparatus itself, thus separating the spectator from the reality of the representational situation, thereby making that spectator more available for reaction to the subject-placement cues provided by the fiction and its vehicle.

Just as the lack of sudden changes in sound level duplicates the self-effacing effect of contemporary image-editing, so the reverberation characteristics of standard practice sound place the auditor in a manner quite similar to familiar spectator-placement methods. According to the familiar subject-placement arguments advanced by Pleynet, Baudry, and Comolli apropos of the perspective image, we spectators are built into the picture as source and consumer. Perspective images are always made for us; they present a sumptuous banquet with an empty chair awaiting the honored spectator-guest. Now, in order to achieve the continuous close-up sound quality characteristic of Hollywood's standard practice, the microphone must be brought quite close to the speaker, cutting out unwanted set noises while—and this is the important concern for the present argument—also radically reducing the level of reverberation.

But what is sound without reverberation? On the one hand, to be sure, it is close-up sound, sound spoken by someone close to me, but it is also sound spoken *toward* me rather than away from me. Sound with low reverb is sound that I am meant to hear, sound that is pronounced *for me*. Like the perspective image, therefore, the continuous-level, low-reverb sound track comforts the audience with the notion that the banquet is indeed meant for them. The choice of reverbless sound thus appears to justify an otherwise suspect urge toward eavesdropping, for it identifies the sound we want to hear as sound that is made for us. While the image is carefully avoiding signs of discursivity in order better to disguise Hollywood's underlying discourse, the sound track overtly adopts the discursive approach of low-reverb sound in order better to draw us into a fabricated narrative.

Hollywood cinema thus established, in the course of the thirties, a careful balance between a "forbidden" image, which we watch as voyeurs, and "sanctioned" dialogue, which appears to be addressed directly to the audience. In terms of movement, a similar complementarity was achieved. The image displaces us incessantly, offering us diverse angles on objects located at radically different distances. Our voyeurism consists precisely in this mobility. Yet we flit about at our own peril, constantly risking dizziness. Just as we are about to lose our balance, however, the sound track holds out its hand, offering continuity of scale as an effective stabilizer. Indeed, if we take the risk of flying about at all, it is certainly in large part because we know that our bodies are anchored by sound, and by the single, continuous experience that it offers. It is thus the sound track that provides a base for visual identification, that authorizes vision and makes it possible. The identity of Hollywood spectators begins with their ability to be auditors.

While cinema's perspective image carries a built-in spectator spot, an interpellative position ready-made for the theatrical spectator, the varied-scale editing practices developed during the silent period move the spectator around at a dizzying pace. Far from inheriting a single place, the spectator must fight to integrate the multiple positions allotted by the film into a single unified home. While this wanderlust is partially cured by a learned, and thus historically grounded, ability to insert shots of various scales into a coherent *Gestalt* of filmic space, it is only with the aid of a continuous-level sound track that the spectator finds a comfortable home. By holding the auditor at a fixed and thus stable distance from all sound sources (except those treated, for previously discussed reasons, through a point-of-audition approach), Hollywood uses the sound track to anchor the body to a single continuous experience. Along with the narrow dynamic range allowed for background music, this process serves to constitute more completely the spectator's unconscious self-identify as *auditor*, thus providing a satisfying and comfortable base from which the eyes can go flitting about, voyeuristically, satisfying our visual desires without compromising our unity and fixity.

A New Model of Technological History

To summarize, we may say that the development of a stable Hollywood audio/visual representational system is best understood according to a tripartite historical model:

1. *Multiple identities derived from pre-existing reality codes.* In its early years, sound cinema endeavored to be all things to all people. It

offered the amplification of public address systems, the performers of vaudeville, the diversity of radio programs, the music of "silent" cinema, the acoustics of the concert hall, and the dialogue consciousness of theater. Never imitating all of these reality codes at once, sound cinema nevertheless gained much of its identity from a clear ability to serve purposes and offer experiences defined by pre-existing representational systems. This period witnessed varied attempts, typically modeled on pre-existing representational systems, to represent space through sound.

2. *Jurisdictional struggle.* For a number of years after Hollywood's conversion to sound, cinema remained the site of an ongoing jurisdictional struggle. To which union would sound projectionists and engineers belong? Where would sound technicians fit in the studio structure? By reference to which model would differences of approach be adjudicated? While many solutions were reached through industry-wide compromise (such as the adoption of the intelligibility-oriented theatrical reality code outlined above), others required open warfare among Hollywood personnel (such as the late twenties/early thirties battle between sound and image technicians[15]) or the deployment of new apparatus (such as the directional microphones developed by RCA in the early thirties[16]). In some arenas, this jurisdictional struggle was over by the end of the twenties (for example, the decision to base music volume on "objective" stable radio or silent film orchestra levels rather than on the volatile and "subjective" levels of parade music or marching bands), while in others it dragged out well into the thirties (for example, the differentiation between the concert hall as the acoustic model for high music reverb levels and the drawing room as the basis for reduced dialogue reverb—even when both types of sound are represented by the image as produced in the same space). During this period, dialogue volume was commonly modeled on theatrical intelligibility, with primary attention devoted not to space but to speech and to the narrative content of which speech is the primary vehicle.

3. *Development of new reality codes based on technological specificity.* Laboring hard to emulate diverse already-existing representational systems, Hollywood directors and sound technicians discovered only very slowly the special capabilities of cinema sound technology. While point-of-audition sound appeared very early in the history of sound cinema, it did not become integrated into a general system of representation until most of Hollywood's jurisdictional problems had been solved. Indeed, curiously, it never received the kind of careful and extended theoretical discussion devoted during the late twenties and early thirties

to the realism versus intelligibility debate. Nevertheless, the mid-thirties were an important crucible for the development of a new audio-visual identity for cinema subjects, dependent both on homogeneous dialogue levels (authorizing, as we have seen, the classic symbiosis of forbidden image and sanctioned sound, as well as the comfortable fit of varying image scale and stable sound scale), and on point-of-audition sound (enforcing sound-based identification with specific characters). Together, the intelligibility system (borrowed early on from theatrical and telephonic precedents) and the point-of-audition system (elaborated during the thirties out of cinema-specific possibilities) constituted a new mode of cinematic unity and a new subject position for the Hollywood audience.

In order to understand Hollywood's conversion to sound we must grasp the many ways in which Hollywood attempted to model cinema sound on other existing uses of sound. If we want to understand Hollywood's standard representational system, however, we must do more than this. We must reckon, as I have tried to do in this essay, with Hollywood's jurisdictional struggles and with the new sound structures developed by Hollywood during the course of the thirties.

Theorists and historians have always concentrated heavily on image space in their attempts to define Hollywood classical narrative. Perhaps the arguments presented in this article will make it impossible in the future to discuss Hollywood's standard mode of representation without appropriate consideration of sound space.

3

Reading, Writing, and Representing Sound

James Lastra

What we hear from the screen is not an image of the sound, but the sound itself which the sound camera has recorded and reproduced again . . . there is no difference in dimension and reality between the original sound and the recorded and reproduced sound.

Béla Balázs
Theory of the Film

. . . in a photograph, the original is as present as it ever was. Sound can be perfectly copied . . . the record reproduces the sound.

Stanley Cavell
The World Viewed

And it is true that in the cinema—as in all talking machines—one does not hear an image of the sounds, but the sounds themselves. Even if the procedure for recording the sounds and playing them back deforms them, they are reproduced and not copied.

J. -L. Baudry
"The Apparatus"

There is no ontological difference between hearing a violin in a concert hall and hearing it on a sound track in a movie theater.

Gerald Mast
Film/Cinema/Movie

Auditory aspects, provided that the recording is well done, undergo no appreciable loss in relation to the corresponding sound in the real world: in principle, nothing distinguishes a gunshot heard in a film from a gunshot heard in the street.

Christian Metz
"Aural Objects"

. . . it is never the literal, original "sound" that is reproduced in the recording, but one perspective on it, a sample, a reading, of it.

Alan Williams
"Is Sound Recording Like a Language?"

Revealing its mandate to represent sound events rather than to reproduce them, recorded sound creates an illusion of presence while constituting a new version of the sound events that actually transpired. . . . [recordings have] only partial correspondence to the original event.

Rick Altman
"The Material Heterogeneity of Recorded Sound"

That a gunshot seems to sound the same in the different acoustic spaces of the street and the inside of the cinema is a deception. . . . . . . familiarity has dulled the capacity to recognize the violence done to sound by recording

Tom Levin
"The Acoustic Dimension"

Original/Copy: Sound Theory?

Despite their obvious disagreement, these two sets of quotations illustrate clearly that within the study of sound recording, especially as it functions in the cinema, the relationship of original sound to represented sound is a (perhaps *the*) fundamental issue. I have separated the groups according to the position each takes in regard to the original versus copy or original versus "repetition" issue. Writers in the first group clearly assume that differences between the original sound and its copy are irrelevant—some, like Metz, on what appear to be functional grounds, others on what could very broadly (and with caution) be called "ontological" grounds.

It is significant that the apparent struggle between these two opposed theories is not carried out solely within the field of film theory or within academic contexts in general, but within the realms of "practice" and "basic research" as well. A surprising amount of self-conscious theorizing is exhibited by sound technicians in and around the film industry with regard to the problems, goals, and status of the representations they produce. In effect, there is a theoretical struggle at work in the debates among technicians over "proper" technique and its relationship to the form of realism they define as constitutive of the film medium. Indeed, this struggle is indicative of the contradictions within the representational system itself. Although it would be foolish to suggest that "theory" plays the same role in the discourse of researchers and technicians as it does in academic discourse, in each it plays an important role, providing an intellectual framework which allows the participants in that discourse to perceive, understand, and evaluate representations as instantiations of some more general function or phenomenon.

Addressing perceived problems in such theories, Tom Levin attempts to perform a "critical analysis" of the sound apparatus, ". . . in order to understand how sound [like the image] . . . is transformed in the process of its reproduction" (1984, 56). Strengthening his objection to theories which ignore these transformations, he maintains that it is the critic's task to reawaken the "capacity to recognize the violence done to sound by recording" (66). On the need for critical analysis I am sure we can all agree. However, the assumption that there exists a sound which is pure and present, which exists unviolated or wholly prior to the "transformations," a firm ground which is more real than its recording, may itself require some critical analysis. Similar assumptions underlie the Williams and Altman quotations. All assume a standard sound which is transformed or violated in recording, which is "digested," "pre-digested," "blunted," "spit out," "neutralized," "conventionalized," and "homogenized" by the technology "itself," and necessarily by *any* application of the technology (Levin 1984, 67). For all three, recording results in an "essential transformation," a certain "partiality," or a "loss" of the original sound. It is the importance of the notions of the "original," and of a single "technology itself" for theories of sound representation which I will address in this essay.

All three theorists stress the materiality of sound events, understanding by the term "sound" the "entire volume of vibrating air" (Williams, 53–4) within the space of production. By positing such a definition, Williams indicates that every sound is spatio-temporally *specific*, or in a broad sense of the term, *historical*. Given that a sound is inseparable from the time and space of its production, each sound becomes an essentially unrepeatable *event*—an event distinguishable from all others.[1] Levin makes the point of specificity most forcefully in the following quotation:

> . . . if a sound is understood as a volume of vibrating air, then assuming for a moment that sound reproduction were absolutely flaw-less . . . such a 'perfect' reproduction of sound waves in a different volume would effectively constitute a *different* sound. (62)

Williams suggests as much when he points to the existence of "good" and "bad" seats in an auditorium from which to hear a concert—the evaluation deriving from a cultural standard of what the event *should* sound like. Thus the point of audition can clearly divide an apparently "single" sound into a potentially limitless number of different events. The same might be said, by extension, of a photograph. The same photograph might offer a very "good seat" on what it represents from the point of view of a spectator interested in formal qualities, and a very "bad seat" from the point of view of someone who needs to identify precisely the object depicted. "Good" and "bad" are obviously defined by what each feels a proper representation *should* look like in each case. Altman develops this view, describing a situation in which auditors situated in different locations have markedly different experiences of the same sonic event, pointing to the difficulties implicit in any theory which defines sonic identity purely on the grounds of physical characteristics or which discusses these characteristics purely from the point of view of sound production. As he says, "The sounds are different, to be sure, but the *name* of the sounds is not" (Altman, "Heterogeneity," in this volume), encouraging us to recognize that there are no "sounds" apart from the goals associated with their perception.

Metz's claim that "nothing distinguishes a gunshot heard in a film from a gunshot heard in the street" (29), evinces a rather different understanding of film sound. Metz is surely aware that the experience of hearing a gunshot in the street hardly resembles hearing one at the movies. In fact, as Altman points out, they resemble each other in one respect only—in name—an important point, since one cannot even say that the *source* of the sounds is the same. Anyone who has ever attempted to post-sync a gunshot for a film can tell you that there are dozens of acceptable substitutes—many of them more acceptable than an actual gunshot. What Metz is apparently indicating is that in a *functional* sense, or in a *narrative* sense, what matters is the ability to identify the source of a sound. In other words, the sound event must be *legible*—it must be recognizable across a series of different contexts as a culturally defined signifying unit. Against the definition of sound as an essentially unrepeatable *event*, Metz describes sound as an eminently repeatable and intelligible *structure*.

For Metz, it would be fair to say that sound, insofar as it is recognized *as* sound, is always already a social/semiotic phenomenon, not a purely sensual or phenomenal one. It is arguable that the very designation "sound" implies not just *any* sonic phenomenon, but one which already bears the traces of its social pertinence. In other words, the simple fact that something can be identified as *a* sound, as a particular *type* of sound, necessarily involves some social or cultural dimension—the very possibility of its having an identity presupposing its social character. Metz rightly comes under fire for reducing the variety of film sound phenomena to a simply narrative function, but he comes very close, in my opinion, to describing the actualities of Hollywood sound representation—a point I will demonstrate at length below.

While it is easy to understand how every sound is unique, Metz's assertion that nothing distinguishes the original from the copy makes sense only in context. A sympathetic reader might take Metz to be saying, "Given this particular form of narrative whose role is strictly defined within a particular economic system, in order to ensure a particular form of narrative pleasure, sound recordings are constructed in order to ensure maximum legibility so that they may take their place as clearly defined elements in a narrative structure. Given these conditions, to the extent that two sounds can be recognized as deriving from the same source and hence, of performing the same function, they are interchangeable."

Levin is far less sanguine, and somewhat more concise about the effects of Metz's formulation:

> That a gunshot *seems* to sound the same in different acoustic spaces . . . is a deception. If differences remain unnoticed, this is a function of a socially constructed auditory practice which emphasizes the similarity of such sounds in order that they be understood (i.e. linked to a common source) by the hearer. (1984, 62)

Avoiding the thorny problem of whether *learned* perceptual habits are automatically "socially constructed" (let's assume that they are), the term "deception" is probably a bit stronger than most of us would care to use. In fact, although Levin's assertion that "phenomenology obfuscates ontology" when dealing with representations seems an adequate rebuke of Metz's assertions about filmic *motion*,[2] Metz's argument about sound is precisely *not* a phenomenological account, but a semiotic or structural one holding that sound in the cinema is a socially produced phenomenon, as illustrated by related claims in the article "Aural Objects."[3] The use of the term "deception" does, however, point to the sort of stakes involved in the original versus copy or original versus repetition relationship, but to keep those stakes high, Levin and Co. must assume an identity and fullness to the original event which is irretrievably lost in the repetition. In almost Platonic terms, there must be a decrease in both truth and being as one moves toward the copy—necessarily assuming some "real" which was, itself, unmediated.

Original Sound: Recording/Representation

By defining sound recordings as partial, transformed, or to some degree *absent* with respect to the original, Williams, Altman and Levin uphold this hierarchy with different degrees of rigidity. Sensing an almost theological undercurrent to Adorno's argument as he adopts it for his own critique, Levin points out that the "analysis is *not* a nostalgic 'fall' story, but a narrative of transformation"(66). Nevertheless, if the original/copy distinction were not one of absolute and irreversible decline, were it simply a "transformation," why would recognition of similarity between original and copy or repetition be a *deception*? And further, if the identity of a sound and its repetition can only be a "function of a socially constructed auditory practice" producing a *deception*, there must be some non-constructed experience, a pure perception, against which to measure this *as* a deception. If there were no such experience, and we were to assert, as I will, that *all* practices of audition are equally constructed, there would be no valid reason for suggesting that one socially constructed practice grounds the discussion and evaluation of all others.

To be sure, there clearly is a *causal* relationship between the "original" sound and its recording, but there is no logical or essential reason why that particular relationship should be the privileged one in theoretical discussion.[4] Given that these theorists stress the absolute uniqueness of every producing and auditing situation, even the "original" event is hopelessly multiple and differentiated in its "singular" occurrence. Since every two seats in an auditorium, for example, can legitimately be distinguished sonically, there can be no absolutely definable original against which to measure the transformations of a recording. Indeed, the original sound can be posited as a theoretical absolute only through the dogmatic assertion that one socially sanctioned experience of the sound, its "best" presentation, is somehow "logically" the essential nature of the sound in question.[5] In fact, the primary ideological effect of sound recording might be creation of the *effect* that there is an "original" independent of its representation.

The endorsement of symphony listening as the *sine qua non* of sound theory has far-reaching consequences because it assumes that all perceptible differences are always equally relevant. When listening to speech, for example, we register differences through categories such as "accent" and "emphasis," but we always *disregard* certain differences between different performances of the same words or sentences. Yes, there are "material" differences between these performances, and yes, it is significant that we do ignore some differences but not others, but these conventions of speech recognition can hardly be called "deceptions" in a meaningful sense. Likewise, I would not say that a friend who had listened at home, on the radio, to a concert I had attended was deceived in believing that he had heard the same concert because I would have to say the same thing to anyone seated in a different section of the theater, either of whom may have had a "better" point of audition that I.[6] Is it not more of a deception to believe that one of us had an experience which legitimately serves as a reference point for the analysis of the others? We simply heard the "same" concert, differently.

The sonic differences to which we attribute significance are always contextually determined, hence no *single* context provides a reference point for theorizing all others. If the recognition of differences between a sound and its representation (or between two different instances of the "same" sound, since Levin offers this possibility explicitly) were simply a matter of recognizing differences pure and simple, there would be no reason to order originals and representations hierarchically. By definition, hearing a recorded sound is just as unique an experience as hearing one "live"—a situation hopelessly complicated by the use of recorded sounds and electronic enhancement in a live performance. Does the insistence on the original not surreptitiously and needlessly introduce a privileging of presence over mediation rather than simply illustrating transformation?

What is at stake, finally, is the importance granted the original sound in any theory of sound representation. In the pieces Levin refers to, Adorno is discussing *symphonies* (a highly conventionalized form of sound practice) and the alterations to musical *structure* wrought by recording and broadcasting over the radio. Adorno defines serious music by its structure—by the specificity of its part/whole relationships, (Adorno 1945; 1941) hence, any acoustic transformation which affects the *perception* of that structure is, by definition, significant. However, crucially, he is nowhere talking about the "technology itself" and what it does to sound in general. One could easily conclude that for Adorno, there is *no* essential transformation of *popular* music through recording since "loss of tone colour and intensity, a reduction of the overtone series, a compression of the dynamic range, an overemphasis on melody, a de-emphasis on accompaniment, an exaggeration of contrasts, etc."[7] are *already* structurally a part of popular music. These attributes may, in fact, be enhanced by recording.

Sound recording is important to Adorno when, through transformation, technology impedes both the presentation and the perception conventionally felt to be appropriate to a particular social or cultural sound practice—the symphony. And he seems very right. He does not, however, say that this is only "technology's" fault. I feel no hesitation in suggesting that Adorno would have been just as concerned had a new fad in architecture produced *concert halls* which caused similar transformations of the music. In fact, listening from the lobby of a hall accomplishes many of these same transformations. I'm certain that Adorno would find the lobby as poor a point of audition as the individual living room. The question, for Adorno, is not one of "original versus copy." A poor original is no better for him than a copy if it similarly distorts the work. It is not a question of technological mediation, but of degenerative mediation, whatever the source.

Adorno is concerned with the perceptibility of pertinent elements, given the dictates of a particular culturally defined form—the network of interlocking cultural practices that shapes our relationship to the staging, presentation, perception, categorization, and evaluation of a particular set of sounds, and therefore determines which elements are *pertinent* to this particular use. However, the desire, in music listening, for the most delicate of differences to be audible is not a general model for how we deal with sounds. Like all forms of audition, music listening ignores certain features of a sonic event in favor of others. In addition, serious music is normally presented in locations designed specifically to hide certain kinds of imperfections and to enhance the overall quality, further complicating the situation. Is lush tone color truly a characteristic of the "music" of the romantic period, or is that a property of the concert halls constructed to produce or enhance this effect? Where is the "original" here?

These problems begin to disappear, however, when we simply recognize that sound recording is better thought of as sound *representation* than as sound *reproduction*. Although the recording of serious music tends toward the latter, it is not difficult to see that reproduction is simply a special case of representation, with no essential priority. The relationship of copy to original is only one possible concern we could have about a representation (albeit a rather obvious one) and is not in all cases the most important relationship a representation can have to what it represents.

All recordings do transform, in some measurable way, the sounds they represent, but they do not always transform them to the same degree or in the same way. In fact, in certain situations the resultant transformations might actually be a benefit, even for music. It seems arguable that Adorno might even *praise* recordings if, once certain technical failures had been lessened, they facilitated a new, more analytical appreciation of the classics. I can imagine that given his interest in critical analysis and in pedagogy, he might consider a recording superior to a concert situation because it isolates and makes available for repeated listening what would otherwise be a fleeting experience. At several points he does mention the transformations of listening in a generally negative way, but I feel fairly certain that he would not necessarily be opposed to them. They need not entirely serve any single ideological master.[8]

So it should be clear that absolute fidelity to the "original" sound is only one obvious, possible goal for representing sound. Now, I take it for granted that people in a movie theater are never *actually* fooled that they are present at an "original" sound event when it comes over a loudspeaker—as much an institutional effect of going to the movies as it is a matter of the technological factors of sound recording. The fact that filmgoers take a recording of a gunshot to function *within a film* as a gunshot is no more or less a deception than taking a flat in a theater for the rear wall of a room. It is, as Levin says, a "socially constructed auditory practice" suited to a particular cultural form which is supported by a whole network of other socially constructed practices (like facing the stage, or not talking during a performance). Altman and Williams have taught us to hear how *all* sound recordings are *staged* representations (i.e. socially constructed). For the moment, then, let us simply ask whether the decision to perform an orchestral work in an auditorium, and the ability to hear differences from performance to performance, are somehow *not* socially constructed auditory practices, or in other words, *conventions*? Is the performance of a musical piece in an auditorium not itself a *mise-en-scène* of sound possessing each and every attribute that is used to differentiate the reproduction from the "original"? Ultimately I will show that the attributes claimed to be indicative of the "copied" sound are, in fact, structural necessities of *any* staging of a sound, even an "original" sound, and in fact are necessary prerequisites for the identification of any sound as being an "original." All sounds, recorded or live, are equally "inscribed."

The Technology "Itself"

The force of Levin's critique derives from his assertion that, despite effective studies of the uses of technologies and the ideologies implicit in these uses, what still remains to be done is an analysis of the transformations produced through the technology "itself"—that is, independent of any particular use of it. In order to make this claim, Levin must assume the existence of *"the technology of sound itself"* (1984, 66) as an object which can be theoretically and practically abstracted from the network of relations and practices which situate it. It is significant, and perhaps symptomatic, that he defines "technology" as an object, rather than as a set of cultural and social *practices*, as I tend to do.[9] Through a discussion of Heidegger, Levin claims that the cinematic apparatus is part of the larger process of objectifying through the structure of representation (*Vorstellung*) which Heidegger sees as characteristic of modernity. However, I do not believe that Heidegger's texts so easily support the conclusion that it is the *device*, the technical object *itself* that frames the world in an objectifying manner. Although I would agree with Levin that "irrespective of the particular content of the image, the photograph is a representation already interpreted, selected and ideologically 'framed' by its very technology" (65), this does not mean that at every historical moment and in every historical use the "very technology" is "the same."[10]

A Japanese interlocutor uses Heidegger's own example of a non-Western alternative, *Rashomon*, to claim that even here, "the Japanese world" has been "especially framed for photography" (Heidegger 1971). Framed *for photography* and not *by* the camera. Levin seems correct in assuming that, as a product of the dominant structure of representation throughout

Western culture, the camera will no doubt be formed to its purposes, but it is not entirely defined by them, nor is it ever entirely self-defining.

The very term "photography" implies a representational image, of an object, in focus, with a more or less rectangular shape. Yet numerous existing photographs—defined as images made on light-sensitive paper (and let's even assume, with a camera) don't fit this "normal" understanding of the term "photography." Would the technology "itself" objectify the Japanese world if, for some reason, the camera never showed the actions pertinent to the narrative? If the camera strayed toward the crew? If the film were exposed so that only very vague shadows were produced? Heidegger is here claiming that the entire process of staging a narrative with actors for a camera, destined for a large audience, objectifies the world by making it subservient to the demands of a particular representational structure inappropriate to it. What this entire industrial *mode* of production (the photography industry as well as Hollywood International) requires is the production of the world as object for consumption in a form (the photograph) which is universalizing and trivializing in the same measure.

A symptom of the generalized technicity typical of modernity, photography "frames" reality as entirely commensurate to human understanding and as manipulable to human need. In the vocabulary of Heidegger's technology essay, it constitutes the world as "standing reserve." Technology, therefore, does not "itself" enframe objects, because it, too, is something of an expression of the dominant historical configuration he refers to as *Ge-stell*, a positing of the world which frames it as available for human purposes. Any relationship (not only those mediated by a technological instrument) which seeks such mastery of the world is indicative of technicity. It is the historical configuration of reason which dictates that the technology be used in a particular way.

In the case of photography (and by extension, sound recording) the production of a representational image understood as "a systematic structure, a model or formation (*Gebild*) devised by man serv[ing] to explain that which it represents,"[11] seems to embody the "frame-up" that Levin decries. Thus understood, the term "photography" refers not simply to a device, but to an entire system of relating to the world as object-commensurate-to-man, implying a vast network of practices surrounding the use of the device in order to produce images which represent, and explain through representing.

When we say "photography" we refer to just such a network of interrelated practices whose parameters are defined by standards such as "professionalism," and so forth. Because of this fact, when Levin refers to a recording of a symphony I can assume that such a recording was made with microphones directed at the orchestra rather than at the audience, from a distance, rather than from the bell of the third trumpet, and in a relatively unobstructed space, rather than from under a chair in the last row of the balcony. Much of the work of "representing" a sound occurs prior to, or independent of (but compatible with) the technology which does the representing.[12]

Levin asserts, in response, that "it is not enough to consider a variety of sound practices because no matter how radical and innovative they may be, they are ultimately *put in an apparatus* which spits them out again in a digested, blunted, and conventionalized form" (1984, 67, my emphasis). I hope I have illustrated, however, that there is no identifiable "thing" which could be "put in" an apparatus, because there is no thing-to-be-represented outside of the goals of the very act of representing. Any act of representing, even by means of technology, arranges its object before it in such a way as to make it representable. So, in representing music, you represent not just "music," but music presented in such a way that it can be represented "accurately" (to choose one standard). The concert hall itself is an apparatus which "frames" music in a certain way, facilitating the appreciation of its defining features and helping to define its "essence." The original is "formed" by the hall apparatus, and this forming is an essential first step in presenting the object ("music") *for representation.* The act of representation, by selecting only certain objects or objects in a certain form, or from a certain point of view, *pre-structures* its objects *for the device.*

Original/Copy: Sound Practice?

I have effectively polarized the sound theorists cited at the outset according to the general schema event versus structure, original versus copy, and unique versus conventional. By turning to an early, transition era debate over the representation of film sound space I believe we can clarify the conflict a little. From the point of view of the studios, the basic technical and aesthetic task of a film sound system was to record and reproduce precisely synchronized, intelligible speech and music in a form which could be mass-produced. Despite the fact that the majority of early Vitaphone films were based on the synchronous recording of *music* (and that Warners may have initially had no plans to make "all-talking" features), all sounds were functionally subordinate to speech in an important sense[13] or were treated as species of a more general, speechlike situation, the most important aspects of a sound being its origin, identity, and comprehensibility.[14] The essential problem was to produce the effect of appropriate and recognizable sounds emanating from the objects on the screen, as if the sounds were, like the voice, a property of the depicted object.[15] However, the model of realistic representation which guided research and the goals of practice (at least as it was given expression in various technical journals) stressed absolute fidelity as the ultimate goal. In effect, these two implicit models of the sound apparatus are in conflict with one another on many fronts, and suggest that arguments about "the" apparatus outside of a historically limited network of practices is an unjustified simplification and one which will lead us to make precipitous claims about "its" essential nature. There is always a dialectical relationship at work between a technology and the particular representational mode within which it functions.[16]

Two models of sound recording dominated, and to a remarkable degree continue to dominate thinking about sound representation. Very broadly, these could be called the "fidelity" model and the "telephone" model. The former stresses the importance of representing a spatio-temporally specific production of sound, the latter stresses intelligibility or legibility at the expense of specificity, if necessary. A recording of an orchestra, for example, tries to preserve the cavernous space within which the sounds were produced, while a telephone, being designed with a very different social function in mind, would never be suitable for this. However, a "fidelity" recording could very easily represent one of the "worst" seats in the house from which to experience a sound event such as a concert, while still remaining "faithful" or specific. A telephone, in contrast, while sacrificing specificity, renders speech rather clearly. For each model, the very conception of what a sound "is" differs in important ways. The "fidelity" approach assumes that all aspects of the sound event are inherently significant, including long or short reverb times, ratios of direct to reflected sound, or even certain peculiarities of performance or space. The "telephonic" approach, not literally limited to telephones and voices, assumes that sound is internally hierarchized—some aspects are essential while others are not. As with our theorists, the relevant terms of comparison are uniqueness versus recognizability, or event versus structure.

Within the classical Hollywood style, there exist types of sound representations that correspond to both the "telephonic" and "fidelity" modes. Schematically, dialogue recording tends almost uniformly, from the early thirties on, to minimize the amount of reverberation, background noise, and speech idiosyncracies, as it simultaneously maximizes the "directness" or "frontality" of recording, and the intelligibility of the dialogue.[17] Even when a speaker appears to turn away, a high level of direct sound often implies that he or she is still speaking "to" the auditor, because speech is understood not simply as an abstract sound, but as a sound with a specific function—a narrative function.[18] This form of recording differs markedly from what Rick Altman has dubbed point-of-audition (POA) sound.

POA sound (like the POV shot) represents the experience of hearing within the diegesis, normally the hearing of a character. Sometimes this is indicated by muffling sounds, as if hearing them through a wall, by including a Doppler effect to indicate the rapid passage of a sound source, by an increase or decrease in volume indicating the approach or retreat of the source, or perhaps by giving a clear sense of the acoustics specific to a particular location. All of these different phenomena can be assimilated under the rubric of what Altman designates "spatial signature"—those indicators of the spatial and temporal specificity of sound production and reception which characterize any recording as unique. It is quite significant that in both the case of the POV shot and the POA sound, a representation of a space taken to be "real" within the diegesis is at stake.

I would suggest that in Hollywood films visually represented space, when not explicitly marked as a POV shot, is primarily a marker of the narrative or enunciative level of the presentation. In other words, its dimension, angle, framing and so on are not understood as someone's actual vision (narrator or character), but as a means of narrative emphasis. Unlike the POV shot, which is marked as a unique perception in a specific, diegetically real space, a typical shot can usually be replaced by another shot representing a noticeably different view of the space—its index of substitutability is much higher since it presents *narratively* important information rather than *perceptually* specific information. It is indicative, however, that sound technicians who call for perceptual fidelity in sound and image representation seem to employ an implicit "invisible witness" model of cinematic narrative. Such a heuristic seems obviously to encourage one to think of filmmaking as a stringing together of unique perceptions, as I will attempt to show below.[19]

Now, while POA sound is not *equivalent* to sound bearing a spatial signature (since all recordings include "signature" in one way or another) it is one clear instance wherein the spatial characteristics of sound are "allowed" to manifest themselves (often, significantly, for *narrative* purposes). In general, close frontal miking of actors, which minimizes reflected and indirect sound, became the norm for dialogue since, as one researcher put it, "In no case did an increase in reverberation cause an increase in articulation [intelligibility]" (Steinberg, 132). Or as another phrased a related observation, "The quality of a recording is effectively independent of the reverberant characteristics of the set if the microphone is within approximately three feet of the speaker" (Hunt, 482). Together, the two quotations indicate that a "good" recording could be associated with recognizable speech sounds, and dissociated from any strict sense of fidelity.[20] In related studies, other researchers sought to quantify "Good Voice Quality,"[21] or intelligibility ("articulation"), extending their (historical) standards of correctness through the apparatuses of science, bringing them to bear directly on the voices and bodily techniques of performers.[22] Other researchers from the period asserted that "naturalness" seemed to be equated with the presence of reflected sound, while "articulation" was associated with direct sound (Hunt, 499). In other words, indications of spatial specificity are related implicitly to certain forms of *unintelligibility*, or at least the possibility that fidelity and intelligibility are not necessarily related. Although my argument here focuses heavily on speech, I would suggest that terms such as "intelligibility" have analogs in the case of sound effects as well, where something like "recognizability" or "identifiability" performs roughly the same function—that of comprehension.[23] A recording with a high degree of reflected sound, or some other indicator of spatial signature, is linked to sound considered as an *event*, while closely-miked sound, with a relatively "contextless" spatial signature, is linked to sound considered as an intelligible *structure*—as a signifying element with a larger structure.

According to Carl Dreher there need not be any extreme conflict between the two, however:

> Since the reproduction of sound is an artificial process, it is necessary to use artificial devices in order to obtain the most desirable effects. For example, it is normal procedure to reproduce dialog at a level higher than the original performance. This may entail a compromise between intelligibility and strict fidelity . . . (Dreher 1931, 756)

What is clearly at stake is not the sounds "themselves" but the signs of those sounds—even in the case of supposedly strictly accurate recordings. Nevertheless, the problem of strict fidelity arises again and again in other contexts. John L. Cass, for example, complains that the "illusion" is destroyed when the spectator becomes aware that despite changes in shot scale, the recordist has maintained "close-up" sound, in order to ensure intelligibility. Since "the resultant blend of sound may not be said to represent any given point of audition" the spectator is left feeling that he is hearing "sound which would be heard by a man with five or six very long ears, said ears extending in various directions" (Cass, 325). Here Cass is, of course, assuming that film narration works by the "invisible observer" method. However, narration in film, as Bordwell tirelessly points out, does *not* need the supposition of a flesh and blood perceiver to perceive every element *for* us (Bordwell 1985b, 3–12, 99–113). "Real" space is simply not an issue for most images on the screen—their scale and angle are functions of narrative emphasis, not of more or less precise perception.

Speaking/Signing

In theorizing cinema sound, Altman and Williams generally attend to the auditing or recording as opposed to the production of sound, yet in each there nevertheless remains a certain privileging of sound *production*. By stressing the unique character of every sound event, its essential unrepeatability, we can better understand the phenomena of sound representation and, as Levin quite rightly points out, better specify exactly what material alterations occur in a *particular* representation of a sound, but we are simultaneously encouraged to conceive of sound along the model of speech—as the effect of a singular act and intention, the reception of which is guided by the desire for absolute presence of the "original." What we want, it seems, is not simply to understand or to recognize this speech but to touch what is "behind" the sounds—presumably something which, unsullied by transformation into the common coin of language, is more real. Understood in this way, any recording or writing of this speech disrupts its presence.

Despite recognizing a conflict between the "naturalness" and "intelligibility" of a sound recording, technicians argued repeatedly over the form of "authenticity" appropriate to sound representations. Such conflicts are symptoms of historically changing notions of representational "reference," and the resultant struggles had important effects on representational form, technical practice, and even devices. Indeed, in the debates over what form of "authenticity" representations *should* have, we indirectly witness the struggles of professionalization, and the emergence of a new "science."

Altman has argued that new realisms can emerge only in relation to existing models of reality and of representation (1984). A relationship of "quotation" obtains between an existing realistic mode of representation and an emergent one. Photography, for example "quoted" enough of the codes of painting and other pictorial arts that, while it appeared different, it nevertheless "counted" as a realistic representation of conforming to existing codes of recognition and so on, even as it transformed them. From this point of view it is easy to understand how there can never be any entirely "new" forms of representation—there are simply far too many constraints (in the form of codes of recognition, practices of everyday life based on representations, entrenched ways of understanding representations and so on) mitigating against its acceptance. The relationships of a new form to existing ones allows us to specify historically how and why some new form emerged, noting how it manifests its genuinely novel attributes while still conforming to the established cultural category of "representational image." Thus, the process becomes one of the regulated appearance of certain forms of knowledge *about* the technology rather than the simple emergence of a radically new, but self-defining form.

In the case of the sound film, then, what would be the relevant reality codes to which a recording (and a synchronized print) would have to correspond? Although technicians repeatedly make appeals to the body of the spectator and to real perception, this is surely not the only, or even the primary standard of realism. The theater, telephony, radio, and public address are all potential models with strong relationships to film sound, but perhaps the most important codes for sound come from *silent* cinema. Silent cinema had already established ways of dealing with problems of uniqueness versus intelligibility, with sound "space," and with sound source, and had already defined the roles "speech" should fulfill in a film.

Bordwell has drawn our attention to how aesthetic and technical norms impinge on all Hollywood practice, by shaping the paradigmatic substitutability of various techniques in any particular film. Techniques which perform the same, or nearly the same function in a film are termed "functional equivalents" (Bordwell 1985a, 4–6). So, with Bordwell's argument in mind, we might ask what roles were preordained for sound even prior to its possibility as a synchronized effect. Despite contemporary claims about how the revolutionary technology was to change "everything," sound could never have been adopted if it did not fulfill or was not capable of fulfilling some function already deemed important by Hollywood standards—the short-lived effect of novelty is never a convincing enough argument for people involved in a multimillion dollar business. As Bell technician Harvey Fletcher pointed out in 1929, from the very start, even basic research into sound recording and reproduction was guided by some very industrially determined standards. Although apparently researching "sound" in general, Fletcher makes it clear that even fundamental research worked under the supposition that "sound" was always understood as having a very specific role to play as a carrier of information.[24] Thus, the reproduction of speech was implicitly (and often explicitly) guided by the preordained role of speech as, above all, an *intelligible* conveyor of information. Although specific social *uses* of sound obviously must serve as a starting point for the development of any sound technology and its technical standards, the particular sound forms and uses chosen are nevertheless extremely important. In this case, they meshed well with Hollywood needs.

The absence of a practical system of amplification for the music and sound effects which accompanied silent films encouraged (or required) architects to design theaters whose acoustics were rich in reflected sound and had extended reverb times (long decay). This undoubtedly added to the richness of the music, but, as we all know, such spaces can render speech almost unintelligible. The problem is compounded if a *recording* of speech carries a strong spatial signature of its own. The addition or multiplication of signatures upon what we would normally think of as a single sound not only confuses the *sense* of the sound, but by marking the reproduced sound audibly with the spatio-temporal characteristics of the conditions of reproduction, the "uniqueness" of the original sound *production* is partially eclipsed by its *re*production, splitting the "origin" of the sound (Hopper, Downey, MacNair, Knudsen). In the sound film, of course, origin is largely guaranteed by synchronization. Bordwell and Thompson, usually the most careful of scholars in matters such as these, nevertheless list "fidelity" (of sound to source) as one of the basic categories of film sound (1990, chapter 8). Decades of tin-sheet thunder and coconut shell hooves, however, prove that fidelity to source is not a *property* of film sound, but an *effect* of synchronization. A gun firing on the screen accompanied by any brief, sudden, explosive sound *produces* the effect of source, it doesn't require it as a precondition. Every judgment of "fidelity," however, necessarily requires the predication of a source for the sound, although even the "correct" sound, if out of synchronization, can destroy the very grounds of the fidelity judgment.

In the silent film, however, the situation was different. An intertitle is affected neither by the space of production nor by the space of reproduction. As a form of *writing*, it is (almost) by definition *legible*. For any literate audience member, then, dialogue is 100% intelligible. However, as a form of writing, intertitles introduce another series of dilemmas. Primary among these is their relative separation from their sources. The voice, as writing, is separated spatially and temporally from its putative origin—the moving lips on the screen. This formulation echoes one of the classical ways of distinguishing writing from speech. Aside from the loss of certainty as to source, though, several other breaks intervene. For example, intertitles cannot easily reproduce the "grain" of the voice, regional accents, differences in pronunciation, tone of voice, rhythms of speech, inflection, and so on—all the sorts of indicators we normally use to identify speech as a unique discursive and phenomenal event.

Mary Ann Doane sees the potential break of voice from body as the scandal that both silent and sound films must avoid (Doane 1980b). To "make up for" the "lacks" of the intertitle, the actors adopt exaggerated gestures and facial grimaces, making visible the originally "audible." In a similar fashion, changes in typeface, use of italics, quotation marks, exclamation points, deviant syntax (all of which appear, for example, in *Wings* or *Old San Francisco*, to name just two) as well as the bracketing of intertitles by shots of the same pair of moving lips, served to assign a source to an utterance and to make the utterance as expressive of the character's emotional state as possible. In each case, the characteristics which mark the utterances as unique are indicated by making them visible, or more exactly, legible. Those aspects of a sound which mark it as authentic are never simply self-evident "attributes" of that sound. Only their inscription within a system allowing or requiring them to become perceptible gives them a semiotic import within that system. Thus, the supposed unique attributes of an original sound become significant and, to a certain degree, perceptible as such only through their constitution as *signs*—precisely that which is *not* unique. The potential "scandal" of writing is overcome by . . . more writing. The *iterability* characteristic of writing, which marks writing as *repeatable*, as quotable or citable in an infinite number of contexts, and thus as non-self-identical,[25] is traditionally seen as disrupting the presence or plenitude of speech. (In fact, it is the intertitle's susceptibility to being repeated without alteration in different contexts that is specifically used to mark the protagonist's speech to his several sexual conquests as inauthentic in *Don Juan*, one of the first Vitaphone films.) As I have sketchily pointed out, however, it is writing (as legible mark) which "comes to the rescue" to ensure the uniqueness or unrepeatability of the speech event. As in the sound film, sound "fidelity" is an *effect* of inscription. Ultimately, the intertitle's status as writing is characteristic of sound recording in general and may extend to the "original" events as well.

The task, then, is to illustrate how these silent film techniques weigh on early film practices and then, later, on the recording process, or the inscription of traces in general. As I noted earlier, conflicts over representing sound space were settled *de facto* by the adoption of the standard of close-miking and a certain "frontality." This "solution" ran against a trend in microphone research, however, which sought to allow more and more distant miking to simulate hearing more closely (Altman 1985b). The type of sound recording which results is relatively "contextless" or spaceless—that is, it is a sound whose "quality," to repeat a technician cited earlier, "is effectively independent of the reverberant characteristics of the set" (Hunt, 482). In other words, such sound is spatio-temporally *unspecific* and therefore in some sense more like writing than like speech.

Effectively, this makes of a specific speech, or more generally, sound event, a species of quotation—a transcription removed from its context. A sound thus recorded could be infinitely repeated throughout the film with different images regardless of the space within which the supposed origin is situated, just as the same title card could be reused in *Don Juan*. Such a recording, by stressing the recognizability of the sound outside of a determinate context, falls on the side of writing rather than that of speech, indicating that an analysis of the speech/writing opposition might shed some light on the phenomena of film sound.

If we consider everyday writing situations where the uniqueness of the utterance or simply its source is an issue, there are common ways in which we overcome the iterability of writing and give it the status not of a repetition, but of an original event. How do we make writing like speech? By appending a signature. I'm suggesting that it is not *simply* an accident that markers of a sound's uniqueness have been named its spatial signature. Your name may be written by anyone, typed, photocopied, repeated endlessly, and it will still refer to you. Yet, although typing your name at the bottom of a contract will identify you, will allow your identity to be recognized, it does not indicate your intention to uphold the contract. The contract will never be enacted, will never "happen." Only by attaching your inimitable signature can you indicate your intention, and effectively carry out your act of will. In its purest sense, the signature is an embodiment of writing as a unique event—of writing as speech.

In the difference between the name and the signature we can read the difference between the aural object and the aural event, the sound as recognizable across contexts, as iterable, and the sound as event, as unrepeatable. But it is the uniqueness of the original sound, its historical happening, and this singular event's relation to its representation (its repetition) that needs to be analyzed. The signature, in order to function as a signature, requires the notion of a fully present intention. The idiosyncrasies of the mark are what stamp this form of writing as historical, as happening once and happening at that time specifically. Yet no signature could function if it were not, as Derrida has pointed out *vis-à-vis* Austin, something like a citation (Derrida 1982). Your "unique" signature is only valid through its comparison with some (obviously repeatable) model—it functions as unique only through its being verified as a copy. Signatures, which undoubtedly "work" every day as embodiments of unique intentions, are nevertheless marked already and always by a certain absence, or in other words, the event of the unique signature is marked already by repetition.

The "original" sound event, of which the recording is a "sample," a "reading," "a partial correspondence," functions in roughly the same manner. All theories of sound recording under discussion here characterize the recording as a degraded form of an original event whose fullness can never be captured (ignoring, of course, that *any* experience of a sound is inevitably partial). The recorded sound may be fully recognizable and possess a remarkable degree of fidelity, but it is always a repetition. It is as if, happening later than the original, the repetition has worn away some, weathered a little. Yet is it not through this "wearing away," this non-originality, that we are able to imagine an original? Is it *ever* possible to be present at the original event, fully? Indeed, Williams, Altman, and Levin all tell us from the outset that this is impossible by definition. In fact, even if a sound is never repeated, appears unique, is it not always through the inevitable reference to the horizon of its recognizability *as* unique, marked by the possibility of repetition, by iterability, by a certain form of absence? Isn't Levin's original sound, exemplified by the orchestral concert, *itself* just as firmly inscribed in what he calls "socially constructed auditory practices?" Like an intertitle, or like POA sound, isn't the "originality" or the unique source of the sound an effect, constructed by the emergence or inscription of differential, signifying marks? Is this not already marked by conventionality? Isn't the performance of the concert in this hall, today, in *some sense* a citation?

The "Originality" Effect

The character of this absence is what is finally at stake. It seems as if the non-presence, the general iterability of the sound is a negative characteristic, a barrier to uniqueness, or to fullness. At its most extreme, it seems to deny that specific events "happen" in a historical sense. This, however, is not the case at all. Although the repeatability of a signature seems to indicate that all signatures are somehow *lacking*, it is this absence which is the positive condition of their functioning. Even a signature which appears never to have been reproduced has the possibility of repetition inscribed in it. In essence, for something to be original, its repetition must be recognized as conforming in some way to the original—or the original must possess a certain ideality which is capable of remaining recognizable in various contexts. Ideality then, would *depend* on repetition, would be, in a sense an *effect* of repetition rather than a precondition for repetition (Derrida 1989). Understood in this way, the repetition, insofar as it is recognized *as* a repetition, creates the original. The non-uniqueness or non-presence of the event marks both the possibility of and limitation of ideality.

But let's return to sound for a moment. At an "original" sound event we all recognize that each auditor gets a slightly different sense of the sound, depending on his or her location and the directedness of his or her hearing. But doesn't this recognition itself imply that there is no strictly definable "original" event? That every hearing is in some way absent? In the case of speech, for example, we ignore certain aspects of the event because our hearing is directed toward certain ends, namely the recognition of speech sounds. The directedness of perception is often institutionally and conventionally determined, hence the possibility of a telephone's being engineered to have a poor frequency response. The "wear and tear" on the original sound is compensated for by the pay-off of a culturally and institutionally relevant form of comprehension. We don't think of the sound as absent because the meaning is present. And so it is for most sounds. To paraphrase Ernst Gombrich, there is no "Innocent Ear." There is never a fullness to perception that is somehow "lost" by focusing on a portion of the event, by using the event for certain purposes, or simply by perceiving with some particular goal, say understanding, in mind.

At the risk of reiterating what may now be obvious, I ask you to consider the following, in this regard. Since every sound is defined by the specifics of the time and space of its production and reception, it would be logically impossible to define what any sound "is" outside of a particular manifestation. There is no definition of what a "violin 440 A" is except as an abstraction from particular occurrences—none of which will be adequately covered by this abstraction. Likewise, the spaces and times of production and the types of sounds produced there are, to a large extent, defined by some particular social form of sound production and reception. It seems obvious that what we perceive in any given situation is determined by the "goals" implicit in that act of listening. What counts as a significant element changes as we change our frame. When listening to a friend tell a story, the emphasis is on the comprehension of words, but were we concerned with our friend's health we might pay more attention to the quality of her voice—is it strained, unusually hoarse, tired? Likewise, a recording of a symphony may very well be inadequate for appreciating the sonic complexity to its fullest, but the same recording could function perfectly well if all that were required were the identification of, say, the flute's melody in the first movement, or the recognition of a musical "quotation" from another piece. The point in these cases, which seem to me fully "legitimate" ways of listening, is recognition and association—not musical appreciation *per se*.

Nevertheless, the sense that there is something more primordial than the trace persists. There is nothing particularly striking about this. The historical happening of the sound event, its spatio-temporal specificity, always appears to escape our apprehension. Whether we're in an auditorium, or listening to a relatively contextless, closely-miked recording, or to one which stresses the peculiarities of the room, the event, in its fullness, seems to escape. What is the "real" of which these are the traces?

Perhaps it is in the non-presence of the repetition, of the wearing away of the original surfaces, the decaying remains, that we recognize the possibility of the event itself. Out of the trace, then, is born history . . . or the *possibility* of history. The recognition of absence by which we classify representations *as* representations, recordings *as* recordings is a positive condition of possibility rather than a fault. If we recognize that all realities are constructed realities, this need not open us to the abyss of absolute indeterminacy or relativism. These "absolutes" are just as unattainable as absolute presence. We do, however, open up the possibility of explaining specific effects of "authenticity," or of "immediacy" precisely *as* effects of a general possibility of "writing," and we can relinquish misty assumptions of the ineffable, unattainable, but for some reason all-defining original. We need not relinquish the original, the real, or the authentic, but we must recognize that these experiences and values, too, are products of historically defined conditions, and that their emergence, like the emergence of representations of those phenomena, follows certain rules. We may well ask, then, to what is attributed or denied these qualities of "originality" and "authenticity," and *in whose interests*? Representational reference is finally, as it is in the writing of history, a question of right and law, a question of morality, and a question of social ethics.

What remains is to develop a theory of representation which does not insist on a loss of being between original and copy, a theory which does not seek to define the referential effects of each and every representation by comparison with some logically unattainable ideal, and a theory which avoids falling into any naive sense of equivalence between "original" and representation. Paradoxically, it is to Stanley Cavell's quotation about photography that we return to find an ironic statement of this. By repeating Cavell out of context, perhaps we can create a new intention for his statement. "In the sound recording the original is still as present as it ever was," which is to say, just as absent.

4

"She Sang Live, But The Microphone Was Turned Off:" The Live, the Recorded and the *Subject* of Representation.[1]

Steve Wurtzler

Several weeks after Whitney Houston's teary-eyed wartime rendition of "The Star Spangled Banner" at the 1991 Super Bowl, newspaper accounts revealed that her vocals actually were recorded several days prior to the game.

> Spectators in Tampa heard that taped version, while TV viewers heard the tape combined with Whitney's live vocals, said Super Bowl sound engineer Larry Estrin.
> The technique is "designed to provide the audience with the finest possible performance," Estrin said.
> Dan Klores, a spokesman for Houston, said "This is not a Milli Vanilli thing."
> "She sang live, but the microphone was turned off," Klores explained. "It was a technical decision, partially based on the noise factor. This is standard procedure at these events" (*Daily Iowan* 3/1/91, 2B).

In struggling to reframe the public reaction to this "revelation," the voices from Houston's camp introduce a number of theoretical concerns relevant to an investigation of representational technologies and their ability to construct or to "hail" social subjects. The rhetorical attempt at "spin control" foregrounds the roles played by "technical decisions" and "standard procedures" (representational practices and conventions) in defining and reinforcing the standards by which "the finest possible performance" is judged. It further foregrounds the role of representational practices and technologies (television, public address, sound recording and mixing, and so on) in positing events that exist prior to their representation and in attempting to fix the relationship between spectator-auditors and those events. Despite Klores's insistence to the contrary, Houston's performance was indeed a "Milli Vanilli thing." Like the earlier scandal (when it was discovered that a rock duo had performed songs which were in fact recordings made by others) it demonstrates the collapse of the discursively produced categories of live and recorded.

All representations posit an absent original event whether such events are understood as fictional (*Blade Runner*) or "real" (Coltrane at the Village Vanguard). Representational practices and the discourses surrounding them also strive to specify a relationship between consumers and such posited events. Thus, any representation can be thought to consist of the moment or act of representing, the absent event posited by the representation, and a consumer's encounter with both. The audiophile enjoys a fetishistic relationship to the means of representing, the means of reproduction, as the desire for ever greater fidelity hinges on the perception of an increased access to an original performance event. In narrative cinema, the consumer's encounter with a film is such that dominant aesthetic practices and conventions of film reception similarly strive to elide the act of representing (including the theatrical space) so as to foreground the event posited by the representation (the diegesis).

In a recent article, Paul Théberge suggests that the development and institutionalized use of multi-track recording in popular music might be considered in terms of a transition from an initial period of representation conceived of as the *documentary* recording of a preexisting event to representation as the *construction* of that event. Théberge's study of the rationalization of popular music production provides a useful point of departure for a larger consideration of the relationship between representational practices, the events they posit, and their consumers. A similar trajectory might historically be traced in a variety of representational technologies (including radio, television, and cinema). In each case, however, it is likely that representational practices at any given moment actually involve the coexistence of both the documentation and construction of an original event. At issue is less a series of rigid stages in an evolutionary development than the recognition that within a given signifying practice the relationship between representational practices and the events they posit is neither synchronically nor diachronically constant.

Whitney Houston's performance at Tampa Stadium and other contemporary representational technologies and strategies (including virtual reality and other computer imaging methods, sampling, and lip syncing) point to a third conception of representation that may be added to Théberge's model. In these instances representation is conceived of as the complete dismantling of the notion of an original event. In such practices, copies are produced for which no original exists. Under such circumstances, the binary opposition live/recorded takes on a new importance, in that the live comes to stand for a category of authenticity completely outside representation. The often-tenuous maintenance of this binary opposition allows the notion of fidelity to an original event, or even the existence of an original event at all, to be discursively maintained. In writing about contemporary pop music, Steve Connor notes:

> What is striking is the way in which the metaphysical model of original and copy survives these inversions of priority. The "live" should be seen as a strategic category of the semiotic, even though its function *within* semiotic systems is to suggest that which lies authentically behind the distorting and falsifying operations of signification. The live is always "produced" as an artificial category of immediacy, and is always therefore a quotation of itself; never the live, always the "live." Paradoxically, this desire for the original and the authentic exists alongside the recognition that there never can be such a thing, at least in contemporary rock music (Connor 134).

As socially and historically produced, the categories of the live and the recorded are defined in a mutually exclusive relationship, in that a notion of the live is premised on the absence of recording and the defining fact of the recorded is the absence of the live. Rather than the "death of the aura" at the hands of mechanical or electronic reproducibility, the recorded reinstates the "aura" in commodity form accessible only within those events socially constructed as fully live.

The categories live and recorded can be usefully conceptualized in relation to their spectator-auditors (consumers). The live is characterized by the spatial co-presence and temporal simultaneity of audience and posited event. The recorded is characterized by the event's spatial absence and temporal anteriority. By separating the spatial and temporal parameters, the relationships can be depicted as follows:

	Spatial Co-presence	Spatial Absence
Temporal Simultaneity	LIVE	
	(I)	(II)
Temporal Anteriority		RECORDED
	(III)	(IV)

Some Associated Representational Technologies/Practices

Position I: Public address, vaudeville, theater, concert
Position II: Telephone, "live" radio, "live" television
Position III: Lip syncing, Diamondvision stadium replays
Position IV: Motion pictures, recorded radio and television

Relationship of spectator-auditors to the "event" posited by representation.

Although defined in mutually exclusive terms, the socially constructed categories live and recorded cannot account for all representational practices and they do not exhaust the possibilities of consumers' relationships to posited original events. Representational dominants—that is those enjoying a certain cultural and economic salience—gravitate toward the two categories represented by positions I and IV. These are two privileged arrangements in that both allow a spatial and temporal unity of the posited event either wholly present or wholly absent. The live posits a single, fully present moment, an event characterized by both audio and visual components that preexist representation. In order to posit a similar unified, single event prior to representation, texts and practices that posit events in position IV (necessary to mechanical and electronic reproducibility and thus to the circulation of representations as commodities) strive for the erasure of indications that the text consists of multiple instances or technologies of production. Events occupying positions II and III are neither fully recorded nor fully live. They involve simultaneous presence and absence, a combination of qualities of both the live and the recorded, the immediate and the mediated. As such they problematize the binary oppositions on which dominant notions of representation are based, live/recorded and the related oppositions event/representation or original/copy.

In the case of Houston's Tampa performance, the home consumer, watching and listening to one of the videotaped versions of the performance available in record stores after the Super Bowl, experienced the event as fully recorded—position IV. Consumers at the Super Bowl misperceived the performance event as that of position I—the fully present live. Instead, the event represented by Houston's version of the national anthem was that of position III—spatial co-presence in an image origin (Houston), but a temporally anterior sound origin (recorded voice). The television consumer, although spatially absent from the depicted event, similarly misperceived a temporally simultaneous sound original—position II. It was this misperception, or rather the revelation of such a misperception, that necessitated the spin control.

While Houston's version of the national anthem demonstrates the non-exclusive nature of the live and the recorded as categories, it also demonstrates the ways in which representational technologies and practices posit events and also spectator-auditor relationships to such events. Furthermore, this example indicates that discourses surrounding audio-visual technologies and representations also struggle to fix a spectator-auditor's relationship to a represented event. The remainder of this essay explores these issues in terms of the two entertainment technologies associated with Whitney Houston and the Super Bowl: television and popular music. This, in turn, will provide a framework for a reconsideration of cinema sound and subjectivity.

Television, When the Live Becomes a Degraded Version of the Recorded

Television as a representational technology can be thought to occupy a transitional position in the above chart, in that programming content is characterized by both the fully recorded (position IV) and "live" transmissions in which the representationally posited events are temporally simultaneous with the audience yet spatially absent (position II). Yet, as some theorists have noted, the textual practices of American television present themselves as, or are experienced in ways similar to, the fully present live. John Ellis has observed that even the recorded programs of broadcast television are assigned a sense of spatial co-presence and temporal simultaneity in that, once a particular program has aired in its scheduled time slot, there is little or no chance of viewing it outside of its initial temporal and spatial (channel) context.[2] Rick Altman builds on this observation and its significance for audiences: "Whether the events transmitted by television are live or not, the television experience itself is thus sensed as live by the home viewing audience. . . . Television programming itself thus takes on the attributes of irreversible reality" (Altman, 1986b, 45). Certain representational practices, as well as the presence within the televisual flow of both representations of position II events and recorded programming made pseudo-live by scheduling patterns, address the television consumer as if the programming were similar to, although not identical with, the discursively produced live. Altman's essay clearly outlines a variety of television sound conventions that contribute to the medium's high degree of discursivity. Such a discursivity directly addresses a spectating-auditing subject, and thus indirectly posits a discursive instance characterized by temporal and spatial contiguity.

Live television broadcasts of, for example, football games feature pre-game images of the announcers directly addressing the audience from the broadcasting booth or on the field. Such images are also often used when coming into and out of commercials. This practice fixes the announcers in space, that is, it positions them as occupying the same space as that of the visual event. Thus, a sound representation (play by play and color commentary) is firstly anchored to a body, a visual representation of its source (the voice is provided with a point of origin), and secondly this audio source/origin is presented as spatially contiguous with the event/origin posited by the images of the game. The highly discursive, direct address of the "descriptions and accounts" that follow position the spectator-auditor in a relationship of temporal simultaneity and spatial contiguity (through the discursive act) with the representationally posited event. This convention also characterizes news broadcasts (another instance of the "live" position II event) which place Andrea Mitchell in front of the White House, Cokie Roberts in the Halls of Congress, or Tom Brokaw at the base of the Berlin Wall. Television conventions thus spatially nudge absent narrators (as sound origins) toward a spatial co-presence with events (image origins). When this process breaks down, when TV threatens to become radio (for instance, CNN's live feed from Beijing is cut off by the Chinese government), the on-site reporter calls in over telephone lines (for instance, Bernard Shaw under a table in Baghdad). With no access to a signifier of spatial presence, the "live" sound is accompanied by a snapshot of the voice's body, a map, or both—all of which function as conventionalized representations of sound source.

While representational practices of American television rely on co-presence implied by highly discursive strategies and conventionalized methods to posit an audio source spatially contiguous with image events, other techniques are used to compensate for the spatial absence of television's posited event. In the case of sports broadcasting, the multiple cameras used to cover an event entail a kind of fragmented spectatorship that overcompensates for the spatial absence from the event by providing a spatial or perceptual abundance. This spatial augmentation of vision accorded to the spectator by the representation is further enhanced by the temporal violation, or transcendence of duration, through instant replay or the associated technologies and practices of stop action and John Madden's "Coach's Clicker."

Over time, as such conventions of the televisually posited live come to constitute the way we think of the live, attending the game (spatial co-presence and temporal simultaneity) becomes a degraded version of the event's televisual representation. This degradation of the live is itself compensated for by the use of Diamondvision and instant replays on elaborate stadium score boards (showing, for example, extreme close-ups of Whitney Houston's tear-streaked cheeks). In other words, the degradation of the live is compensated for by the inscription into the "real" of its representation.

Contemporary Popular Music—Copies Without Originals

Just as televised sports events have led to the perception that the live is a degraded version of the represented (thus inverting the hierarchical oppositions entailed in live/recorded or event/representation or play/replay or original/copy), so too has a similar inscription of the recorded into the live characterized contemporary popular music concerts with important implications for the ideological work done by representational technologies and practices.

Andrew Goodwin proposes three reasons why popular music audiences continue to attend live concerts: the "abstract visual pleasure of the spectacle," the authentification of musical competence, and the opportunity to consume a star presence (Goodwin, 45). The continued popularity of live concerts can also be seen to result from a representational crisis within popular music. As Théberge documents, during the 1960s and 1970s, the use of multi-track recording technology by popular music producers gradually shifted from the documentation of a studio performance to the construction of an illusory performance event. Studio looping, digital drum machines, and the use of technology such as the digital sampling music computer to encode, store, manipulate and reproduce sounds within almost limitless parameters have moved audio representation ever further from a notion of a preexisting original event. Contemporary popular music is characterized by "the increasing problem of distinguishing between originals and copies on the one hand, and between human and automated performance on the other" (Goodwin, 39). Dominant sound recording practices for popular music arguably might be seen as following a three-stage trajectory: firstly, recording conceived as the documentation of a preexisting event; secondly, recording conceived as the construction of an event; and thirdly, recording conceived as the dismantling of any sense of an original event and the creation instead of a copy for which no original exits.

The live concert is one practice through which a notion of a fully present original event is reintroduced into popular music. By acting out the production of sound in an event spatially co-present and temporally simultaneous with consumers, the concert reinscribes a notion of a performance that exists prior to its audio representation, while the popular music industry capitalizes on an "aura" made commodifiable through the mass production of audio texts.

However, the production of live popular music concerts is increasingly characterized by the simultaneous presence of "live" performance, audio playback of prerecorded material, and large screen video representations of onstage events. The practice of lip syncing at concerts has recently generated popular disdain. The "scandal" involves the discovery that recorded performances are presented as if they were live. The popular outrage is often rhetorically framed around notions of creativity and artistic integrity, but also at stake is the integrity, or rather the existence, of the live's status as a fully present event. The disjunction between spatial co-presence and temporal anteriority reveals the artifice of representation and shatters the posited "unity" of the live event.[3]

The incorporation at contemporary popular music concerts of the "live" production of music, lip syncing to prerecorded sound, and large-screen video representations of the ongoing event poses a series of challenges to notions of the centered subject and the binary opposition, live/recorded. Such an "event" speaks of the fragmented, decentered subject privileged in discourses of postmodernism even as the collapsing of oppositions such as live/recorded or original/copy testifies to the "eclipse of the real" and other postmodernist tropes. The apparent collapsing of distinctions between live and recorded, and the difficulty of theorizing a subject effect for the popular music concert, result from the simultaneous presence of two, by definition, mutually exclusive categories: the live and the recorded. Even though the live concert struggles to reinstate a notion of the fully present original event in popular music, the co-presence of the live and the recorded contribute to a potential crisis in our notions of a real that exists prior to representation.

The "Live" Album

The popular music industry's practice of releasing "live" albums also seeks to reinstate the distinction between events posited as live and as recorded. The "live" album presents itself as a recording of a performance event. Its name promises an ontological link to an absent event even while it allows endless repeatability in virtually any spatial context. That repeatability testifies to the consumers' inevitable lack of access to a temporally prior, spatially absent original. The recorded concert is treated like a narrative, in that a clearly marked beginning (introduction of performers) and end (encore) mark the boundaries of the live event, and the concert's internal narrative order (progression of songs) is respected such that temporal ellipses or reordering are disguised so as to signify authentic duration. Yet, while the "live" album presents itself as the product of a *documentary* use of recording technology to represent its preexisting event, the use of contemporary recording technology also functions to *construct* the commodity's sound. Overdubbing vocals, adjustments to balance, multi-track mixing and other technologically produced enhancements all function to construct the "live" album as a representation.

Like the event it posits, the "live" album incorporates versions of previously released material, songs familiar to consumers in different, prior forms. Critical evaluations of live recordings often hinge on comparisons to these "original," massively reproduced recordings. The "live" album frequently is judged positively if the increased "presence" signified by it is perceived as invigorating the studio-produced original or approximating the "aura" of nonmediated performance. If the "live" album is judged negatively, it is often because of the "loss" of sound quality, the failure of the "live" to conform to the representational standards of the mass-produced "original" versions. Again the live is conceived as a degraded version of the recorded.

Thus, popular music's "live" album refers to a plurality of original events: firstly, the space and time of the recorded performance event (often plural in that the "live" album is frequently constructed from several different concerts); secondly, the "original" studio-recorded versions of mass-produced commodities, themselves constructed and referring to a performance that has never existed outside of its assembly through multi-track technology; and thirdly, the recording studio event at which multiple concert recordings are remixed, "sweetened," overdubbed, and otherwise augmented to construct the commodity "live." The success of the "live" album hinges on posing an ontological link to the first event, presenting itself as an enhanced supplement to the second, and eliding the work done by the third.

Although the popular music "live" album (by positing multiple and conflicting original events), potentially challenges the notion that live and recorded are mutually exclusive opposites, the hierarchical binary is reinstated through criticism, promotion and other discursive means. The repeatability of the "live" album, that which insures its status as commodity, hinges on a series of absences, lending a commodifiable "aura" to an inevitably lost, yet plurally posited notion of nonexistent original event(s).

Early Synchronous Sound Films—Recording as Documentation

The history of cinema sound can be productively reconsidered in light of the above discussion of popular music and television. Prior to the innovation of synchronous sound recording and reproduction, motion pictures were characterized by a disjunction between posited sound and image events. The event posited by the image was spatially absent and temporally anterior to film-goers (position IV on the chart above). But the audience occupied a different relationship to the sound accompaniment, whether provided by an orchestra, an upright piano, live narration, or the mighty Wurlitzer. The event posited by sound was that of position I (temporally simultaneous and spatially co-present).

Such a situation poses a potential conflict for notions of centered subjectivity, in that the spectator-auditors of "silent" films were simultaneously hailed by two representational practices discursively constructed as mutually exclusive—that of the recorded and that of the live. They were differently hailed as spectators and auditors. Such a disjunction threatens to foreground the act of representing at the expense of the event posited by the representation. The shift to synchronous sound reproduction might thus be seen as a re-inscription of a unified subject position (the linguistically unwieldy "spectator-auditor") spoken by a representational form (sync sound films) in which both sound and image posit an event characterized by spatial absence and temporal anteriority.

Synchronous sound films initially relied heavily upon recording conceived as the documentation of preexisting events. Films produced by both the Fox Film Corporation and Warner Bros./Vitaphone involved the recording of situations culturally considered position I events (direct address speeches, both high- and low-culture performance events). The Fox Film Corporation's initial use of the Movietone sound-on-film system to record and reproduce the remarks of international leaders relied on highly discursive, performance acts to foreground the fact that both the reproduced image and sound originated from a single, identifiable source at a specific, depicted time. The direct-address speeches of government leaders and literary personalities such as George Bernard Shaw and Arthur Conan Doyle, whether released as autonomous short subjects or incorporated into Fox's Movietone Newsreel, underscored the ability of the new technology to document events discursively "known" to be fully present. The representation of the speaker's body as the source of the sound, through the synchronization of recorded voice with moving lips, posited an event, preexisting its representation, present in all of its fullness. At times, intelligibility of the recorded voice was deemed less important than the ability of recording and reproducing technologies to posit such events. For example, an excerpt from a speech by German President Hindenberg appeared untranslated in the October 25, 1930 edition of Fox's Movietone News. At stake in this Fox newsreel segment are the posited event and the technology's ability to record and reproduce it, rather than the untranslated, linguistic content of the speech on German patriotism.

The Vitaphone shorts produced and distributed by Warner Bros. were often characterized by a similar concentration on the recording and reproduction of discrete, highly discursive scenes, for the sake of signifying a fully present sound and image event and the technology's ability to reproduce it. Unlike the Fox-Movietone shorts, the Vitaphone short subjects were more prone to document performance events than public address events (with the notable exception of Will Hays' speech welcoming Vitaphone). Through their reliance for subjects on both vaudeville and "high art" performances, the Vitaphone shorts initially featured recordings capable of foregrounding a specific origin for both sound and image. Like the Fox direct-address short subjects, the early Vitaphone shorts were usually characterized by a high degree of discursivity, with performers directly addressing the recording technology as audience surrogate.

After these initial synchronous sound films, Hollywood conventions of sound recording and reproduction involved a shift in emphasis, from recording thought of as the documentation of a preexisting "event" toward recording conceived of as the creation and construction of a pseudo-event.

Hollywood Sound Practice—The Sound Perspective Debates

While the conversion to synchronous sound recording and reproduction potentially unified the film spectator-auditor's relationship to the event posited by the film text (as a position IV sound and image event), the conversion to sound involved the combination of two distinct representational technologies. As such, synchronous sound films still had the potential to posit two different specific events prior to their representation—a sound original and an image original. Mary Ann Doane surveys some of the representational techniques used by Hollywood to disguise the work done in constructing an apparently unified representation from two distinct technological systems (blooping, sound analogues to continuity editing, the perceived necessity for a constant signifier of sound space [room tone], staggering sound and image cuts, and so on). Doane finds in these techniques a series of conventionalized responses to the ideological demand to disguise the work done in constructing the Hollywood sound film, to efface the act of representing in favor of the events posited by the representation (Doane 1980a).

Doane also addresses the hierarchical conception of sound events that privileged dialogue, particularly the *intelligibility* of dialogue, over other sound phenomena. For Doane, such a practice is complicit with ideological notions of the individual as the center and origin of meaning, although, as in the early sync-sound shorts, also at stake in privileging dialogue in synchronization with its sources is the positing of sound and image events as identical:

> The need for intelligibility and the practice of using speech as a support for the individual are both constituted by an ideological demand. Yet, it is an ideological demand which has the potential to provoke a fundamental rent in the ideology of the visible. This potential finds expression in the arguments concerning sound perspective which appear with regularity in the technical journals of the early 1930s. (Doane 1980a, 52)

The 1930s debate among engineers and Hollywood sound technicians involved, on the one hand, those who advocated a strict matching of sound perspective with image scale and, on the other hand, those who advocated a sound track of relatively uniform sound level that privileged the intelligibility of the voice over the matching of sound and image perspective (see Altman, "Sound Space," in this volume). As Doane and Altman have shown, this debate on Hollywood sound practice can offer a privileged historical instance in which can be read the process of establishing realistic representational conventions. Also at stake, however, is the potential disjunction between spectator positions with respect to the posited sound and image events.

Notions of the ideological effect of motion picture images, as developed by Baudry and others, posit a direct connection between motion picture

image-producing technologies and Renaissance codes of perspective—
both of which, so the argument goes, address or position a centered
subject. Thus, the positioning of a cinema subject is threatened by a sound
film practice that privileges intelligibility of the voice over the matching
of sound and image perspective. Equally at stake is the cinema's ability
to posit a single event as the origin of both audio and visual representation:

> Renaissance perspective and monocular vision organise the image
> which positions the spectator as the eye of the camera. But that
> position is undermined and placed in doubt if the apparent microphone
> placement differs from that of the camera and fails to rearticulate the
> position. . . . The effect of spatial depth conveyed by the image is
> destroyed, and it is this illusion of a certain perspective and a certain
> spectator position which is broken by the early sound films. (Doane
> 1980a, 53–54)

But is such a potential conflict between a spectator hailed by the image
and an auditor differently positioned by the sound such a threat to the
cinema's subject effect? Perhaps a variety of coexisting, even diametrically opposed representational techniques can produce the same effect in
different ways, so that subject positioning by the cinematic apparatus is
always only approximate and overdetermined. Two equivalent processes
are at work in the sound perspective debate. In one, the sound film posits a
single, original, unified audio-visual event that precedes its representation
(here, sound and image perspective roughly coincide). In the other, the
disjunction between sound and image perspective is "healed" through the
very *discursive* nature of a hierarchical sound recording, mixing, and
reproducing practice that privileges intelligibility of the voice.

At the level of ideological effects—subject positioning and the positing
of an event preexisting its representation—the two approaches to sound
perspective are not entirely at odds. In response to Doane's paper, Jean-
Louis Comolli posed the following:

> Why is it that the intelligibility of dialogue is so important a technical
> problem, demanding so much care and attention on the part of the
> sound engineer? It is not simply in order that the dialogue be clearly
> understood by the spectator, it is also, more interestingly, for reasons
> relating to the co-presence of the characters and the spectator. In fact,
> intelligibility of the dialogue allows these words and voices to be heard
> as though one were there with them; there is a direct interpellation of
> the spectator who is set on the stage on which the dialogue takes place.
> (Comolli 1980, 57)

One must interrogate the notion of "direct interpellation" posited by Comolli for the apparent inevitability of effect it implies, and for the fact that this interpellation is based on a single material quality of film sound convention to the exclusion of coexisting heterogeneous practices. Yet, with these concerns in mind, Comolli's notion, that an overtly discursive sound practice (a sound quality labeled "for-me-ness" by Altman 1986a) has the ability to signify a relative spatial co-presence between auditor and representationally posited sound event, has important implications for a discussion of representational practices and subjectivity.

One way to account for the potentially disjunctive positioning of auditors and spectators by the Hollywood sound film is through a notion that such positioning is always only approximate. While the traditions of Renaissance codes of perspective, when used in a painting, can be thought of as "speaking" a specific, unitary subject position (in front of the painting with the representation organized around this single view), the assemblage of any Hollywood scene from a variety of camera positions clearly does not "speak" a spectator thrust with each cut into a new subject position, much less "subjectivity." Conventions of continuity editing (including those mobilized to disguise such shifts in perspective) "speak" instead a coherent and approximate relationship between film spectator and depicted space or events. Similarly, Hollywood conventions of sound practice might be thought of as "speaking" not a single, specific position for its auditor (as the early synchronous shorts do), but an approximate relational position to a depicted sound space. When combined through a series of procedures that attempt to erase the material heterogeneity of the sound film, such approximate spectating and auditing positions strive for a kind of general, relational consistency (a spectating auditor or auditing spectator), rather than a specific identifiable position. This position, so important to the cultural label "realistic," hinges in part on the sound film's ability to posit a single, unitary audio-visual event that exists prior to its representation.

This notion of an "approximate subject positioning" as the ideological effect of sound film technology and Hollywood representational practice hinges on the hypothesis that a variety of sound techniques potentially erase what might be seen as the fragmentation of the subject by the Hollywood sound film. Among such techniques and practices are the two approaches seen as mutually exclusive by the 1930s sound perspective debates and by contemporary sound film historians. Rather than diametrically opposed techniques, sound representation with a high degree of discursivity and a fidelity of sound and image perspective are analogous in that both practices are capable of positing a similar "presence" of audio-visual event.

Hollywood Sound Practice—Nondiegetic Music

Even if we were to posit such an "approximate" subject effect for the Hollywood sync-sound film, this would not exhaust the potentially disjunctive roles played by sound conventions. The presence of nondiegetic music in Hollywood films involves a pervasive representational practice that problematizes both the cinema's ability to specify a unitary, centered subject position and its ability to posit an original event that precedes representation. Not only does a nondiegetic score specify a subject position different from that of the synchronous recording of voices (whether privileging intelligibility or sound perspective), but it also posits no time or space of origin, no event or source.

Three accounts of the presence of nondiegetic music in "realistic" films suggest themselves. First, the pervasive use of musical scoring can be seen as something of an aesthetic "survival" from preexisting representational technologies and practices. From this perspective, Hollywood's use of nondiegetic music is a holdover from the silent cinema, theatrical melodrama, or both. This explanation hinges on the observed tendency for representational practices associated with new technologies to borrow from and build upon the conventions of realism characteristic of other, previous systems of representation (Altman 1984).

A second account of nondiegetic scoring views the practice as not threatening, but rather constituting, the cinema's ability to posit an autonomous centered subject. By invoking the Lacanian paradigm of the formation of subjectivity, this perspective suggests that Hollywood's sounds-without-origins provide the spectator-auditor with an illusory access or return to the prelinguistic plenitude of the Imaginary. By providing something of a "sonorous envelope," the nondiegetic score invokes through displacement an aural spatial plenitude, analogous to the experience prior to the formation of subjectivity. From this perspective, the nondiegetic score of the Hollywood film functions as an aural method of suturing the absences/lacks experienced by a spectator-auditor who is differently hailed by image and sound (when sound and image perspective don't match), confronted with her or his discursive inadequacy (Kaja Silverman's notion of the "foreclosed site of production"), or confronted by the lost object (the absent "real" of cinema). The nondiegetic score's work of suturing spectator-auditors back into the Imaginary compensates for the fragmented subject positions posed by the co-presence of recording practices that alternately provide a continuous level sound track, match sound perspective to image perspective, and/or include instances of "point-of-audition sound." Thus nondiegetic music acts as a [Lacanian] Imaginary string linking together sounds and images which posit a variety of conflicting original events. This account of nondiegetic music also looks to the influence of representational conventions from prior technologies. In considering both phonograph recordings and early radio's use of disembodied voices lacking spatial signature, Amy Lawrence has attributed to these technologies and practices a suturing process similar to that outlined above (Lawrence 1988).

The Lacanian master narrative of the formation of subjectivity has a certain seductive appeal in this context. It certainly has the power to explain the shared cultural desire for the "real," for that which is absent from representations. The Lacanian Symbolic, like representation, consists of spatial absence (subject/object splits involve a loss of spatial co-presence) and the initiation of a notion of duration (hence temporal anteriority). The Lacanian Imaginary, like the Live, is knowable to us only in its absence. Thus the Lacanian paradigm relies on the same order of binaries that are the subject of this paper. To live/recorded, event/representation, and original/copy we can add imaginary/symbolic.

A third account of the apparently disjunctive nature of nondiegetic musical scoring uses this pervasive sound convention to interrogate the whole notion of film's subject effect. From this perspective, the nondiegetic score is evidence of the cinema's inability to "speak" an autonomous, centered spectating-auditing subject. Instead, films, like television and contemporary popular music, "speak" a fragmented subject ever in the process of formation, multiply hailed by different discourses, representations and the events they posit.

At stake, then, is not the determination of sound's role in perpetuating a single subject effect for cinema. Instead we must recognize that the material heterogeneity of the sound film and the variety of events posited by the Hollywood soundtrack obstruct the hailing of a unified, centered subject. While dominant recording practices for popular music historically followed a path from recording conceived as the *documentation* of an event, to the *construction* of a pseudo-event, and finally to the *dismantling* altogether of the notion of an original event, these three stages simultaneously coexist throughout most of Hollywood's synchronous sound period. In "point-of-audition sound," recording practice purports to *document* an event as heard within the diegesis. The dialectical play between the highly discursive privileging of the intelligibility of voice and the practice of matching sound and image perspective *constructs* a pseudo-auditory event. Nondiegetic music *posits no event* prior to representation. As we begin to listen closely to the Hollywood film, it takes a place alongside television and popular music as a representational technology (and set of practices and conventions) that cannot assure us of an original event existing prior to representation, and can only problematically, uneasily, or contradictorily "speak" an autonomous centered subject. These "ideological effects" of texts are thus assigned, fixed, and affirmed by discourses and practices

surrounding representations, rather than by the representations themselves.

Conclusion

Some representational practices problematize a notion of centered subjectivity and the discursively produced opposition between live and recorded, even while informed by an ideological "need" to posit each.
Hence, discourses surrounding representational technologies struggle to
reinscribe a centered subject and the empiricist notion of an original event
that precedes representation. Among such discourses are those that attempt
to establish and maintain the live and the recorded as mutually exclusive
categories. But other texts and practices participate as well. Whitney
Houston's rendition of the national anthem was discursively reframed in
terms of conventional practice, standards of acceptable performance and,
perhaps most importantly, artistic integrity. "She sang live . . . "—the
event happened. Similarly, the live concert, the "live" album, and the
promotional and critical discourses around each, struggle to reinstate a
performance event within a popular music industry that now produces
copies for which no originals exist.

Recent discussions of film theory and its approaches to sound demonstrate how this particular discursive practice struggles to reinstate both a
fixed subject effect for cinema and a sense of an original sound event. Jim
Lastra has tracked the extent to which theoretical work on film sound has
depended on an assumption that an original, fully present sound event
either is directly and completely reproduced by the cinematic apparatus
or is partially rendered or transformed by its recording and reproduction.
Critical approaches to film sound have thus discursively produced and
perpetuated binary notions of live/recorded or event/representation either
by simplistically equating the two terms into a relationship of identity or
by positing the event as the standard to which representational systems
and work are measured.

Similarly, Kaja Silverman's *The Acoustic Mirror* demonstrates the ways
in which "film theory has been haunted since its inception by the specter
of a loss or absence at the center of cinematic production, a loss which both
threatens and secures the viewing subject" (Silverman, 2). In examining a
number of theoretical interventions in debates on realism, suture and
sexual difference, and representation, Silverman demonstrates that much
of the rhetoric of film theory surrounding the absent "real" suggests
defense mechanisms similar to disavowal and fetishism. For Silverman,
much of film theory, through a series of displacements, struggles to
overcome the "crisis" surrounding the recognition that film is structured
around absence: "These orchestrated displacements have as their final goal

the articulation of a coherent male subject" (10). Thus, according to Silverman, film theory, like its object of study, struggles to arrive at a coherent subject effect.

But the discursive production of a live/recorded binary opposition and autonomous subjectivity takes place in more popular discourses as well. The ideological effect of any technology also involves the way that technology and its practices are "known" by consumers, the way it is itself represented and discursively produced as a science and/or commodity. Socially produced notions such as fidelity, "the ontology of the photo image," or "the next best thing to being there," as well as copyright disputes over sampling, the "scandal" of lip syncing at concerts, and the commodification of the "aura," all struggle to fix the "ideological effects" of representations.

Therefore, any ideological effect with respect to subjectivity is not fixed and inevitably determined by technology or representational practices. Though technological design and innovation, and conventionalized techniques are influenced by an ideological "need" for positing a centered subject and an event existing prior to its representation, social subjects are actually multiply produced through a variety of discourses, including those of the live and the recorded.

5

Wasted Words

Michel Chion

The world is in motion and in chiaroscuro. We always see one side of things, always moving, always changing. Their shape dissolves into a shadow, sketches itself in the motion, loses itself in the darkness, or in the excess of light. And our attention is also in chiaroscuro. It comes and goes from one object to another, and focuses successively on the details and on the whole.

Films seem to have been invented in order to represent all of this. They show bodies in light and shadow, they leave objects and find them again, they isolate them with a dolly-in, or relocate them with a dolly-out.

There is only one element which film has not been able to treat this way, and which today still remains constrained to perpetual clarity and perpetual stability. We must always hear every word, from one end to the other, in order that no word be lost, that each word be understood one after the other. Why? What would it matter if we lost three words in what the hero says? Yet this has remained almost taboo for film. We are barely beginning now to learn to limit the clarity of dialogue.

Let us begin by remembering that silent film was not, in spite of its name, deprived of language. The latter was present on two levels: explicitly in the text of captions, which alternated with the images; implicitly in the very way these images were cut, shot, and edited to constitute discourses in which a shot or a gesture was the equivalent of a word or of a syntagma. "There is the house. Peter opens the door," they said.

This use of the intertitle represented a type of constraint, that of breaking the continuity of images, and it implied the conspicuous presence in film of a foreign body, of an impurity. But at the same time, it allowed a great deal of narrative flexibility: the intertitle could be used for locating the time and setting, as well as for summarizing part of the action, or for giving a distancing opinion of the characters and, of course, to transcribe approximately the spoken dialogue.

In general, of course, the text gave only a summary, an interpretation of what was being said. It did not offer itself as an exhaustive transcription. This text could choose the direct style, but also the indirect style ("she tells him that . . ."). In short, it had at its disposal the entire narrative arsenal of the novel.

Sound put an end to all of this, at least in the beginning, when it reduced the text present in the film to a single formula: dialogue spoken in the present tense by the characters. And to this day, this is how most films function.

This development did not occur all at once. During a transition period of five or six years, various forms were tried and tested until nearly all films were based on dialogue.

In my essay *La Toile trouée*, about speech in cinema, I suggested distinguishing three uses of speech in films, which I termed *parole-théâtre, parole-texte, parole-émanation*: theatrical speech, textual speech, and emanation speech (Chion 1988, 92ff).

In theatrical speech, which is the most common case, characters exchange dialogue that is integrally heard by the spectator. In special cases, we can hear their internal voice in the present tense, analogous to a theatrical "aside." But in these cases, the text which has been heard remains one of the concrete elements of the action, powerless over the reality revealed by the image.

Textual speech is able to make visible in the images that it evokes through sound. That is, to change the setting at random. This great power is generally given only to certain privileged characters, in films which use this type of speech, and only for a very limited time. Rapidly, this image-creating mode of speech stands aside and is replaced by the type of speech spoken by the characters. The few examples of films using textual speech abundantly are famous: Sacha Guitry's *Roman d'un tricheur*, for instance, and certain of Woody Allen's films. However, brief moments of textual speech may be found in many films.

The third type of speech is even rarer. It's what we might call emanation speech, where speech is not necessarily completely heard and understood. In any case, this type of speech isn't tied to the heart of what might be called *action*, in a general sense. Speech becomes therefore an emanation of the characters, an aspect of themselves, like their silhouette: significant but not essential for the mise-en-scène.

In theatrical speech, mise-en-scène (in a general sense, from screenplay to editing by way of stage business, lighting, camera movements, and so forth) is conceived almost unconsciously—shall we say—in order to make the speech of the characters into the central action, in the process making us forget that it structures the whole film. This explains the paradox according to which certain films which we remember as action films, like many American films, are actually nine times out of ten dialogue films, but which treat the dialogue as action. The most striking example is *Rio Bravo*, directed by Howard Hawks, but also the films of Alfred Hitchcock, in spite of his reputed contempt for dialogue.

The principle of talking while doing something, in classical cinema, helps to restructure the film according to and around speech. A door which is slammed, a cigarette which is lit, a camera movement or a reframing, everything can become punctuation, and therefore a heightening of speech. This technique makes it easier to listen to the text, while focusing attention on it.

In this type of cinema, even the moments when characters are not talking make sense precisely because they are moments of interruption in a verbal continuum. The *kiss*, for example, interrupts speech and breaks up the confrontation, thus settling the verbal impasse—an effect much more inherent to film than to theater or opera.

But emanation speech, in which speech is relativized and decentered in relation to the film, is the rarest case, and sound film has barely used it, for complex reasons which we will attempt to evoke. Still, we find emanation speech, for instance, in the films of Jacques Tati, and in another manner in the films of Tarkovsky and Fellini, as well as in isolated sequences of other films.

In one way, these three types of speech could be used in silent films: textual speech, theatrical speech, and also emanation speech, since characters spent a lot of time talking and much of what they said was not translated. The content of their speech, therefore, did not force the mise-en-scène and the interpretation to value it word for word. With sound, this freedom disappeared little by little. While increasingly adopting and subtly restructuring itself around theatrical speech, film was aligning itself on the model of a verbal and linear continuum.

Filmmakers were conscious of this risk, and many tried, from the very beginning of the talkies, to relativize speech, in other words to try to inscribe it in a visual, rhythmic, gestural, and sensory totality, in which it would no longer remain the central and determining element.

We are aware that this question has many aspects: technical, historical, aesthetic, linguistic. Let us make clear that for some time now it has been possible to achieve a "verbal chiaroscuro," either through direct sound or by post-synchronization. By verbal chiaroscuro I mean an image of human speech, in which at one moment we understand what is said, and at another we understand less, and at times nothing at all.

It has been possible for a long time, for example on a shoot, to take two simultaneous recordings of the same voice, one clearly defined, the other less so. Then, by mixing, it is possible to move continuously from one to the other and back. However, this is done quite rarely. I am not suggesting that this process can be carried out without technical difficulties. Yet the preservation of dialogue intelligibility involves no greater technical difficulties.

For the time being, it will be most helpful to review various isolated attempts at relativizing speech, primarily during the early years of sound cinema.

Rarefaction

The simplest approach involves rarefying the presence of speech. This is what René Clair attempted, notably in *Sous les toits de Paris* (1930). In principle, this option allowed the conservation of many of silent film's visual values, but it also involved two problems: on the one hand, situations must be specially created in order to explain, more or less artificially, the absence of the voice; on the other hand, we sense a feeling of silence and emptiness between the few spoken sequences, which begin to sound like a foreign body within the film. For example, this is what we feel in the dialogue scenes of one of the few modern films which adopts René Clair's ideas. I am speaking of Stanley Kubrick's *2001, A Space Odyssey* (1968), where speech is concentrated in just a few localized scenes.

Proliferation and Ad Libs

The second method achieves a similar effect by using a contrary approach: by accumulating words, by superimposing them, and by proliferating speech, lines annul each other, or rather annul their influence on the structure of the film. Many characters talk at the same time, quickly link their replies, or say things of "no importance." In his film *La Tête d'un homme* (1933), filled with various sound experiments, Julien Duvivier tried to treat one of the scenes on the model of a collective chattering, a proliferation of speech surrounding an event: in this case the breakdown of a car, simulated by the police in order to allow a suspect to escape, so that they can follow him to the culprit.

In this scene from *La Tête d'un homme*, the relativization of speech is reinforced by the counterpoint between speech and the image, which doesn't show the speakers. But when we see Duvivier's film in its totality, we feel that this scene is not integrated fluidly into the rest of the film, which treats dialogue in a more traditional fashion. Later, filmmakers will employ this process only for specific types of scene, especially meal scenes, during precise moments. These moments resemble imitations of the theater, when the text calls for "crowd noise," with a large number of ad libs.

This process is especially clear in the eating scenes from Jean Renoir's *La Chienne* (1931), Ingmar Bergman's *Hour of the Wolf* (1968) and Ridley Scott's *Alien* (1979). In all three films, the meal scenes in question involve particular moments which break with the rest of the film, and last only a few seconds. Later we will see how Federico Fellini has generalized this concept in a particularly personal manner.

Mixture of Languages and the Use of a Foreign Tongue

Some isolated films have relativized speech, simply by using a foreign language not understood by most of the spectators, or sometimes by mixing various languages, which is to say they relativize languages with respect to each other.

In *Anahatan* (1953), Josef von Sternberg uses Japanese actors who speak in their own language, and who are neither subtitled nor dubbed; the voice-over of a narrator—Sternberg himself—summarizes the story and the dialogues, and distances us from the characters. As in a silent film, we need the help of a second text in order to understand what the characters are saying.

In *Et la lumière fut* (1989), Otar Iosseliani does the same thing with African characters. In a scene from *Death in Venice* (1971), on the beach of the Lido, Luchino Visconti uses the situation (an international beach for rich foreigners) in order to mix languages: Hungarian, French, English, Italian. The same thing occurs in Jacques Tati's *Playtime* (1968) and in certain of Fellini's films.

Narrative Commentary over the Dialogue

In certain films, a narrative voice-over partially covers the dialogue spoken by the characters, thus relativizing the dialogues and their content. For example, this technique is used in Max Ophuls's *Le Plaisir* (1952).

Submerged Speech

Selected scenes in certain films are based on the idea of a "sound bath," into which conversations dive and then surface again. With this method, the filmmaker uses the situation itself as an alibi, either in a crowd situation or a natural setting, to reveal and then conceal the words, thus relativizing human speech while locating it in space.

In Tati's *Les vacances de Monsieur Hulot* (1953), the sound bath in which speech is immersed is itself often made of speech, but of heavily reverberant speech that is difficult to understand and whose sources are usually invisible: in this case, children playing and screaming, never seen throughout the film.

Loss of Intelligibility

Sometimes there is not only a flux and reflux of speech, in the sonorous totality, but precisely the localized awareness of a loss of the voice's intelligibility, which we continue to hear by itself.

In his first sound film, *Blackmail* (1929), Hitchcock tried a famous experiment with the loss of the voice's intelligibility, in order to express the subjectivity of the heroine. The previous night, she had killed a man who tried to rape her, and now she fears that her guilt will be discovered. She hears a neighbor speaking about the crime; in her chatter we hear only the word "knife," the weapon of the crime. This attempt at a "close-up" of a word, like the close-up of a face, was very courageous, but it remained quite isolated. Even Hitchcock himself repeated the experiment only once or twice, in *Rope*, for example.

What is the problem with this approach? In this blurring of the voice, speech is transformed into a sonorous haze interrupted by only a few clear passages. We thus hear only a technical process, instead of a subjective experience. Notice that the visual equivalent of the same process, where haze is used to express loss of consciousness, has become an established rhetorical figure.

One aspect of the problem lies in the particularity of our auditory attention, as compared to our visual attention. As easy as it is to eliminate something from our field of vision, by turning our head or closing our eyes totally or partially, it is quite difficult for the ear, and cannot be done in the same selective manner. Even the sounds that we don't listen to actively, our ears listen to nonetheless, inscribing the sound on our brain as on a tape recording, whether we listen to the sound or not—even in our sleep or under hypnosis.

In a few scenes of *M* (1931), Fritz Lang also attempted a transition from verbal clarity to verbal haze, but more as a dramatic process for linking scenes, with no reference to a notion of subjectivity. In this example, the two scenes are linked by the idea of the sonorous haze, moving first from clear to hazy then from hazy to clear. Here we have the equivalent of the optical process. The loss of intelligibility is the result of three factors. The first two are acoustic: the voices become more distant and increase in reverberation. The third is a psychological factor: a character becomes nervous and talks in a confused fashion. However, this process requires an extreme psychological situation, and cannot be used at random.

Decentering

In conclusion, we will cite a more subtle mode of relativizing speech, which does not touch on the acoustic nature of speech, but which uses the entirety of the mise-en-scène. In "decentering," the clarity and intelligibility of the text remain untouched, but the mise-en-scène is not centered on speech, and therefore doesn't induce us to listen to the dialogue. Speech goes one way and the rest goes the other way. In Fellini's *Casanova* (1976) or in Tarkovski's *Stalker* (1979), for example, we understand almost everything acoustically, but the cutting and the interpretation don't emphasize the content of the lines. The impression is completely strange and novel.

Had I been able to see *Nashville* (1975) again (unavailable in France at this time), I would have liked to show how Robert Altman achieves a similar effect in a different manner. Regarding the relativization of speech in this film, Rick Altman has written a very interesting and suggestive article, containing fascinating developments on this topic (Altman 1991a).

Of course, by decentering I don't mean what is traditionally considered as subversive deconstruction, for example in the films of Jean-Luc Godard. In my opinion, what Godard does with the text in many films does not involve this notion of decentering. For Godard, even if the text is more or less hidden by other sounds or by heavy reverberation, speech remains the center of attention, the main structuring element. Godard is like a little boy, who derives pleasure from doing the opposite of what others are doing. Yet by accomplishing the opposite, he succeeds only in reproducing and reinforcing the familiar dialogue-centered structure, but in an inverted fashion.

What we might call *decentered speaking cinema*, making heavy use of emanation speech, is something else again—a decidedly polyphonic cinema. We find prefigurations and examples of this not only in the films of certain auteur directors, but also in contemporary action films and special effects movies. In the latter, the use of varying sensory effects and the presence of certain sensations and rhythms create the feeling that the world is not reduced to the function of embodying dialogue.

In a certain sense, this new decentered speaking cinema is like the silent cinema, but with the sound. It could give rise to the third period of narrative cinema.

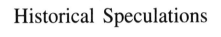

Historical Speculations

Introduction: Sound/History

Rick Altman

For once, let us begin at the beginning. Of all the basic assumptions on which cinema history is built, none is more deeply ingrained than the apparently tautological notion that cinema history is the history of *cinema*. But what is cinema? Rarely are such naïve questions asked, because the answer is so obvious. By and large, we know just what cinema is, and what it is not, so much so that it has not seemed necessary to theorize cinema's identity. Yet the media industry has shown much less assurance than critics about the nature of its products, often openly revealing hesitations about their identity.

If cinema could be defined solely from the standpoint of the image, then it might make sense to base a definition entirely on the image apparatus. Seen in this manner, cinema has for a century followed a more or less straight-line trajectory. An entirely different figure appears— zigzagging and indirect—when we take sound into account, for cinema's sound identity has undergone constant redefinition, through regular redistribution of the dividing lines among media. With the apparent retrospective illumination provided by an era of relatively stable cinema identity (from the thirties to the fifties), we easily conclude that cinema has always been clearly identified and that the media have always been neatly differentiated. When we take a *prospective* look at the early cinema industry and its products, however, we find an entirely different situation. The media that we now take to be so well differentiated from cinema are one after other the other conflated with cinema, to the point where it becomes impossible to identify cinema as an independent phenomenon, separate from other media. While this process affects the image as well, it is especially evident in the domain of sound.

With 20/20 hindsight, we are typically convinced that we understand what constitutes a medium or a technology. In fact, however, representational technologies are constantly in the process of being redefined. Today's wide-screen and multiple-channel technologies are not the same as those introduced in the fifties, which in turn differ from the wide-screen and multiple-channel approaches pioneered in the late twenties and early thirties. Yesterday, the term "film" meant one thing; today it means another. If we want to understand how cinema works, we must guard against projecting today's definition into the past. Instead, we need to learn from the past an object lesson about cinema's tenuous and volatile identity. Derived from multiple image and sound technologies, film has an admirable ability to blend in with whichever of these technologies serves a particular aesthetic or economic purpose.

We will understand these chameleonic talents better through a survey of some of the media that have played a part in cinema's self-definition, with an emphasis on the early years of film history, where the interpenetration of cinema and other media was at its height. At the conclusion of this overview, I will suggest how an understanding of cinema's problematic and fluctuating sound identity might lead to a new model of cinema history.

1906: Cinema as Photography

In spite of the familiar cliché whereby "the silents were never silent," most of the early nickelodeons treated the newfangled film medium as nothing more than moving photographs, sufficient unto themselves and requiring no musical accompaniment. An automatic piano or phonograph was almost always present, but typically used on the street to attract trade, in the manner of a carnival barker. A pianist was often on the scene as well, but he (or, more likely, she) was there to accompany the featured illustrated song. The theater operator, according to a contemporary set of instructions for running a nickelodeon program "is required to call the accompanist as the [film] performance nears the close, that the intermission music may start promptly at the close of the pictures" (Gardette, 79). Everything was accompanied, in these early days, *except* the film. For at this point in its history, film was just that, a spool of Eastman or Pathé film capable of registering moving photographs. Though in this early period sound and image were simultaneously present in the theater, they had not yet come together to produce the familiar audio/visual phenomenon we now call cinema.

1907: Cinema as Illustrated Music

It didn't take very long for filmmakers to figure out that film was just as good as song slides at illustrating familiar songs. Here we first encounter the notion that film is not just photography, but a combination of image and sound. More and more films were shot in view of a specific accompaniment. This was the heyday of the Passion Play, with its multiple openings for church music. The operetta was soon recorded on film, with a film version of Lehar's *The Merry Widow* opening in New York nearly concurrently with the stage version (Kalem, 1907). Old favorites like "Only a Bird in a Gilded Cage" (Edison, 1909) or "The Spanish Cavalier" (Edison, 1912) offered additional opportunities for musicians, as did Fourth of July releases like "The Star-Spangled Banner" (Edison, 1911) and "The Battle Hymn of the Republic" (Vitagraph, 1911). In terms of content as well as programming, films like these were produced to take the place of the song slides with which cinema had long shared the bill, thus revealing that, in spite of its growing tendency toward narrative fiction, cinema was at this point still not entirely differentiated from the song slide tradition.

1908: Cinema as Vaudeville

For many years, the exhibition practices of vaudeville and film were closely intermingled. By adopting moving pictures as one of its acts, big-time vaudeville had turned into so-called small-time vaudeville; conversely, nickelodeon owners at pains to differentiate their programs from the other nickelodeons on the same block had begun to introduce live acts on the cinema bill. Still, in 1908, there was one way to distinguish clearly between the vaudeville and film worlds: whereas vaudeville thrived on name acts, contractually guaranteed billing, and star system salary scales, film never even so much as alluded to the names of its actors, writers, or technical personnel.

Enter Cameraphone, 1908. Now, it had long been the dream of filmmakers to add sound to the film-viewing experience. Edison had paired the phonograph with the Kinetoscope; Gaumont had attempted to sync disks to film; many others had labored to link moving images and recorded sound. When the Cameraphone Company offered its new sound-on-disk system to "Owners and Managers of Vaudeville Theatres," it revealed no interest at all in this distinguished lineage of attempts to produce sound films. For Cameraphone had no stake in realizing some inventor's pipe dream. Instead, it sought to sell a recognizable product to the well-known impresarios of the vaudeville world.

What difference does it make that Cameraphone saw its product not as sound film but as a new form of vaudeville turn? If Cameraphone had been selling films, they would have been designated as comedy, drama, adventure, chase, or perhaps musical novelty. No mention would have been made of the actors or technicians. Because of the widely divergent vaudeville tradition, however, Cameraphone covered the pages of national publications with the names of its headliners: Eva Tanguay, James Harrigan, Alice Lloyd, Blanche Ring, Vesta Victoria, and many others. Soon, in response to strong popular demand, Cameraphone began to diversify its offerings, producing dramatic subjects as well as straight vaudeville turns. Now, in late 1908 and early 1909, the importance of Cameraphone's early self-definition as canned vaudeville has its most important effect: fully integrated into the film exhibition world, Cameraphone carries its vaudeville-based star orientation with it. Strange to say, the Hollywood star system is not the product of turn-of-the-decade machinations of Biograph and Vitagraph, but a perfectly predictable import from vaudeville, vehicled by the neither-fish-nor-fowl Cameraphone, the film that thought it was vaudeville.

Tradition has it that early sound film systems were no more than inventors' oddities. Rarely has film scholarship been so wide of the mark. "We have no hesitation" says the editor of *Moving Picture World* on March 6, 1909, "in prophesying that before long hardly a moving picture theatre in the country will be without the talking or singing phonograph as part of its entertainment" (261). A week later, another editorial drives the point home: "The combination of the phonograph or graphophone with the picture machine has now advanced to such a state of perfection and is being promoted by so many well financed concerns, that it is destined to occupy an important part in the moving picture field" (*Moving Picture World*, March 13, 1909; 293). A year later, this assurance had not dwindled (though notice the subtle change in the language, confirming the now independent existence of sound film as a separate concept): "In our opinion the singing and talking moving picture is bound sooner or later to become a permanent feature of the moving picture theater" (*Moving Picture World*, May 7, 1910; 727–28). In 1909, Frank L. Dyer, Vice President of Edison Manufacturing and President of the Motion Picture Patents Corporation, confidently predicted that talking pictures would soon reach the complexity and success of the legitimate theater (*New York Dramatic Mirror*, May 1, 1909; 36).

With a hundred theatres equipped with Cameraphone apparatus by the end of 1908, and many more serviced by the dozens of competing sound film systems, it seemed that sound film could hardly be far off. Such are the complexities of film history, however, that it would take nearly two decades to install a durable sound film system. The star system, however, was installed permanently within months after Cameraphone's decision to record vaudeville on film.

1911: Cinema as Opera

For the first of many times, the film industry in 1911 recognized its ability to record the stage action of famous operas, with local orchestras taking on the challenge of playing the accompanying score, now provided along with the film by the producing company. Pathé launched the mode with its version of *Il Trovatore*, with the Verdi music arranged by Charles P. Muller for a small orchestra or even for a lone pianist. When Edison produced *Aïda* later in the year, Pathé countered with a spectacular version of *Faust* (earlier produced in a shortened version by Edison). As long as film was just photography, popular music, or vaudeville, it could hardly attract the carriage trade. Through repeated early teens attempts to record opera, classical novels, and successful plays, film successfully redefined itself as a very proper medium indeed. Viewed retrospectively, cinema's identity at this point in its history seemed foreordained by its technology; considered prospectively, cinema was still actively seeking to establish its own identity in a profitable manner, based on social and commercial affinities rather than solely technological ties.

1916: Cinema as Cartoon

It is a clear sign of film's chameleonic tendencies that it could simultaneously play host to grand opera and to lowly cartoons. Other industries are defined by their products: some make breakfast cereals, others make toothpaste. Now, on the surface of things, it might appear that the film industry is appropriately defined by its products: not biodegradable plastic bags, but films. In fact, however, we make more sense of the film industry by understanding it as a complex of related production strategies. Just as minimal wartime retooling made it possible for a can factory to make grenades or for a camera manufacturer to fabricate bombsights, so Hollywood easily slid from silent snapshots to merry melodies and from chase films to newsreels. Because its production system could reproduce epics just as easily as interviews, the film industry found it not only possible, but economically desirable, to pass rapidly from opera to cartoons and back.

In mid-1911, Horsley began distributing the Nestor Film Company productions of "Mutt and Jeff Talking Pictures." Based on the familiar comic strip characters, these films offered an unexpected solution to the dialogue problem: they simply included written-in speech balloons like those found in the contemporary funny papers. Never what we would call headliners, these films nevertheless fared passingly well over the years. In fact, they did so well that, in 1916, a certain Charles F. Pidgin attempted to patent a method for producing filmed cartoons without resorting to animation or drawings. Pidgin's "invention" provided for each character to inflate, at the appropriate moment, a balloon carrying the words to be spoken. As Pidgin's patent application put it:

the words constituting the speech of the actors or characters are placed on balloons of oblong shape adapted to be inflated to a relatively large size and normally occupying a comparatively small space with the words entirely visible. . . . The blowing or inflation of the devices by the various characters of a photo-play will add to the realism of the picture by the words appearing to come from the mouth of the players. The balloons may be made of rubber or any other suitable material and the words or other characters, constituting the speech may be applied to or placed on the balloons in any desired manner, and a suitable valve will preferably be provided for maintaining the balloons or other inflatable device in an inflated or expanded condition.[1]

Unfortunately, Pidgin provided no instructions about how to manipulate multiple balloons in the actor's mouth during long conversation scenes. I am pleased to report that Pidgin's invention was approved, receiving U.S. Patent number 1,240,774 on September 18, 1917. Let it not be said that the U.S. Government ever harbored any prejudices against Pidgin English.

1922: Cinema as Radio

Few will dispute the notion that radio is one thing, television a second, and film yet another. This assumption of course overlooks the extent to which television was referred to as radio throughout the twenties. It pays too little attention to the attempts of RKO Radio Pictures to capitalize on its connection with the parent Radio Corporation of America. For years, every RKO Radio Pictures advertisement played up radio iconography, as if the film were somehow received over the "ether," as early radio buffs put it. In fact the RKO logo still perpetuates this connection.

Today we look back on the radio towers in RKO's ads and smile at their naïve rhetoric. But in 1922, it was anything but rhetoric. How would you synchronize a human voice or a phonograph record to an otherwise silent film? In 1922, you might have done it in the manner invented by Harry J. Powers, Jr., for Chicago's Rothacker Film Company. Inspired by the actors-behind-the-screen approach widely used in the late first decade of the century and in the early teens, but concerned to develop a greater economy of scale, Powers looked to the synchronization opportunities offered by radio broadcasting in order to produce sound films. Today, we can confidently affirm that radio and cinema are different media, but in 1922 the borders of the media remained an open question. Radio was not born ineluctably separate from cinema; instead, they grew apart historically.

But in 1922 they had not yet definitively separated, as demonstrated by

American Cinematographer's contemporary description of the Rothacker process:

> A motion picture is produced in the studio as usual, the scenario writer having supplied speaking lines and sound effects as though the production were to be given behind the footlights. A number of theaters are equipped with radiophone receiving instruments and projection machine synchronizing apparatus. The movie company, possibly composed of the same persons who made the original film in the studio, is assembled at the radiophone broadcasting station. Out at the theaters the overture has overtured and the audiences settle back for the evening's feature movie-speakie. Buz-z-z goes the signal at the broadcasting station and in all the theater projection booths. The master projection machine begins throwing the photoplay upon the screen at the broadcasting station and simultaneously, to a fraction of a second, the silversheets at the various theaters are illuminated with the shadow drama. And at the broadcasting station the movie actors are re-enacting the drama, speaking out their lines, word for word, just as though the many different audiences were seated down in front instead of in many different theaters many miles apart. The actors watch the film being screened by the master projector very closely lest they supply the speakies too swiftly or too slowly for the movies.[2]

Today, we would call this approach to synchronization a *simulcast*. The very existence of the word appears to sanction this practice, while Rothacker's 1922 experiment somehow strikes us as pitifully misguided. We laugh when the Chicago Tribune film critic, describing the sound system for the opening of *Don Juan* four years later, explains that the sound comes from "a miniature broadcasting station perched up in the projecting room" (Russell). The problem isn't restricted to Chicago, though. It resides instead in our own tendency to draw barriers around the media, to assume that cinema's identity is once and for all determined and no longer subject to history.

Just what did Vitaphone mean when it compiled its first program of film shorts? A look at the history of radio in 1925–26 makes it quite clear how Vitaphone defined "film" at this point. On January 1, 1925, an all-start cast of Victor recording stars, led by tenor John McCormack, gave a live concert over a chain of AT&T-controlled radio stations spearheaded by WEAF (affectionately known as the tollbooth of the air, because AT&T insisted on identifying radio broadcasting as "radiotelephony," in order to circumvent an agreement whereby RCA could monopolize radio while AT&T would have a free hand with telephone). With AT&T contributing the air time, the Victor artists were not paid, thus arousing the ire of the ever-vigilant Equity union. For the first half of 1925, and then again in the beginning of 1926, this arrangement was perpetuated on a weekly basis. While Equity pressure had caused McCormack to withdraw, top talent nevertheless continued to contribute. The quality of the performers, the protestations of the union, and the resultant publicity combined to concentrate public attention on these weekly concerts.

It is thus no surprise that Warners should model their first variety film program on Victor's successful radio program, right down to their signing of John McCormack. Though McCormack eventually did not appear in the opening Vitaphone program, Warners' advance announcement of the new process leaves no doubt about their intention of recreating Victor's radio show: "At a phenomenally small cost," explained Albert Warner, "the unquestionably planned and perfected radio music program will begin a new era for moving picture patrons throughout the country" (New York Times, April 26, 1926). In 1908, Cameraphone recorded vaudeville in order to sell film. In 1926, the system has changed; now it was radio that film must emulate. But not just radio.

1926: Cinema as Phonography

Histories of cinema typically treat Hollywood's conversion to sound as the culmination of a long march toward today's technology. Edison dreamed of linking the phonograph and the moving picture. DeForest invented the Audion tube and the sound-on-film recording process. Scientists at Bell Laboratories perfected the sound-on-disk process. Warner Brothers took a chance on the new system and produced *Don Juan* and *The Jazz Singer*. Case and Sponable made the sound-on-film system commercially viable. Fox used their new system for its Movietone newsreels. All the other companies followed suit. In a word, this is the standard story.

It didn't happen quite that way. While during the post-war period DeForest seems to have been driven by a desire to perfect a sound-on-film system, Bell Laboratories had more important fish to fry. With new sound apparatus in every domain (microphones, amplifiers, recording methods, loudspeakers, and much more), Bell made a frontal assault on two important and lucrative fields: public address and phonography. The appearance of the Orthophonic Victrola in 1925 brought these efforts to a successful conclusion. For the first time bringing together the benefits of electrical recording, matched impedance, and the folded speaker horn, the Orthophonic Victrola was rightly hailed as a revolution in the phonograph field. In fact, Bell licensees Victor and Brunswick were so convinced of the revolutionary nature of the new system that they made a point of selling off their entire stock of existing phonographs before marketing the new victrola. Then, in 1926, they began an all-out media blitz in favor of the new phonograph.

When Bell, Western Electric, and Warners got into the sound film business, their actions were almost entirely unrelated to DeForest's sound-on-film experiments. On the contrary, *Don Juan*, the Vitaphone shorts, and *The Jazz Singer* were an outgrowth of the record industry. By and large unaware of the specific background of the Warner Brothers experiment, the critics of the period were nevertheless not fooled by the new medium. With the Vitaphone process, said a New York Times reviewer, "the eye as well as the ear is engaged in the business." That's right: "the eye as well as the ear." For this reviewer, the recorded sound is clearly primary, with the image added on to provide illustration. A Chicago critic was more specific: Vitaphone sounded like "a telephone plus a phonograph plus a radio" (Ashton Stevens in the Herald-Examiner, quoted in Weaver, 29).

A year later, the headlines were all garnered by *The Jazz Singer*, but the reviews remained the same. "*The Jazz Singer*, primarily, is scarcely a motion picture," says John S. Spargo of the *Exhibitor's Herald*. "It should more properly be labeled an enlarged Vitaphone record of Al Jolson in half a dozen songs" (Spargo). Bert Ennis was even more straightforward: "when it comes right down to it, what is a talking picture but a phonograph record with plenty of amplification behind it?" (Ennis, 43). MTV, move over. Music videos were hardly the first to conceive of cinema as illustrated phonography.

1929: Cinema as Telephony

As developer and monopolistic exploiter of America's telephone network, AT&T had everything to gain from identifying the Vitaphone system with its familiar telephone technology. Against all logic, a 1929 advertisement campaign sought to capitalize on Vitaphone's popularity in order to solidify Western Electric's overall reputation. "It pays to go to theatres equipped by the makers of your telephone," the ad proclaims. On the left a series of drawings of microphones establishes continuity between the familiar telephone mouthpiece and the condenser microphone used in Western Electric's film sound system. On the right a similar set of drawings ties the familiar telephone receiver to Western Electric's loudspeaker horn. Every version of the ad seeks to transfer satisfaction with AT&T's telephone network to the Vitaphone system, and from there to the rest of the Western Electric realm. "This same organization which brought the telephone to its present excellence," the ad affirms, "will likewise constantly seek to improve Sound Picture apparatus still further" (*Photoplay*, September 1929; 13).

In fact, Western Electric's attempts to position Vitaphone as illustrated telephone are not entirely without logic. Throughout the twenties, Bell Labs labored hard to discover the exact properties of sound that make speech comprehensible. Originally conceived as an aid to AT&T's telephone operations, this research eventually proved instrumental in Western Electric's attempts to master theater acoustics. Stressing intelligibility over realism, Western Electric's sound system brought to film sound precisely the same narrow frequency response and dynamic range that made the telephone a communications triumph—and an aesthetic washout.

The list could go on. The important point is that film is not a unified object, nor cinema a homogeneous medium. Viewed retrospectively, cinema may appear to have a stable technologically defined identity, but considered prospectively, cinema takes on a series of disparate identities, its sound-based affinities with other media often challenging its apparent image-based unity.

Typically founded on a particular understanding of their object of study, approaches to history cannot withstand a radical redefinition of that object. It is thus no surprise that the reconsideration of cinema identity offered here should have far-ranging consequences for the writing of cinema history in general. These will be best understood through comparison to the current dominant mode of cinema history writing. As I see it, this mode of historical explanation is built on three simple principles:

1) The principle of *identity*. Each representational technology is identical to itself. For example, a camera obscura is always a camera obscura; that is, in order to be termed a camera obscura an apparatus must minimally perform certain functions deemed constitutive of the stable notion known as "camera obscura." In the same way, cinema is always fundamentally identical to itself. While historical changes are possible, they in no way undermine the transhistorical definition of cinema's identity.

2) The principle of *functional equivalence*. By performing a similar function, one technology or technique may effectively substitute for another. This principle, as extensively employed by David Bordwell in *The Classical Hollywood Cinema*, emphasizes the ability of one system successfully to carry out functions defined and initially performed by another (Bordwell, 1985, especially pp. 5, 248, 303–04).

3) The principle of *succession*. Characterized by metaphors of parentage, birth, and inheritance, the historical accounts constructed by practitioners of the identity and functional equivalence principles are commonly built around a notion of bequest, with each representational technology simply bequeathing its structure and function to a fundamentally similar mode of representation.

However logical these principles may appear, however traditional they may have become in the fields of philosophy, literary criticism, and political science, they fail to provide an appropriate basis for recounting the history of representational technologies. The complexities of historical interaction are better served by the following principles:

1) The principle of *identity redefinition*. According to a constantly varying scale of material, social, and technical needs, apparently identical systems regularly take on new functions and thus new historical roles.[3] In addition, as we have seen in the case of early cinema, the retrospectively defined identity of a particular system often appears fragmented when considered prospectively. With the ascendancy of sound cinema over vaudeville, for example, Cameraphone lost its chance to be defined as a type of vaudeville; instead it has been seen as a (failed) attempt to create sound cinema. But in 1908, no such conclusion could be drawn. Nor, I am suggesting, should it be drawn today. Only by recognizing the tendency of representational technologies to take on multiple identities, constantly redefined, can we understand the complexities of the historical object. For representational technologies are just as subject to the vagaries of reception as are literary and filmic texts; that is, they may be interpreted or defined in more than one way, according to diverse "use formations."[4]

2) The principle of *functional near-equivalence*. Bordwell rightly recognizes the desire of artistic and technical personnel to provide more efficient or more versatile equivalents of existing techniques and technologies. While providing improvement in one area, however, such efforts invariably cause disturbances in another, precisely because of their non-equivalence in that other area. The combination of a longing for true functional equivalents and the impossibility of creating them is one of the prime movers of history. The problems that enter through the back door of non-equivalence are just as important as the fully equivalent front door improvements. For example, the adoption of Wollaston's meniscus lens was important for reducing the exposure time of early photographs, yet while increasing available light, the new lens simultaneously introduced chromatic aberrations, causing a disparity between the focus of visible yellow light on the ground glass and recordable blue light on the plate.[5] All changes in representational practice conform to this model: equivalence and improvement in one area are accompanied by a zone of non-equivalence in another.

If cinema had a single identity, with a single defining principle, then it might be possible to envisage a linear history involving successive functional equivalents (or progressive developments of, say, the attempt to create a viable sound film system), but cinema's successive conflation with other media has created multiple sets of conflicting desiderata, thus precluding true equivalents. Each attempt at producing an equivalent system stems from a desire to maximize one particular set of values; judged from the standpoint of a conflicting value structure, however, the new system always reveals a lack or excess not present in the old system.

3) The principle of *jurisdictional struggle*. According to the principle of identity redefinition, new representational technologies are subject to multiple definition, with the models provided by competing reality codes. Whereas the principle of succession assumes a stable situation, in which the shape of the future is assured by the political structure of the present, the approach that I am proposing here assumes a constant skirmishing over questions of investiture. Not just "who will be the next sovereign?" but "what body may decide who shall rule?" Not "what decision will be made?" but "according to what principle will the decision be made?" Not the language of hereditary monarchy but that of revolutionary freedom.

Practically speaking, the tendency of representational technologies (especially during their formative years) toward multiple definition has regularly led to quite literal jurisdictional skirmishes. The rise of the nickelodeon, for example, was heavily marked by repeated battles, on the local or state level, over the legal definition that would be attached to moving-picture shows. In the watershed year of 1908–09, for example, films were classified as a circus in Delaware and as an exhibition in Arkansas (until April, 1909, when they were reclassified as theater). *Views and Films Index* says they are "neither a book nor a drama, but . . . a photograph" (March 21, 1908; p. 6), while in the *Ben Hur* trial they are characterized by the U.S. Court of Appeals as "stage representations".

It is hardly surprising that Essanay's 1910 contest to name the new medium should conclude with an overt compromise: the *photoplay*. Why not the vaudesong, the pictobook, or the dramatone?—because of copyright decisions, the need for easily reproducible subject matter, evolving standards of narrative as an entertainment vehicle, and many other reasons too complex to evoke here. Whatever the answer given, the problem is clearly defined in terms of a territorial struggle in which existing systems battle for supremacy over a new medium. The important novelty in the approach I am suggesting here is contained not in this or that particular explanatory sentence, but in an overall argument structure that turns on jurisdictional concerns, on an ongoing struggle to define the representational technology and its products in a particular manner.

Traditional accounts of Hollywood's conversion to sound, for example, foregrounded the history of attempts to perfect sound cinema, the finances of Warner Bros., or the heroic innovations of the first sound directors. An account more attuned to the problem of jurisdictional struggle would stress instead the multiple identities of film sound in the mid-twenties (as radio, record, public address, theater, telephone, and so on), the near-equivalences characteristic of each attempt to translate silent practice into sound, and the constant battles over who should have jurisdiction over jobs and decisions. Who should play the disks in the theater? The projectionist, a musician, an electrician, or a stagehand? Who should apply the sound insulation to studio sets? Should the needs of sound men or the desires of cinematographers have priority during a take? Somehow it seems appropriate that *Photoplay*, the very magazine that took Essanay's 1910 contest name, should run its own contest to name the talkies. Eschewing the obvious *phonoplay, Photoplay* instead opted for audien, a term so unfamiliar today as to suggest that, in 1929, Hollywood was simply not yet fully ready to define its project. The jurisdictional phase of the conversion to sound had not yet come to a close.

Legal jurisdiction, union jurisdiction, aesthetic jurisdiction—these and many more are implied by the notion of jurisdictional struggle, with the complex social investments that each of these implies.

If all we were trying to explain were the image, the identity/functional equivalence/succession model might prove acceptable. As soon as we grant a hearing to the cinema sound track, however, an entirely different decision must be rendered. Film sound's multiplicity of related technologies and connotations, the impossibility of satisfying all interested parties with any proposed functional equivalence, and the constant need to adjudicate among differing sound sources, values, and industries lead directly to a new understanding of the way in which history must be configured, as long as sound is to be part of the figure.[6]

6

Historical and Theoretical Issues in the Coming of Recorded Sound to the Cinema

Alan Williams

The period of the transition to sound film offers a splendid example of historical overdetermination. Separating out the various cultural, economic, and technological determinants involved is a complicated and delicate task. This essay will examine several problems related to the adoption of synchronous sound technology. In some of them, issues of historiography and film theory intertwine, and only tentative answers can be suggested for complex questions. One takes the transition to sound so much for granted: things happened the way they did, therefore they *must*, it seems, have happened the way they did. There is no ready way of conceptualizing the role of historical contingency in the process, nor of thinking precisely about the extent to which it may indeed be true that recorded sound came to the commercial cinema because it was, in fact, inevitable.

Teleologies

To consider the latter question is somewhat unfashionable because it invokes the idea of teleology. From the point of view of many film scholars, it would be idealism pure and simple to argue that there is something intrinsic to the cinema that calls for the addition of recorded sound to the recorded images which first defined the medium. Here, however, one must make the distinction between cinema as technology and as institution. However much we must avoid teleological thinking about the former, the latter often seems to call for it. In this area, as in so much else, contemporary thinking reacts against the legacy of André Bazin, who once described the transition to sound cinema using a religious metaphor. So-called "silent" cinema—it was almost never truly silent—

is the "Old Testament" of the art form; by implication, sound filmmaking is the New Testament, and sound technology the Savior (Bazin 1967, 23). Bazin viewed cinema history as characterized by an ever-increasing drive toward realism; the advent of the talkies fits so well into his thinking that he simply takes it for granted in his essays on film history.

In the post-Bazinian era, this schema has been denounced without being replaced by anything significantly more satisfactory.[1] Broadly speaking, the "realism" of narrative cinema, both "silent" and sound, is held to be an illusory construct created through conventions, the multiply-determined product of a need for unity and transparence on the part of the viewing subject. The logical consequence of this view, however, is a new teleology based on the cinema's elaboration of an increasingly convincing simulacrum of the real, the desire for which is grounded in human psychology in the same general way as is Bazin's idea of a fundamental need for realism.

The problem for any such view of film history is that sound cinema seems to have had little appeal for spectators—beyond its curiosity value—for more than twenty-five years after it became technologically practical. The first successful public presentations of synchronized sound processes were made at the Paris Exposition Internationale in 1900. The modern reconstructions of several of the films presented there seem crude enough in terms of sound quality and image manipulation (there is no editing), but one does understand the words, and certain sound effects (dancing feet on a stage, for example) have real impact. No one seems to have complained, in any event, that these early sound films were fundamentally unsatisfactory from the point of view of realism. Nor were there such complaints about the Pathé Frères and Gaumont processes test marketed in the decade that followed. Public reaction to them, however, was so tepid that the French producers gave up their pioneering efforts entirely, only to become victims of German and American patent holders in the late 1920s.

Until Vitaphone, in fact, the history of sound filmmaking is the history of repeated failure, not of technology but of marketing. Even Thomas Alva Edison, with his great resources and flair for publicity, failed miserably at it. Edison's technology, it is true, was surprisingly primitive. The electrical recording and amplification systems which came later almost certainly produced better quality sound, but if there were an innate vocation of the cinema to be an art of the real, or of spectators to demand an aural complement to cinematic duplication of the Lacanian mirror-stage, surely these cannot have been terribly strong—at least not before 1927. It is often argued that the problem of attracting audiences was mainly technical, due to inadequate amplification and synchronization. But the early Gaumont sound films were presented to audiences of 5000 (!) patrons at the Gaumont Palace in Paris, using an amplification system based on compressed air. And Lee DeForest's Phonophone process, virtually immune to synchronization problems, was extensively test marketed in the early 1920s. One journalist titled his review of this direct ancestor of modern sound-on-film processes: "New Talking Picture Is Shown—But What of It?" (Geduld 1975, 98).

If there was an evolutionary pressure at work in cinema history which eventually culminated in the general adoption of synchronized recorded sound, this trend arguably has little to do with demand, the sphere of consumption, and much to do with the logic of industrial production. For what the triumph of Warner Bros.' Vitaphone finally accomplished was to complete a process begun long before: the progressive mechanization of the cinematographic spectacle. Years before the 1895 debut of the Lumière Cinématographe, Emile Reynaud's Optical Theatre projected moving images (painted, not photographed) onto a screen. The Lumière apparatus did not immediately drive this competition out of business but did exert considerable economic pressure, because Reynaud's spectacle was *incompletely mechanized*. Not only were his images painted rather than photographed (thus taking much time and skill to produce), but each projection was in the fullest sense a performance, in which sequences of images were run forwards and backwards, at varying rates (and hence required a well-trained, adept operator).

Emile Reynaud had, as did the Lumières, a musical accompaniment played on a piano. The intervening years before Vitaphone had further mechanized the film show in virtually every respect except for that. For example, most films had some form of color. At first, as in Reynaud's spectacle, color was hand-painted by brush onto individual copies, but soon stencil processes such as Pathécolor and the cheaper methods of tinting and toning became widely adopted. There remained great variability—even among individual copies of the "same" film—until the general adoption of "natural" (completely mechanized) color processes.[2] The coming of synchronized recorded sound to world cinema essentially completes the mechanization of the medium. And with full mechanization comes the most pervasive, general change brought about by the conversion to sound: increased standardization. Silent film presentations had been notoriously variable. Works could be projected at different speeds, with operators advised in some manuals of their trade to vary the rhythm of projection within a given film. A single work could exist in different versions: black and white, or colored by one of several methods; long, short, or medium length; accompanied by large orchestra using carefully planned cue sheets, or by a single drunken pianist. Between individual films, there were enormous variations, perhaps most notably in running time. Acting styles, set design, and other elements of film style also varied widely—far more than they would with the arrival of the talkies.

This tendency toward mechanization and standardization outlines a teleology considerably less mystical than the Bazinian one or its possible successors.[3] It also helps explain why pressure for the adoption of recorded sound came persistently from the production sector of the industry, and not from exhibition. The new technology engendered a radical rebalancing of power relations within the industry: whereas before the talkies the luxury and particular style of a cinema theatre and the popularity of its musical performers were often more important (and directly controllable by the exhibitor) to total revenues than the films themselves, after the transition to recorded sound the films, and almost only the films, counted. Warner Bros. owned few cinemas, which largely explains why it, of all studios, was the pioneering force in the drive to mechanize cinema sound. But exhibitors did in fact make windfall profits from the talkies when they finally arrived. And this is one of the great mysteries of this part of film history. Why, with no previous indications of dissatisfaction, did audiences suddenly embrace the talkies, acting as if they had been dissatisfied with "silent" cinema for a long time?

We can only speculate on the answer to this question, but such speculation is not necessarily fruitless. It is worth remembering that the partisans of the "art of silence" denounced the coming of the talkies as cutting down in its prime a "mature" art form. This may have been, precisely, the point. If mass culture works as a kind of corrupt, speeded-up parody of traditional, elite culture, then one would expect change precisely at a point of "maturity," where novel effects within an established system of conventions become increasingly difficult. What is surprising about the demise of the "silent" feature is how *soon* it occurred, and not *that* it occurred. And this problem introduces the other major mystery of the history of sound cinema: why did momentum for change grow irresistible in the wake of one specific film, a work which is widely considered so clumsy and unconvincing as to be unwatchable today?

Why *The Jazz Singer*?

If *The Jazz Singer* had not existed, culturally inclined historians would be tempted to invent it. Few films crystallize the contending forces in a given historical moment as clearly as this one does, and few have had more direct impact on what happened to the medium after them. It had, perhaps most crucially, the distinction of combining two film forms that until then had been kept distinct. These corresponded to the two uses that Warner Bros. envisioned for Vitaphone: canned musical (and other) stage performances, filmed with synchronous sound; and "silent" narrative films accompanied not by a live orchestra but by a recorded one (with, as in standard live accompaniments, selected sound effects). These were, perhaps not coincidentally, the two formats through which Lee DeForest had exhibited the Phonophone, and while Warners stuck with them as separate entities it had only somewhat more success in marketing its process than had the inventor. In *The Jazz Singer*, the barriers come down and the two genres contaminate one another, with cataclysmic results. Many modern viewers experience the transition from the musical numbers to the silent narrative as almost physically painful, and from the latter to the former as liberating, like a chance to breathe anew. Did contemporary audiences feel the same way? Almost certainly not, but it seems likely that the film's curious structure invited its viewers to participate in a kind of do-it-yourself test or referendum on the uses of the new medium. The crucial difference between *The Jazz Singer* and all previous attempts to market recorded sound was this co-presence of two kinds of discourse *within a single work*.

But there is another, somewhat less obvious aspect of the film's persistent duality. As Robert L. Carringer has astutely argued, if one removes the sequences about Jackie Rabinowitz's relations with his family, "what we are left with—the drive to success, the relentless pace of the chorus line in rehearsal, the show-must-go-on motif, the miraculous last-minute leap over film and circumstances, the resounding triumph at the end—are the main plot elements of one of the most successful genres in the studio's history, the backstage musical of the thirties" (Carringer 1979, 27). In this way the film looks forward in cinema history; but in another way it offers the beginnings of a farewell to another kind of cinema, and another sensibility. The other parts of the film form an equally recognizable, if abbreviated version of a major film genre: family melodrama, written and executed in the hyperbolic, ultra-sentimental style that characterized the melodrama in cinema before the talkies.

Jackie's feeling for his mother, for example, is evoked on the sound track by a full-blast rendition of the love theme from Tchaikovsky's *Romeo and Juliet*. In these parts of the film Jolson's gestures, such as clasping both hands together over his heart, could have been taken from an old stage melodrama handbook for actors—not from a handbook written for players in the late twenties, however: by the time of the film, this kind of playing and subject matter was considered horribly outdated by most opinion leaders in the theatrical communities of major cities. As many reviewers and later commentators have pointed out, the film coarsens and all but caricatures its already not terribly subtle source, the Broadway hit by Samson Rafelson (Carringer 1979, 20–28). But it does this primarily in its domestic melodrama sequences. This sort of story, and performance style, had been a staple of Hollywood since well before World War I, but by the late twenties it was on the wane.

What is important about this is that the sync sound performances are persistently associated with the backstage musical strand of the film. Even the two performances (out of eight in the film) by Jackie's father are made major turning points of the stage musical plot, and in other ways recuperated by it. The first, "Kol Nidre," is later sung by Jackie as his farewell to his heritage just before (in film, though not fictional time) he goes on the Broadway stage to sing "Mammy." The second is a performance by Cantor Rabinowitz which Jackie attends unbeknownst to his father—not at all by coincidence the "Yahrzeit," a secular work sung in commemoration of a death (the son's symbolic death in the eyes of his father). (For further details on these and other religious and ethnic aspects of the film, see Carringer, 1979, *passim*.)

And if the father's performances are made to function as aspects of the son's tale, Cantor Rabinowitz attempts, at one highly charged moment, to have his own say about his son's singing. It is often said that the only dialogue in *The Jazz Singer* got there virtually by accident (Jolson's supposedly irrepressible urge to improvise), but there is ample reason to doubt this. Jackie's father's reaction to his rendition of "Blue Skies," in any event, is not written on a title card: aghast at the desecration of his house by "jazz," he cries "STOP!" It seems one of the most momentous spoken words in all of sound cinema, wrenching the film out of its most developed music-with-speech sequence and back into the traditional discourse of "silent" cinema. It is as if the older man is also saying stop to the sound recording machines, and they obey. In this way and in others as well, the film persistently associates the old cinema with the Rabinowitz family, and the new one with Jack Robin, as Jackie is called in the other parts of the film. If one identifies with the leading character's desire to succeed, to please audiences, to find freedom outside of what is presented as a quaint but stifling immigrant tradition, as the film throughout invites one to do, then one is led also to prefer the medium by which "Jack" finds fulfillment: the talking picture.

The Impact of the Talkies

People involved with film production everywhere felt their world shake with the sustained popular success of *The Jazz Singer*. Frances (Mrs. Sam) Goldwyn reportedly called the film's Los Angeles premiere "the most important event in cultural history since Martin Luther nailed his theses on the church door" (Berg, 89, 173). The standard textbook account is of massive disruption: producers panicked; careers were ruined; no one knew how to use the new technology, and so sound recordists became *de facto* directors; the art of the film took a giant, if temporary, step backwards, particularly in editing and camera movement. Some specific points in this account are clearly in need of revision. The power of the sound engineers, for example, seems to have varied from company to company and even project to project, and a strong-willed producer, director, or cinematographer could often obtain spectacular movement out of the primitive early sound cameras. However, most scholars accept the basic story of panic and drift.

In this context, the account given in Bordwell, Thompson, and Staiger's *The Classical Hollywood Cinema* is refreshingly counterintuitive. In a (significantly) brief chapter of that massive work, David Bordwell argues that recorded synchronous sound produced only certain "adjustments in film style. . . . Sound cinema was not a radical alternative to silent filmmaking; sound as sound, as a material and as a set of technical procedures, was inserted into the already constituted system of the classical Hollywood style" (Bordwell *et al* 1985, 298, 301). Although certain qualifications of *The Classical Hollywood Cinema*'s account of the transition will be suggested here, the usefulness and significance of the book for an understanding of the period is great. Bordwell's central thesis seems unassailable (though its terms are limited to a relatively narrow definition of visual style). But how is one to reconcile his vision of industry calculation and stylistic continuity with the more popular image of near-revolution (or reformation)? On the most important level, there is really no problem at all: Bordwell is working with relatively large temporal units, as many modern historians do, and from his perspective continuity and calculated adjustment emerge against a background of temporary "noise" (the two years or so of the heart of the transition).[4]

Even more important, *The Classical Hollywood Cinema* does not construct its model of "silent" cinema using the films most film scholars know from the period.[5] The accepted canon of "silent" masterpieces has inevitably tended to center on works *not* like the talkies, presumably to give audiences habituated to sound some reason to want to see something else. But films like Howard Hawks' *A Girl in Every Port* (1928), or—to give a European example—Henri Fescourt's *Les Grands* (1924), really are stylistically very much like talkies without the sound—more so than many better-known "silent" features. They do not, for example, have the dissolves within continuous scenes accepted by audiences and filmmakers before recorded sound but virtually prohibited afterwards. But this small example raises an interesting point: the possibility of confusion about what the "real" silent cinema was like suggests that there may well have been greater heterogeneity, more stylistic options within the classical system before the talkies came. If sync sound did not fundamentally *change* the textuality of Hollywood films, it did arguably make the system stronger and more normative.

Why would this have occurred? An extremely useful avenue of approach to the question was indicated by Sergei Eisenstein in his "Statement on the Sound-Film": "every ADHESION of sound to a visual montage piece [shot] increases its inertia as a montage piece and will increase the independence of its meaning." He worried that this greater inertia and semantic independence of shots with synchronous sound would be "to the detriment of montage," and indeed montage as he knew it largely died with the coming of the talkies (Eisenstein 1928, 258). Whether these characteristics of the sound film were the *only* reasons for the decline of Eisenstein's and other alternative approaches to cinema is a complex historiographical issue, as we will briefly see in the next section. But inertia (phenomenologically, the sense of weight and "presentness" of the image) and semantic independence not only work against montage in the strong, Eisensteinian sense; they also pose problems for continuity editing, making it more difficult to end shots unobtrusively and connect them "transparently" to other shots. Furthermore, "silent" cinema had a fundamental source of continuity which was largely absent from sound film, except at points of narrative discontinuity (for example, scene changes or temporal ellipses) or heightened emotion: the musical accompaniment, which appears to have acted like a secondary narrator for the spectator. With the talkies, musical continuity all but disappeared at the same time that the individual shots acquired greater inertia and semantic independence. And so it is no wonder that the "rules" of the continuity system which is the fundamental basis of classical Hollywood style suddenly seem to be in force with greater vigor in the early days of the talkies.

The narrowing and increasing codification of visual style does not, however, entirely account for the widespread intuitive sense of an enormous break with the coming of sound to the American cinema. But the purely technological transition to sound cinema, and the stylistic adjustments to it, are by no means the only factors at work in film history between 1927 and the early 1930s. The adoption of sound recording causes other historical currents to surface, or to intensify. Although Hollywood film (visual) *style* may have changed relatively little, film content is another matter entirely. Pressures for change that had been building over the years seem to have been released with the coming of recorded sound, and American filmmaking quite strikingly all but abandoned an *ethos* which had been a major component in its definition in earlier years.

For the coming of the talkies coincides with the decline of traditional stage melodrama in mainstream commercial cinema, virtually the last place where it still thrived. This is the melodrama of D. W. Griffith, of pure maidens tied to railroad tracks, of spectacular confrontations between good and evil. Melodrama in this historically specific sense was born in the aftermath of the French Revolution and shared for most of its history the Revolutionary ideal of *sensibilité*. Characters poured out their feelings to one another and to the audience, baring their souls in moments of moral transparency. Contrary to modern, dismissive stereotypes of the genre, good did not always triumph over evil; it was the battle that mattered most, and the lessons that could be learned from it.

Nothing intrinsic to the new machinery obliged filmmakers to reject this kind of story and manner of storytelling—particularly the expressive gestures and eye-catching, non-naturalistic settings—when the industry converted to sound. Nothing, that is, unless one assumes that pressure inevitably existed to employ extensively the most obvious kind of synchronous sound, human speech. Assuming this pressure existed, then the melodramatic tradition was almost automatically imperiled. There was little talk, and a great deal of music and sound effects, in traditional melodrama, which is what made it an ideal match for "silent" cinema. One is tempted to argue that it is precisely melodrama, and the melodramatic esthetic which characterizes so much of pre-talkie world cinema, that kept the silent film viable as an entertainment form. From this point of view, when the former ceased to appeal to audiences, the latter was doomed, and all it took was the right sort of push to bring the edifice crashing to the ground. As it happened, that push was given by *The Jazz Singer*, but if it not been made, some other, similar work would probably have done the job as well.

Whether one wishes to make the decline of traditional melodrama a primary factor in the transition to sound or not, it remains a key element for the explanation of many aspects of the transition. For example, the decline in the careers of certain stars of silent cinema, such as John Gilbert or Ramon Novarro, is said to have occurred because their voices "recorded badly." This is at best an obscure notion, except in the cases of players such as Vilma Banky who had such thick accents that their lines were difficult to understand. Listening today to Gilbert or Novarro, one is struck by how *well* their voices recorded. And even foreign accents were not an insurmountable barrier to success in the talkies, as Garbo's case demonstrates. Leaving aside the truly vocally impaired—probably only a handful of players at most—the "bad voices" of the most notorious Hollywood stars were probably in part a product of their association with melodramatic *sensibilité*.

It was, most notably, certain of the men who suffered, those whose acting was expressive, whose screen personas were somehow feminized, in the terms of the new film culture. For them, perhaps, *no* voice would have "recorded well." It is, for example, around the time of the transition to sound that male characters begin to cry far less frequently—and that crying begins to signify, not admirable sensitivity, but hysteria and sexual ambiguity. Perhaps the most striking symptom of the decline of the melodramatic sensibility in American cinema is this change in male gender definition, but it is not the only sign of transformation. Women characters, too, underwent a similar but less complete sea change. Wise-cracking, irony, and self-control characterized many of the new female roles and star images, but some of the older sensibility survived in the generic ghetto of the "woman's picture" and in the larger category of family melodrama. Is the decline of traditional melodrama causally linked in some way to the transition to sound cinema? The new, post-melodramatic males and females would have seemed strange indeed and difficult to comprehend before the talkies, their behaviors grounded in a denial of what made the "silent" film tick: bodily expressiveness. The liberation of speech brings with it the repression of the body; whether this is technologically and psychologically inevitable or, on the other hand, historically contingent (the expression of the transition from one sort of social structure to another) deserves to be the subject of debate and further research.

Hollywood and the World

It is too rarely remarked that the shape of the transition to sound in the rest of the world seems to have been rather different from what happened in the United States. In Europe, the coming of sound brought relative stylistic uniformity to a diverse set of textual strategies produced by a remarkable variety of art movements, tendencies, and stubborn individualists. In France, for example, this period coincides with the death of the "Impressionist" film art movement, as well as the near-total decline of the extra-industrial avant-garde or experimental cinema that had proliferated during the years between 1924 and 1929. In Germany, only a few Expressionist works were made with the new technology.[6] And in the U.S.S.R., the first sound feature—Ekk's *The Road to Life*—is also the first manifestation of Soviet Socialist Realism (or classical Hollywood style in the service of the Party).

As the last case should suggest, here we encounter the crucial historiographic problem that the transition to recorded sound occurred at a moment of great social and political change throughout the world. There is no immediate, local connection between the final stage of the basic mechanization of the cinema and the consolidation of Stalin's power in the Soviet Union, which finds expression (among many other places) in the adoption of Socialist Realism as the only sanctioned method of filmmaking. Or rather, there is no connection except that the new medium offered a powerful pretext for imposing uniform adherence to a new "line," and that it makes film production more capital-intensive and thus a more pressing target for administrative centralization. What the Soviet example shares with the more typical disruptions linked to the market economy is a demonstration of what we might call the "earthquake theory" of film history: upheavals such as the coming of recorded sound intensify and help direct the progress of trends already in place. In continental Europe, for example, these included the weakening and fragmentation of the post war avant-garde movements.

Everywhere, the coming of sound appears to have reduced diversity and acted against those who would oppose the classical Hollywood cinema with an alternative of their own. Was this uniquely the result of something intrinsic to sound recording technology? This seems unlikely. But it seems defensible to attribute the worldwide imposition of classical Hollywood style in at least some measure to the peculiarities of the development of sound technology and of spectator psychology. With early equipment, maximum intelligibility was obtained only with direct recording of dialogue; "dubbing" was not a satisfactory option for roughly a decade. Those films which succeeded best at the box office were the ones which continued (and perhaps also marked the consolidation of) the classical Hollywood style. And yet Hollywood itself was suddenly in a position of competitive international inferiority in the production of precisely this kind of product, because of the linguistic specificity of its films. American producers experimented with producing multiple, foreign language versions of their films, but these proved unprofitable in most markets and were almost completely abandoned by 1932.

Why the multi-language system of production was so spectacularly unsuccessful is a matter of no small interest to students of film sound. It cannot be exclusively the fault of the American studios' desire to make such projects very cheaply; the German mega-studio UFA made a similar effort (mainly directed at the French market) with much greater financial and artistic resources, only to fail more slowly and less dramatically at it than American studios such as Paramount and MGM. One reasonable hypothesis might be that recorded speech, as opposed to written titles, fatally introduced an element of cultural and social specificity into narrative film that simply hadn't been there before. Spectators reading title cards to themselves provided their own voices for them. Suddenly, with the talkies, there were *other* voices, having clearly identifiable social origins. Once this happened, the cultural and social sensitivities of different audiences would have become vastly more easily to disturb, since film stories with spoken dialogue took place in a world more solidly grounded in the experience of everyday life—as opposed to fantasies about it. Postsynchronization—which even in the most proficient hands reintroduces an element of the abstract, "neutral" voices of silent spectatorship—

would later emerge as a kind of perfect compromise between the painful cultural specificity of recorded speech and the abstract, spectator-generated "voices" of silent titles. By the late 1930s, dubbed films would help Hollywood regain its world hegemony. The exact role of sound technology in this is, evidently, a potentially fruitful ground for historical and theoretical reflection. (For a related commentary in this area, see Williams 1981.)

Thus, for a while at least, sound cinema brought a measure of protection to the formerly all too porous non-American market. Having created a great public demand for a certain type of product, the talkies also (temporarily) weakened the most efficient producer of that product in most of the world. No wonder that new production companies throughout the world rushed to supply the works that the U.S. could now provide only in English. Ambitious European producers no longer were obliged to remain in the "art cinema" niche of their own markets, and production capital migrated to where rates of return were the highest. This, perhaps acting in tandem with the greater "inertia" and semantic independence of images with synchronous sound, would have all but doomed both the radical avant-garde and the commercially oriented "art cinema" in Europe— though the exact relationship between these two determinants remains to be specified. All of which is to suggest that if *The Classical Hollywood Cinema* is right, and sound recording in and of itself changed Hollywood filmmaking relatively little, it nonetheless helped change the rest of world cinema in a quite fundamental way.

7

Translating America: The Hollywood Multilinguals 1929–1933

Nataša Ďurovičová

". . . by now it has become impossible to dub in the dialogue of a sound film."

—Istvan Fodor, *Film Dubbing* (1975)

"America is the original version of modernity. We are the dubbed, the subtitled version."

—Jean Baudrillard, *America* (1988)

A test case of historiography in film studies, the history of sound has been what we might call a growth industry. It has developed essentially in three theoretical directions: economic histories that emphasize the role of determinants like financing, quotas, patents and distribution practices (Gomery 1980, Josse, Thompson); technological histories that consider, for instance, links between broadcast and film sound reproduction in revising the history of miking (e.g. Altman 1985b and 1986a, Pereboom); and aesthetic histories, that is, polemics variously engaged with the heritage of Bazinian ontological determinism, and, in particular, with debates over the ideological foundations of the aesthetic ideal of "realism" (Altman 1980c, Doane 1980b, Metz, Williams). What all three directions have in common—as goal and as outcome—is to account in a systematic fashion for the dominance of "the classical model," each choosing a different starting point to chart the relations between stylistic, technical and technological conventions and the most economically viable modes of film production. In a common "catch-22" of system-building, however, these approaches are prone to subsume to their overall model, as a structurally contained "differentiation," any phenomenon that strays too far from the theoretically established norms of change.[1]

The peculiar historiographical problem I want to consider here presents itself in a set of films known as "multilinguals" or "foreign language versions" (hereafter abbreviated as FLVs). These films (mostly, but far from exclusively, of American origin) were made mainly between the years of 1929 and 1933 by a given country in one or several languages other than its own, in a production process that involved reshooting the entire "original" film with actors fluent in the relevant language. When acknowledged at all by recent histories, these films appear as little more than eccentric holding actions, freak experiments, glitches *en route* to the technological solution of the language barrier. As soon as dubbing and subtitling become commonplace, the foreign language versions vanish— so the argument goes. These ". . . special language versions had a short life (1930–31), and served only as the transition to the dubbing process still in use today."[2] The brevity of the phenomenon is taken as a proof of its insignificance.[3]

Even if we were to settle for the barest and most functional reading of the FLVs, understanding (with Douglas Gomery or Kristin Thompson) the enormous additional expenditure and the deviation from standardized production methods, as the films are reshot time and time again, simply as a series of risky but necessary experiments in the service of a rapid innovation and diffusion, there would be more to say. The multilinguals would still remain as fascinating traces of the complexity and turbulence brought about by the transition to sound, bearing testimony to the full range of sound track options. Yet it is out of this very disturbance that the American cinema's relationship to the non-"American"-speaking world has emerged, even as other arrangements between language, economy and power (for instance that of Germany to other European and Asian countries) were being negotiated and established. Problems related to the multilinguals—how to regulate the transposition of languages—continue to this day to worry classical Hollywood cinema's dissemination to all non-American speakers: to subtitle or not to subtitle, to lip synch or not.[4] The history of FLVs thus properly comes to an end, and can be profitably taken up now, at the moment when English, in its increasing dominance of the global mass media, is about to render obsolete the very idea of a "foreign language."[5]

As soon as the prospect of sound cinema began to be developed systematically, it became evident to all the major studios that while sound in general would be a costly but profitable investment, the newly revealed problem of language would seriously endanger the American cinema's world markets, which by 1929 generated between thirty-five and forty percent of a major studio's profits.[6] This problem was, for instance, the key topic of several Academy of Motion Pictures debates in April, July and September of 1928. Perhaps more importantly, in the already ongoing confrontations with countries outside the USA, language would prove an exceptionally fierce instrument. Since 1921 in Germany, and since roughly 1925 elsewhere, quotas against the extraordinary expansion of American cinema were being widely implemented; this was the case not only in most European countries but also in other parts of the world, for instance in Japan, Brazil and Australia (Thompson 118). The manifest goal of trade regulations was to protect the economic survival of the domestic producers (if not exhibitors—who of course regularly sided with the American interests). Despite the concerted efforts of many countries to stave off the flood, the USA maintained anywhere from fifty to eighty-five percent of market share in most countries through the end of the 1920s (Thompson 219–221).

But the crude terms of economic competition, which the Americans were winning so overwhelmingly by flying the tricolor of universality, electoral democracy, and advanced capitalism (roughly "you asked for it, now we give it to you") were occasionally recast—and translated—into other social discourses. In mid-1925 (just as the campaign for quotas was beginning in the British press), *Variety* reported a series of attacks on American cinema by G. A. Atkinson, the BBC's first film critic and influential drama reviewer for the *Daily Express*, a paper owned by Lord Beaverbrook, himself a major shareholder in British film productions. For Atkinson the corrosive nature of American cinema, and its incompatibility with British national culture, resided in its insistence that all human values—loyalty, patriotism, romantic love, respect for elders—have a direct cash exchange equivalent: no sentiment is too sacred to be compared with the pleasures of the commodities displayed (Atkinson 1925a, 1925b). To this attack, two kinds of responses were published in *Variety*. One simply accused Britons of a symmetrical hypocrisy (roughly 'who are you to teach us morals when your pubs are full of women guzzling beer while nursing their infants?'[7]). The other, more intriguing line of argument claimed that far from a decline into wealth-induced decadence, America's post-war prosperity enabled a more scientific and hence more candid approach to theological and psychosexual problems of the new age as reflected in its screen dramas—a kind of financially empowered upward mobility of the spirit.[8] The author of the latter reply was none other than B. P. Schulberg, the head of Paramount's west coast studios, which stood to benefit greatly from any increase in the guiltless leisure consumption of British masses.[9]

Although neither sound in general, nor linguistic translation proper, is at stake yet, the debate does clearly revolve around the broadest domain of national identity, namely the *cultural* idiom, and, more particularly, its locus and its translatability. While Atkinson wishes to underline Britishness as a distinct and nationally shared discourse (with, say, morality, customs, tradition as signifier and idiosyncracy, uniqueness, non-translatability as its final signified), Schulberg's argument implies that Americanness is not merely an alternative, competing cultural idiom (scientific view of sexuality as signifier, progressive and upwardly mobile social structure as signified). Rather he presents Americanness itself as the very signifier of universal human evolution, subsuming under it all the local currencies of cultural exchange, a limitless melting pot of mores, nations and classes.

If the Atkinson-Schulberg letters respectively assent to and reject Hollywood's position on America as a distinct nation-state within the domain of the English language, a remark made about a year later hints at a similar idea, though one bearing on the industrial rather than on the linguistic site of cultural production. Explaining to the Paris press the exceptional popularity of Hollywood films abroad, United Artists' president Joseph Schenck points out that not only are the American masses already a mixture of all "races" and therefore representative of the entire world, so too is the cosmopolitan world of the Hollywood studios already a cultural microcosm gathering the best and the brightest from all continents. American films cannot fail, therefore, to be the most universal form of art. Europeans are, however, welcome to send over their all too locally colored films—as these always "provide a stimulus to our own production" (*Variety* [November 9, 1927], 10).

It is, then, this Velveeta cheese vision of culture—integration and leveling of differences, followed by a homogenous spread over the entire world—that confronted, around 1928, the ancient and unwieldy formation of language, the domain where a nation's and a subject's identity lock into each other under the regime of the Symbolic (as it finds its expression in the nation-state). From now on, even in Great Britain—linguistically the most "neutral" domain—the discourse surrounding the American cinema ceases to be able to claim unchallenged that Hollywood simply represents a transnational, "modern" contemporaneity. It must, instead, acknowledge that this cinema, too, represents the interest of one particular ideological and cultural formation. But how can—and will—this formation be translated for the benefit of its innumerable foreign recipients?

One possible starting point for tracing out this process of translation may be jazz—the sound track of the Roaring Twenties, the signature melody of pure modernity that perhaps more than any other cultural idiom mediated the reception of America abroad. Hence the European success of *The Jazz Singer* (rather than *Don Juan*) as the icebreaker for Hollywood sound, and the innumerable jazz revues whose enormous popularity underwrote the wiring of the theatres between 1928 and 1930.[10] It could profitably be argued, in a low-Adornoesque vein, that it was jazz, with its predictable harmonic structures, improvisational forms based on repetition, and emphasis on rhythm—that is, its abstracting tendency—that provided the perfect transitional cultural form. The history of *language* reproduction needs, however, to be separated at this point from that of sound in general. Although the addition of music to film was simply part and parcel of the problem of sound reproduction in general, the question raised by language was twofold: how to *re*produce it (technology of speech recording and transmission), but, to an equal degree, how to *produce* it? That is, how to find the proper bodies to generate the proper voices, how to find the proper *sites* from which the proper noises would emanate?

Obviously this was also a problem for English-speaking cinema on the home front. Beyond the apocryphal stories of John Gilbert's voice not being "right" for his body, or of silent careers crashing at the sound of an accent (Walker) the quest for the proper site of language led most of the major studios temporarily to turn their back on California and to concentrate on developing facilities on the East Coast, in closer proximity to New York's language-producing industries: legitimate theatre, publishing, and broadcasting. While the first attempts to make French talkies were undertaken at the British Elstree studios, the German UFA's first full-scale sound film, *Melodie des Hertzens*, was set and partially filmed in Hungary. Displaced in a comparable but more complex fashion, the American FLVs are, I think, attempts simply to *locate*, and progressively to *fabricate*, "the proper body to make the proper noise."[11] The complete history of the FLVs would then comprise the redefinition of this sought-for body as a conceptual (synthetic) rather than a physical (organic) entity, and seek to map the routes by which language's origin shifted from a geographic site to a technological space.

This transition needs to be understood as meandering rather than linear, grounded as it is in an apparent technological redundancy. Even the briefest account of the transition to sound is bound, after all, to include prominently the sound-on-disk (Vitaphone) versus sound-on-film (Movietone) debates. Even though the drawbacks of the sound-on-disk method were evident enough (especially problems in distribution and exhibition), by 1928 the technological principle for matching a separately recorded sound track to a separately shot image track was readily available (Lewin; Wolfe 1990). So why was it necessary to move in the direction of acquiring the foreign body *as a whole*—to undertake, that is, the costly and complicated experiment of the FLVs at all?

On June 6, 1928, *Variety* reports that Paramount's chief special effects designer, Roy Pomeroy, on internal studio loan to head the newly formed sound department, is continuing his work on a separable sound strip, so that Emil Jannings, the studio's exclusively German-speaking star, could record the sound track for his next film in the several languages in which he is fluent. The same article mentions, however, that Jannings is also in the process of learning English, so as to be able to satisfy his American audiences. It is thus evident that while sound track inter-changeability and even the possibility of proper lip synchronization is considered as within reach, Janning's own spoken English, no matter how meager, is not thought to be supplantable by another recorded voice.[12] A characteristic voice is apparently deemed necessary to render a character "site-specific," as if to reinforce the proper social space around the figure and guarantee in turn the continuum of that space. Such a continuum might indeed be the experiential and phenomenal underside of the commonly denigrated "canned theatre" effect. In this light the economic extravaganza of FLVs may be the result of a specific aesthetic assumption—to be contrasted with those underlying a second, more technologically de-manding solution to the problem of the inseparability of body and voice. This latter solution involved, instead, rear projection behind speaking characters, "welding" together two unrelated spatial planes so as to create the illusion of a continuous filmic space (a procedure to which I shall return later).

What precisely, then, was the *modus operandi* of the FLVs? Standard Hollywood studio procedures had by the late 1920s developed the well-known (and much admired) system of divided, vertically managed and highly specialized labor tasks, delegated to studio employees at all levels and fairly strictly monitored—whether they were among the crafts person-nel, featured actors or even stars (Bordwell, Staiger and Thompson 1985; King 1986). In its attempts to combine the industrial imperative of effi-ciency with the linguistically motivated need to duplicate the performance, the FLVs met these practices about halfway. In counter-current to a number of European stars leaving the US because of their difficulties with sound, MGM and Universal in late 1928 began importing foreign actors and directors, mostly from France and Germany, with the specific goal of organizing them within parallel foreign language departments on their own lots. At about the same time, Paramount made, instead, a hugh investment in the sophisticated studios at Joinville outside of Paris (with a $10,000,000 annual budget), where Robert Kane began producing FLVs for Paramount's substantial European markets.[13] While some French-language originals were made to satisfy French quota regulations and to gain a foothold in the initially undersupplied French market, the main emphasis was on the serial remaking of previously released American films in anywhere from three to fourteen language versions, ranging from German to Polish to Japanese. On sets copied from the American originals and manned by expert technical and managerial crews (mostly, if not exclusively, American), troupes of actors from Germany, Czechoslovakia or Sweden would enact, in virtually identical costumes and with identical movements, usually guided by a director from their own country, the same comedy, drama or mystery, with the (union-required) French extras milling about in the identical background spaces. The surreal atmosphere thus generated on the sound stages and in the suburb of Joinville was the target of much vitriolic comment from the French and international cultural establishment—most notably in the Soviet political *flâneur* Ilya Ehrenburg's book-length essay *Fabrika snov (The Dream Factory)*—and continued invariably to provoke violent sentiments whenever referred to in the numerous autobiographies of the many Joinville veterans. Minus the grandly cosmopolitan air, the procedure of "reading off" the staging, acting and editing of the first version while filling in the specialized bodies was also followed by UFA in Berlin, as well as by several smaller European production companies such as Osso, founded by Paramount's former French head Adolphe Osso (Chirat).

The overall strategy of the FLVs, characterized by Ginette Vincendeau as a temporally foreshortened variant of the remake, seems to me more readily understood as following a hybrid logic, that of a theatrical performance from which all leeway for both rehearsal and improvisation—that is, all threat of inefficiency—has gradually been removed. Some problems of this procedure also characterized the production of contemporary American stage-to-screen dramas.[14] However, the conceptual idiosyncracy of the FLV format is most apparent if we consider that the mechanical reproduction of a performance (in some sense at the origins of cinema proper) is here reduplicated by yet another round of "imitation performances," themselves more or less mechanically repeating each other, with the original *découpage* as the "master text."[15] It is as if sifting away even the last trace of any nonstandardized, subjective element in acting was the necessary compensation for the time lost in production due to the duration of speech and its recording.[16] In Paramount's extreme variant of FLVs the national becomes gauged simply as the difference between the least possible and the least necessary inflection of the basic text: the ideology of culture is reduced to a contrast between different-sounding languages. In Paramount producer Geoffrey Shurlock's memorable formulation, the issue was to decide "whether the undoubted theoretical advantage of having every person in the company—from the director and the star to the meanest assistant prop-boy—working, speaking and *thinking* in the same language is great enough to be of practical value, or not" (10).

To understand more precisely how this non-standardized dimension of a *particular* cultural context, a dimension always at least potentially accompanying a theatrical performance, was affected by the copying of the *découpage*, it is necessary to take a close look at a "matched set" of FLVs—for instance *The Lady Lies*, made in 1929 at Paramount's Long Island studios, then reshot (along with four other language versions) in Swedish at Joinville in late 1930 as *Vi Två*.[17] Directed by Hobart Henley, *The Lady Lies* is based on a highly conventional romantic stage comedy by John Meehan. Claudette Colbert is a salesgirl turned mistress of a wealthy widower (played by Walter Huston) who, fearing social pressure from his puritan relatives, refuses at first to marry her, but succumbs, after more pressure, this time from his two teenage children, making Joyce an honest woman after all. Filmed entirely on a sound stage, with the exception of a single cutaway exterior shot (reproduced exactly in the Swedish version), the film has all the earmarks of the "canned theatre" style: minimal camera movement, predominantly theatrical rather than analytic space, conversational rather than action-oriented dramaturgy. One can only speculate whether it was the film's banality, or instead some more specific inscription of universality, that made it eligible to be reshot in five different language versions.

It is possible that the initial decision to transpose the film to French may have been motivated by the one brief allusion to national origins: early in the plot Colbert, employed by the Maison Yvonne Fashions (with outlets in New York and Paris) speaks one brief sentence in her mother tongue, almost a sound effect of sorts, in the flow of her otherwise impeccable American stage English. According to Raymond Chirat's catalogue, the French version, with Jeanne Helbling in Colbert's role, is set in Paris instead of America, thereby grounding and naturalizing the film for its French audience. By contrast, what is curious about the Swedish version is that, rather than receiving a similar contouring to *its* audience's nationality, minimally demanding in terms of production effort, *Vi Två* reverts to its American emplacement. Paramount had clearly intended to market the film as an essentially Swedish product. While Meehan does get screen credit as the author of an original play, none is given for the Swedish adaptation or supplementary dialogue (which would flag the derivative character of the enterprise); neither is the name of a cinematographer listed (most likely the Britisher Harry Stradling). By contrast, the names of the well known Swedish director, John W. Brunius, and the extremely popular male lead, Edwin Adolphson, both feature prominently.

The sets are a close (if somewhat cheaper) replica of the Long Island sets both in terms of the basic floor plan and class references, although even the last remnants of a play with offscreen space have been eliminated here (an ornate staircase is thus replaced by a simpler door)—with one striking exception. In the opening sequence of the American version an open window allows us to glimpse city lights—the vaguely New Yorkish skyline into which the heroine at a later moment threatens to hurl herself lest the marriage not come off. The Joinville set (constructed presumably for the French master set-up) shows instead, undoubtedly by mistake, a background of absolutely iconic, almost René Clair-like Parisian rooftops.

Yet in the Swedish version we are meant to be in Manhattan again: the children have been sent to boarding school in Maine; the brother comforts his worried sister by a song accompanied by a ukulele (an instrument unthinkable in the hands of a Swede); the vicious snob of a cousin is once more characterized as "blue blood Henry Tuttle of the Salem Tuttles"; the Swedish actors address each other by Anglo-Saxon names, glazed, naturally, by their Swedish accents. Joyce thus becomes *Y:oys*, Charlie Rossiter, *Š:órli*, and so forth: here even phonetic transcription can only approximate an effect whose main interest is its non-conformity with normative phonetic systems. Indeed, it is precisely the names that immediately betray the enterprise, as if the actors' bodies were chafing against the characters. This is not exactly a problem of translation—for while it is extremely faithful, it is also quite skillful, colloquial and fluent. What ultimately makes the film so difficult to watch (and what, by extension, may have complicated the reception of the Paramount versions in general) is rather that the sense of comfort with which the Swedish actors speak their lines is essentially incompatible with the manifestly non-Swedish social mannerisms, surroundings and psychological types of the characters. The effect has nothing to do with "bad acting"; neither is the problem here "theatrical acting," in the sense of stylized performances (as we could point to in the case of German cinema). Certainly it is in the theatre that we may most readily find a model for a foreign text in translation, "set abroad" but played for a "domestic" audience.[18] Yet it is precisely in contrast to a stage performer, says Siegfried Kracauer, that "the film actor must seem to be in his character in such a way that all his expressions, gestures and poses point beyond themselves to the diffuse contexts out of which they arise. They must breathe a certain casualness marking them as fragments of an inexhaustible texture" (Kracauer, 95). In the American version, for instance, Claudette Colbert's one French aside could be taken to be such a gesture: the connotations evoked by that narratively useless remark, delivered offscreen, could have indeed been considered exemplary of the "fragments of an inexhaustible texture" Kracauer had in mind.[19] This carefully achieved trace of spontaneity, binding the performer's and the character's traits together into the kind of unique unit required for the construction of a star (Paramount's plan for Colbert, just imported from Broadway) is missing in the Swedish version.

Another instance of a problematic (mis)match of role and performer is the character of the daughter, Jackie: while played by a quite young girl (eleven or twelve years old) in the original version, in the Swedish version she is played by Anne Marie Brunius (the actress herself being, moreover, the daughter of the Swedish director) who appears to be in her late teens. The choice alters the tenor of the father-daughter attachment (the key obstacle to the new romance of the father with the shopgirl) into a relationship that invites a more manifestly incestuous reading than one would make room for in the plot's highly conventional melodramatic frame; but given the "foreign" (that is, American) setting, the effect of this inflection—even though it originated with the Swedish cast's purview—is paradoxically to render the *American* fiction slightly perverse, odder, and finally more noticeably alien, counteracting the entire effort of the FLV enterprise. In Metzian terms perhaps we could characterize the problem as the imaginary not "taking" sufficiently. Constantly (made) aware that the Symbolic presented on the screen is not quite the proper one, the spectator is encouraged to identify with the narrative through some of the conventional strategies (for instance structures of exhibitionism/voyeurism), but prevented from identifying with it fully insofar as the secondary relay, the diegesis, is insufficiently unified.[20] Ironically, then, it seems as if "Americanness," instead of simply providing a neutral and effective matrix of style which could be inflected for the proper "local" form of foreignness, emerges as doubly visible, a kind of negative imprint of its own origins.

While the Joinville FLVs represent one attempt to construct a synthetic transnational diegesis, there existed a second, radically different strategy for mixing and matching of social with linguistic spaces. In the wake of the late-1920s vogue of exoticism, and influenced by the enormous success of travel documentary features like *Nanook of the North, Grass, Chang, Rango* and *Simba*, several studios pursued this direction by sending out their cameramen to shoot abroad; MGM for instance assembled tens of thousands of feet of footage shot in Europe, in exotic landscapes and under water, and deployed the stock shots in effect as (unacknowledged) montage, intercutting them with studio-originated action. While there is some indication that RKO in particular attempted in a similar fashion to combine shots of the different foreign actors in close-ups with a basic "master" *découpage* of the plot, an even more innovative strategy, experimented with by both Paramount and RKO, was the so-called Dunning process. This special effects procedure involved rear projections and matting which would permit the unification of two disconnected spaces in the same *frame*.[21] Paramount's primary goal seems to have been to use the process for what might be termed "foreign *land* versions," exotic travelogue plots such as *The Four Feathers* (1929), in which shots of African landscape would eventually be processed so as to incorporate action filmed in California (*Variety* [November 10 1928], 4). The newly formed RKO, on the other hand, apparently hoped to use the process to resolve the language problem. An English version would be produced in Hollywood and the print subsequently mailed out to its studios or affiliates abroad, where suitably shaped foreign actors would literally step into the cut-out slot freed up by their American models (a procedure similar to the traditional fair attraction where a customer's face completes a cardboard figure so as to be portrayed by an itinerant photographer). The main problem of the Dunning method was the difficulty in fully eliminating the black lines around the actors' bodies—a residue, as it were, of the insufficient integration of the corporeal and the social spaces, a trace, precisely, of the boundary between the acoustics of emission and those of resonance.

These two specifically American experiments thus represent a stage in the attempt to recapture the linguistically differentiated world markets while relying on techniques reproducing body and voice as an organic unit (be it via foreign language reenactments or via special effect substitutes), that is, while starting out from an essentially theatrical concept of the actor. Neither of them, as we know from hindsight, was successful.[22] Specialized forms of FLVs, for instance Fox's continued attempts to produce Spanish-language (that is, Latin American) versions of their standard releases, or films like G. W. Pabst's *Kameradschaft* and Jean Renoir's *La Grande Illusion*, where German, French, and even English is used simultaneously in the same space, could of course be found at least into the 1930s. By and large, though, the alien speaking body—be it in its tangible or its representational form—virtually vanished from the parameters of the American studio lots and screens. The process of its elimination and replacement by a synthetic "transnational" body involved, however, several quite different strategies, each fraught with its own controversies. An overview of these should serve, temporarily at least, to block out the terms of the re-establishment of the American-language cinema's hegemony within and over the diversity of non-American (film) cultures.

The tactics for making American films linguistically acceptable abroad fall into two categories: subtitling (preservation of the original sound track, supplemented by written text) and dubbing (substitution of the original sound track). It is not difficult to imagine why the first alternative would have seemed a less than acceptable solution. Returning to the barely eliminated format of textual supplement defeated the very purpose of sound film. The problematic nature of this new layer of information and its relation to the image is evident, for instance, in the considerable variety of solutions (indicative ultimately of the fact that control over one dimension of the filmic text had returned to the hands of exhibitors— where film sound had been before the emergence of sound film). At times subtitles were handed out as separate programs (not unlike an opera's libretto today), or were projected on a separate screen adjacent to the main one; or else films were screened with two different sets of subtitles printed onto the image.

Another key factor working against an all-out acceptance of subtitling as a mode of linguistic compensation points to the need to refine further the categories of reception so as to differentiate between various *functions* of language in films on the one hand (its communicative value), and between various *groups* that were concerned about the coming of sound on the other (language's symbolic value).[23] While the American industry initially estimated the written subtitles to be unacceptable on grounds that they were cancelling out the novelty of characters talking in a language comprehensible to the average spectator,[24] the very fact of a character speaking in *any* language that was not the spectator's own came to be of paramount importance to the cultural establishment in a number of countries.[25] As early as 1929 Mussolini's government decreed that all films projected on Italian screens must have an Italian-language sound track. Far from allowing for a competition with domestic products on the basis of linguistic parity (as FLVs were intended to do), the state's intervention "leveled" all non-Italian films into an equally deficient status (rendering, say, a Dutch and an American film equidistant from the Italian spectator—even though the legislator's primary target was obviously the expansive American culture).[26] In Italy dubbing immediately became a powerful state weapon in the re-emergent nationalist movement that only a few years later would alter the European cultural and political landscape.[27] The substantial cost of dubbing (lower than an FLV but much higher than a subtitled version [Thompson, 160]) led the American producers, in turn, to attempt a maneuver that would remain a cornerstone of the US-Europe film flow. Applying to participate in a Milan film fair and competition the year before the first Venice festival, the MPPA's goal was to convince the Italians of the *artistic* value of the American "original versions," which would eventually lead them to relinquish dubbing altogether (*Variety* [February 7, 1933], 17). Here "Americanness" emerges, probably for the first time in the context of cinema, as an explicit and specific national formation. Not only identified in terms derived from high art practices, this quality was evaluated on criteria established within the framework of a refereed competition rather than measured by box office success as the guarantor of aesthetic validity.

In France, the debate over dubbing brought into play yet another set of issues intended to ascertain a film's proper national identity and reception. Paramount's activities at Joinville, coupled with the efforts of MGM's French department in Hollywood, made it evident that, in order to redeploy the notion of "Frenchness," the nation must contend with it as a fluctuating rather than static nexus of body and space.[28] While in Italy the attempt to control the sound track was geared toward reception (making sure the spectator was hearing nothing but Italian coming from the screen, regardless of whether the sound track itself was produced in Berlin, Paris or Los Angeles), in France the preoccupation was with the credited origin as much as with the final effect.

It appears that already in late 1929 unionized orchestra musicians began demanding that the supplementary musical tracks being added to silent films not be imported along with the film but instead be recorded in France (*Variety* [November 28, 1928], 6). Opposition to dubbing was formulated along similar lines. While a debate seems to have been going on about the relative merits of the French productions shot abroad (in Berlin but especially in Hollywood), one condition quickly became unnegotiable. In response to the first systematic attempts of the Americans to dub in foreign languages (a practice preferred by studios that had no production facilities overseas), the film actors' union threatened a strike, demanding that appearance on camera be the prerequisite for "loaning out" an actor's voice.[29] What mattered, in other words, was that the national cinema be defined in terms of the origin and site of its production by insisting on the preservation of the organic body/voice unit of the actor. It is not quite clear just how extensive and successful the dubbing strike itself was. But in contemporary legislation regulating film imports, meanwhile, the preoccupation with the "organic" origins of the national cinema is reflected on a different level. In 1931 a maximum of seventy-five out of two hundred French films produced abroad could be postsynchronized outside of the country; a year later the law was modified to require in principle that *all* dubbing be done in France. The organic unit(y) thus posited between language and land was established as an important guiding rule for all subsequent delineation of the national cinema's identity.[30]

In contrast to Italy and France, Germany's entrance into the sound film market in general, and into sound film competition with the USA in particular, started from a position of relative strength, thanks to the severely enforced quotas as well as the complex overlap of the two countries' patent rights. In the first round of negotiation with Western Electric to settle an impasse over these rights, J. Otterson proposed that the organizing principle ought to be a division of the world according to linguistic spheres of interest: the English-speaking world, the German-speaking world, the "free market zone" (Josse, 272). While this rule of thumb was subsequently modified, it is clear that the strength of its base guaranteed German an unprecedented linguistic parity: indeed, with respect to the smaller European nations, the threat German sound film posed to other national cultures was analogous to that of the USA as perceived in Europe. In Germany itself, the production of FLVs apparently continued into the late 1930s, while dubbing and subtitling seem both to have been possible until April 1933. From this moment on the first of Hitler's *Entjudung* decrees, aimed specifically at the mass media, required that no Jewish personnel be employed in any position in either German or foreign-owned media industry. As *Variety* reported, this new law applied to a majority of American employees, leaving unfinished several dubbing projects. Having complied, Paramount found out subsequently that the "Aryan" dubbers assigned to complete the sound track for *The Sign of the Cross* substantially altered the script by revising several dialogue sequences into heavily anti-Semitic harangues (*Variety* [April 18, 1933], 6, 16). Much like the Maria-robot in *Metropolis*, the synthesized body here became virtually co-extensive with its ideological function.

Even the sketchiest overview of the function of the FLVs lets us glimpse, then, the dense and unstable network of economies set in place by the Americans' effort to establish a feasible exchange rate between cost and national culture. In addition to its potential histori(ographi)cal value, this account does, however, ultimately also beg a theoretical question. The thrust of recent theoretical writing on film sound has been to identify, characterize and so deconstruct the contribution made by the conventional use of the sound track to the effects of "full presence" and the so-called "unified subject"—the ideological, institutional and aesthetic cornerstones of the classical cinema (Doane 1980a and 1980b, Altman 1980c, Metz, Alan Williams). The argument is roughly that the practices involved in recording and editing sound in classical cinema (dialogue and noise, although not necessarily music) (1) serve to conceal the origin of the sound as being separate from the image, and so (2) invite the spectator to disavow the split, to posit him- or herself as a unifying surface for the disparate impulses by taking up the position of "reverse specularity," through which "the cinema appears to assent to the unity of the human subject only in order to establish its own unity" (Altman 1980c, 71).

Mary Ann Doane refines this position by considering the various types of space—and by implication the types of body and pleasure—called into play by the cinematic institution: the acoustic envelope of the auditorium itself, the spatial orientation of the spectator toward the screen, and the space of the diegesis (Doane 1980b). Her argument carefully links the perceptual and psychic transactions taking place in each domain as they attempt to reconcile the technological and psychological apparatuses into an effect of unity (even while capable of exploiting the tensions arising from this impossible task).[31] In Doane's psychoanalytically inflected model, these transactions are ultimately grounded in the sheer pleasure of hearing, in what she, after Lacan, terms *the invocatory drive*, "with its elements escaping a strictly verbal codification—volume, rhythm, timbre, pitch" (43), elements that in part provide a hallucinatory satisfaction pertaining to early childhood memories, those of the maternal voice (in competition with the "verbal" track of the paternal voice, agent of the Symbolic).

In light of the complications accompanying the Hollywood cinema's "acquisition of language(s)," this theoretical argument—emphasizing the sound track's importance for the effect of unity that underwrites the smooth operation of the cinematic apparatus—needs either theoretical revision or historical modification. If Doane, Altman and others are right, it is the FLVs that would appear to be the most appropriate—even necessary—strategy in order for the American cinema to have remained the universal "good object" abroad as well as in this country.[32] Meanwhile, subtitling and dubbing—the two dominant strategies securing the Hollywood model's universal availability—each disturb this ideal acoustic/linguistic state. While subtitling does preserve the powerful link between body and voice of the actor (without which the identification of a star is in danger[33]), and so leaves intact the acoustic unity of the diegetic space, it—or more precisely the gap between that space and the spectator which the subtitling cannot close—severs the spectator from the "narcissistic" pleasure of identification with the body on screen. Dubbing, on the other hand, betrays the body/voice connection so fundamental to our sense of reality that its breach belongs to the basic register of horror cinema (Linda Blair "dubbed" in a male voice speaking Latin is instantly deemed in need of an exorcist: Altman's vivid metaphor of cinema as ventriloquist almost ceases here to be a metaphor). The dubbing mix also tends to alter, even destroy, the sound perspective and depth, those acoustic properties granting stability to the spatial relationship of the spectator and the screen—a relation which in turn underwrites the "hallucination of a fully sensory world" (Doane 1980b, 45).

What to make, then, of the classical Hollywood cinema's capacity to reappropriate the "alien" spectators for the effect of plenitude and presence?[34] What to make of its capacity to override that slight but decisive misalignment of subjectivity to which the displaced sound track has permanently relegated them? How to account, in other words, for the fact that this alienation effect, properly speaking, did not block the capacity of the non-American spectator to be fully absorbed by the imaginary of the American cinema?

By way of a provisional conclusion, let me suggest some possible lines of thought following from these questions. One bears on the Hollywood actor, or more properly (given the synthetic character of the figure on screen), on a new construct of the human body in fictional space, and on this construct's capacity to compensate for deficiencies in the "foreign" spectator's acoustic, social and/or psychic language room. While the major name attractions for the FLVs came from the legitimate theatres of their countries of origin (recruited on the strength of the same logic as Broadway stars to Hollywood—for example, Edward G. Robinson, Ruth Chatterton, Claudette Colbert), their "name value" turned out to be considerably smaller than that of the American stars with their enormous studio-designed "build-up" (in *Variety*'s parlance). While in the domain of theatre national identity may have been the condition of stardom, in the domain of cinema the line was drawn not between competing national public spheres but rather between a collective, "public" experience of the stage space and a "private" (if mass-produced) experience of the lit screen. Language, in its role as the agent of familiarity, immediacy, spatial contiguity and secondarization was thus being displaced by the auratic character forming the core of the star phenomenon. The American cinema's capacity to recover from the "loss of words" abroad is an index of its capacity to grasp, and work with, the constitutive role of distance for fantasy.[35]

Overcoming the resistance of which the foreign language versions offered a first and last sign, the admired and feared "international dream factory" may have become instrumental in making the world dream in Hollywood's English idiom—or dream *for* that English, the stars' lips coming to mouth the shadow of that wish, beyond the inefficient cacophony of the world's separate tongues.

8

1950s Magnetic Sound: The Frozen Revolution

John Belton

In the mid-1950s, the wide-screen revolution transformed the nature of the traditional motion picture experience. Screens became larger and wider and curved across the front of the theater, obliterating the old-fashioned proscenium and engulfing audiences within a semicircular ring of images. Sound spread from one central speaker behind the screen to additional behind-the-screen speakers on the left and the right, issuing forth from as many as five behind-the-screen speakers and from dozens of "surround" speakers mounted on the side and rear walls of the theater auditorium. The clearly delineated segregation of spaces which had characterized previous conditions of motion picture spectatorship gave way to an illusory integration of spaces in which images and sounds from the "fictional" space of the motion picture appeared to enter the "actual" space of the audience; the audience, thus surrounded by images and sounds, felt itself to be a part of the space depicted on the screen. Distraction, which (for Siegfried Kracauer) epitomized the motion picture experience of the movie palaces of the 1920s, in which the architecture of the theater encouraged the spectator's eyes to wander from the screen to the surrounding decor, gave way to "participation," the new entertainment catchword of the 1950s, which was used to describe the audience's absorption into the spectacular display of sound and images arrayed before (and around) them (Kracauer 1987).[1]

But the revolution was not entirely successful. Though old narrow-screen aspect ratios were overthrown forever, stereo sound failed to unseat mono (except in a few large, first-run theaters which were equipped to run both). The magnetic movement began in the post-war era (*circa* 1946) when several studio sound departments, drawing upon confiscated German technology, began to convert their production and postproduction facilities from optical to magnetic sound (Mullin; Ryder; Lafferty, 170–219). Magnetic sound provided an unprecedented fidelity, a dramatically expanded frequency range, a significantly improved signal-to-noise ratio, and a larger dynamic volume range. However, the magnetic revolution proved to be more of an in-house shake-up than an industry-wide transformation. Though it briefly disrupted established sound recording, editing, and mixing practice, it had little impact on what spectators saw and heard in movie theaters.[2] This was due, in part, to the fact that films continued to be released with optical rather than magnetic tracks in order to conform with existing theatrical practice where optical playback was the standard. As a result, whatever improvements in sound quality that magnetic recording and re-recording introduced were lost when the magnetic track was finally converted to optical sound for release prints, though magnetic recording and mixing did cut production costs considerably.[3] In the related field of radio, a similar course of development took place. The broadcast industry had converted to magnetic sound several years before the film industry, but this new, improved sound was received and played over low-fidelity AM equipment in the home (though a small percentage of audiophiles with FM sets experienced considerably superior sound reception in the late 1940s and early 1950s) (Fortanale and Mills, 121–123).

In 1952–54, however, an assault on the twenty-five-year-old exhibition standard of optical sound took place in the form of stereo magnetic sound, which was a prominent feature of Cinerama, CinemaScope, and certain other wide-screen processes such as Todd-AO, as well as an element of several 3-D systems. The opening of *This Is Cinerama* in 7-track stereo magnetic sound in the fall of 1952, of *House of Wax* in 3-D and 4-track stereo in the spring of 1953, and of *The Robe* in CinemaScope and 4-track stereo in the fall of 1953 (as well as 32 other stereo releases in 1953) heralded a new, albeit short-lived, era in sound motion pictures. But this attempt to establish a standard, 35mm, magnetic stereo format did not succeed, and it was not until 1975 that a 35mm stereo sound system began to gain wide acceptance through the efforts of Dolby Labs to market a 4-track *optical* stereo sound system (Hodges; Larry Blake).

This essay explores the apparent failure of the stereo magnetic sound revolution of the 1950s. It looks at the demise of 35mm stereo systems from the perspective of the conflicting demands of a diverse motion picture marketplace in which the differing needs of producers, exhibitors, and spectators came into conflict over the issue of stereo magnetic sound. It will demonstrate how the compromises which resulted from this conflict led to the institutionalization of a two-tiered exhibition system in which the (theoretically) radical realism of large-screen (and large format) motion pictures with stereo sound was rendered "elitist" and "unrealistic," while the old-fashioned format of monaural, optical sound became the bearer of a redefined realism, anchoring the spectacular, new wide-screen image in the familiar conventions of a pre-wide-screen sound, which had achieved a certain identification with realistic representation over the past twenty-five years. In the process of sketching out this argument, this essay will consider the advent of magnetic sound from the perspective of theories of technological change and the demand for greater realism implicit in those theories. It will also examine the interdependence of realistic representation and the conventionalization of aesthetic devices introduced by new technologies.

Did 1950s Stereo Sound Really Fail?

The "failure" of 35mm magnetic sound to become an industry standard has been regarded, by myself and others, as one of the great setbacks of the wide-screen revolution, unnecessarily depriving motion picture spectators of high quality, state-of-the-art sound in the theater, and delaying "the process of motion-picture engineering" (Belton 1988, Handzo). Not only is the appeal here to "progress" suspect, but so also is the notion of "failure." It is not entirely clear that magnetic stereo "failed," or, if it did, how extensive or complete that failure was. Several recent histories of Twentieth Century-Fox's innovation of CinemaScope (again, including my own) have termed Fox's experiments with stereo sound a failure and have attributed this failure largely to economic factors (Belton 1985, Hincha). The story of stereo's demise generally follows a predictable course. Small exhibitors reluctantly agreed to install CinemaScope projection lenses and wide screens but balked at the "extra" cost of converting their theatres to stereo sound (Hincha, 48–50). Fox insisted on a stereo-only policy and rented CinemaScope films only to those theaters equipped to show them in stereo. But when other studios using the CinemaScope process began to make prints available in an ersatz optical stereo format known as Perspecta Sound and in monaural optical versions, Fox relented and released films with dual, magnetic and optical soundtracks (Hincha, 50; Belton 1988, 719). As a result of this concession to exhibitor complaints about cost, only one-quarter of all movie theaters around the world ever installed stereo magnetic equipment (Belton 1988, 719).

The majority of theaters chose mono over stereo. But this apparent defeat of stereo was not without qualification. One-quarter of all movie theaters did convert to stereo; by the late 1950s, that amounted to over 10,000 theaters! And most of these were large, first-run houses. These theaters not only conferred prestige on the films (and special film processes) presented in them, but they also generated the bulk of the profits for Hollywood releases. As Spyros Skouras, president of Twentieth Century-Fox wrote to producer David O. Selznick when the latter questioned the necessity of stereo sound, "the relatively small number of magnetic-equipped theatres contribute 75% to 80% of our income from a picture."[4]

Box office statistics on the performance of the first CinemaScope film, *The Robe*, give some indication of how problematic a simple economic determination for the failure of stereo can be. By the end of March 1954, roughly a month before Fox abandoned its stereo-only policy, *The Robe*, playing in 1370 stereo-only sites, had grossed over $24.6 million and had returned over $13 million in rentals to Fox (*Daily Variety*, March 30, 1954: 3). The economic status of the small exhibitor may have determined the failure of stereo, but the economic clout of the large exhibitor accorded it considerable success. As a result, stereo, which emerged as a crucial form of product differentiation, separating the first-class, showcase theaters from the rest, became a fixture of first-run, CinemaScope exhibition until the end of the decade.

When Fox abandoned its stereo-only policy, 35mm magnetic stereo did not so much disappear as begin a slow decline, the victim of apathy on the part of production personnel at Fox and elsewhere and of competition with other magnetic systems developed for wide film formats such as Todd-AO. In response to complaints from exhibitors who had converted to stereo, Fox production chief, Darryl Zanuck, sent a memo to studio personnel encouraging producers, directors, writers, and editors to make full use of stereo sound, noting that it had been used "conservatively rather than in its full potential" and he cited, in particular, the failure to use the fourth, surround track.[5] The problem with stereo's "invisibility," however, was not entirely due to neglect.

After Fox relented on its stereo-only policy, filmmakers at Fox were forced to design films so that they could be played back in either stereo or mono. As a result, sound information that was crucial to the narrative or to the audience's understanding of the film could not be put on the fourth track because not all theaters could play it back; and even if that information were to be mixed down into a monaural track, it would lack the special spatial properties it originally possessed on the fourth track. It would no longer serve the purpose for which it was initially designed and thus, it would have little or no value for either the exhibitor or the audience of non-stereo films.[6] Shortly after Fox agreed to mono releases of their stereo films, the fourth track fell into disuse, neglected for all but one or two minutes of service in a two-hour feature.[7]

By 1958, Fox had even ceased recording dialogue and sound effects in stereo and began to record them in mono, "panning" the sound in the mix to follow onscreen movement (Blake).[8] At around the same time, the expensive practice of producing mag-optical prints for every release began to give way to more and more optical-only releases.[9] One North Dakota theater owner, who felt betrayed by Fox's policy reversal, wrote a letter to the president of Twentieth Century-Fox to voice his anger at the decline of stereo sound:

> Dear Mr. Skouras,
>   In my projection booth I have a piece of equipment between the upper magazine and the projector head that my operator has forgotten how to use. Please advise if I will ever have any use for this equipment or should I throw it all away and just mark it up to experience?—and loss of faith in a man's word.[10]

Skouras had promised that CinemaScope and stereophonic sound would save the film industry and, to some extent, it did. But the original advantage which many exhibitors who had converted to stereo enjoyed quickly disappeared as Fox and other studios cut back on the number of stereo prints struck for circulation.

Meanwhile, CinemaScope's 4-track 35mm stereo magnetic sound was gradually being eclipsed by a variety of 70mm widescreen systems (such as Todd-AO, M-G-M Camera 65, and Super Panavision) which featured six-track stereo sound. Stereo thus continued to be connected not with the average movie-going experience of the 1950s audience but rather with special presentation large-screen processes and with blockbuster spectacles. Stereo films ranged across a variety of genres, from musicals (*Oklahoma!, Carousel, South Pacific, West Side Story*) to historical spectacles (*Around the World in 80 Days, Spartacus, The Alamo, Mutiny on the Bounty, Lawrence of Arabia, Cleopatra*) and biblical epics (*Ben Hur, The Big Fisherman*). Through its usage as an element of spectacle and through its identification with the genres of spectacle, stereo sound became associated for audiences not so much with greater realism as with greater artifice. The next section of this essay examines the relationship of stereo, as a technical innovation, to the traditional attribution of greater realism to new technologies.

Stereo and Greater Realism

Theorizations of technological change in the cinema have tended to posit models of development ranging from simple, sequential, linear accounts of autonomous evolution to complex, quasi-dialectical, non-linear notions of highly mediated process. At one end of the spectrum, André Bazin declared the cinema to be "an idealistic phenomenon" whose development unfolded along a teleological trajectory towards the realization of the myth which had guided its initial invention and subsequent development (Bazin 1967a, 17). Like Icarus who dreamed of human flight, Bazin's cinema was obsessed with the fulfillment of primal dreams which "dwelt in the soul of everyman" (Bazin 1967a, 22). One of these dreams was "the myth of total cinema," which endowed the cinema with the (potential) power to reproduce reality—to reconstruct "a perfect illusion of the outside world in sound, color, and relief" (Bazin 1967a, 20). The course of the cinema's evolution, which passed through successive stages of development from black and white, silent motion pictures to a cinema of sound, color, relief (3-D), and wide-screen, "little by little made a reality out of the original 'myth' " (Bazin 1967a, 21).

At the other end of the spectrum, Jean-Louis Comolli challenged the linearity of earlier historiography (including Bazin's) and called for a "materialist theory of the cinema" (Comolli 1985, 47). Following Julia Kristeva, Comolli argued for "a *stratified history*; that is, a history characterized by discontinuous temporality, which is recursive, dialectical, and not reducible to a single meaning. : . ." (Comolli 1986). Thus, for Comolli, technique and technology did not evolve in a straightforward fashion but moved first forwards then backwards, then forwards again through a series of dead ends and detours.[11] Yet Comolli's uneven or "stratified" history proved ultimately to be driven by the same "myth" or (to use Comolli's terminology) "ideological demand" as was Bazin's (Belton 1987). The cinema's invention satisfied an ideological need "to see life as it is," that is, for a certain realism in representation (Comolli 1985, 55). Its advances in both technique and technology responded to a desire "to make things more real" (Comolli 1986, 437). In other words, for both Bazin and Comolli, technological development resulted in the production of "greater realism."

Technological innovation in the cinema has traditionally been associated with the production of "greater realism." The invention of the motion picture camera enabled filmmakers to create images which they described as "life-size" and/or "life-like;"[12] the Lumières presented their Cinématographe shows as "la vie sur le vif" or "life on the run."[13] With the advent of sound, film could "provide the most marvellous reproduction of life as it unfolds before our eyes."[14] Vitaphone insisted that "The Characters [in its pictures] act and *Talk* like *living people*" (Kreuger, 17). Movietone boasted that it was "More than Sound—Life Itself!" (Kreuger, 10). Launching the wide-screen era, Cinerama declared that it was a medium "that creates all the illusion of reality . . . [that] you see things the way you do in real life—not only in front of you as in conventional motion pictures, but also out of the corners of your eyes . . . [and that] you hear with the same startling realism."[15] Charles Barr insisted that wide-screen processes such as Cinemascope enabled "complex scenes to be covered even more naturally: detail can be integrated, and therefore perceived, in a still more realistic way" (Barr, 157). Stereophonic sound was praised for its realistic sense of directionality; "sound seem[ed] to come from the exact point of origin—made it appear as if the words spoken by each actress came from her lips, giving the whole scene a life-like quality."[16]

In the case of the evolution of sound technology, technical developments in sound recording could be seen as inspired, as Mary Ann Doane has suggested, by a quest for more realistic sound reproduction, that is, by attempts to improve the overall system's signal-to-noise ratio, to make the signal more intelligible and, at the same time, to reduce noise (Doane 1980a, 61). Thus, the introduction of magnetic recording in the late 1940s, of stereo magnetic playback in the theater in the 1950s, of Dolby sound in the 1970s, of digital recordings in the 1980s, and of digital playback in the 1990s mark the progress (to date) of this evolutionary progression toward an ideal, absolute sound lacking any attendant noise.

But "greater realism" was not always the product nor the goal of technological development. As Ed Buscombe has pointed out, early color films were associated not with realism but with its opposite—with "unrealistic" genres—with animated Disney cartoons, fashion shows and/or musical sequences inserted in black-and-white films, with fantasy films, and with musicals (Buscombe, 90). Indeed, realism continued to be signified in the cinema not by color but by black and white, which remained the dominant mode of realistic motion picture representation until the widespread diffusion of color television in the late 1960s. For Buscombe, the demand for greater realism which informed the models for technological development set forth by Bazin and Comolli may have been a dominant determinant of technical change but it was not necessarily the *only* demand satisfied by innovation (Buscombe, 87, 91). Color, for example, provided spectators with "luxury or spectacle;" and, in certain cases, it simply celebrated technology (Buscombe, 90–91).

Significantly, all of the technological developments discussed above were identified not only with realism but with spectacle as well. The attention of the audience was drawn to the novelty of the apparatus itself. The "greater realism" produced by the new technology was understood, it would seem, as a kind of excess, which was in turn packaged as spectacle. Nonetheless, the artifice which underlay the heightened illusion of reality was celebrated, if not always displayed. Thus ads for *Broadway Melody* declared it, as an "all talking, all singing, all dancing dramatic sensation," to be "the New Wonder of the Screen!" (Kreuger, 23). Fox Movietone "dubbed" itself "The Sound and Sight Sensation" (Kreuger, 10). Cinerama, CinemaScope, Todd-AO and other wide-screen processes regularly identified themselves with epic proportions and/or spectacular effects.

In a similar way, stereo magnetic sound was praised both for its realism and its artifice. Scientists celebrated its "greater realism" in relation to monaural optical sound. Thus Fox engineers proudly noted that stereo magnetic sound provided "direction, presence, proper phase relationships of the sound waves, and all the other aspects of the actual sound from the original source."[17] Showmen boasted of its greater artifice. Skouras informed reporters that "in *The Robe* you'll hear angels' voices. And they'll come from the only place where you'd expect to see angels—right above you. And when you see the film and hear the voices, you'll look up for the angels" (Prall, 21).[18]

In spite of the gradual decline of the use of the fourth track during the mid-1950s, Hollywood continued to use surround sound on occasion for special sonic effects. Concerned about his own studio's failure to fully utilize the fourth track, Darryl Zanuck sent a memo to Fox staff praising the work of a rival studio. "In some of the battle sequences [of Warner's *Battle Cry*] it is a tremendous and realistic thrill when you hear the roar of the cannon coming from behind you and then it seems to pass over your head and land on the screen in the distance. They use this about six or seven times . . . and each time . . . it gave a terrific impact."[19] Though Zanuck refers to the realism of these effects, their "realism" is clearly bound up with spectacular display, as Zanuck himself seemed to realize when he mentioned that his wife, who is "usually never conscious of anything of a technical nature and concentrates only on the story or the actors" noted these effects and "discussed [them] after she had seen the picture. . . . I know we have used things similar to this, but this is the first time she has ever noticed them and it came without any coaching from me."[20]

Cinerama pioneered the practice of "travelling" sound which so impressed Zanuck and his wife, and exploited it as a form of audience participation. In an attempt to heighten the participation effect, Cinerama sound recordists regularly mounted five microphones in fixed positions on a support that was itself attached to the Cinerama camera, effectively binding visual and auditory perspective together and putting the spectator in the very midst of the onscreen action.[21] Thus, in the Cypress Gardens sequence of *This Is Cinerama*, the sound of a motorboat can first be heard dimly from the rear of the auditorium, then somewhat louder from the right surround speakers, then, as the image of the boat appears on the screen, the sound follows its movement from right to left across the fifty-one-foot-wide screen. During the Long Island Choral Society's rendition of Handel's Messiah, "as you sit in the theater, the music of the thrilling 'Hallelujah' chorus comes to you from every direction . . . first, behind you . . . then, on both sides of you, as the singers approach the stage pictured on screen . . . and finally, from the great stage itself."[22] Though travelling sound contributed an apparent realism to the scenes, providing exact correspondence between sound and image, it also functioned as a display of what multi-track stereo magnetic sound could do. While undeniably realistic, the practice nonetheless drew attention to itself, violating the timeworn conventions of stylistic invisibility which governed Hollywood filmmaking practice and which insured that the audience's access to the events which unfolded before them would be unmediated (that is, realistic). This self-consciousness remained consistent with Cinerama's overall marketing campaign, which foregrounded the experience of the process and, as the word "Cinerama" in the titles of the first two features (*This Is Cinerama* and *Cinerama Holiday*) suggests, the spectacular effects of the process itself.

Fox and other producers of narrative features in stereo relied upon a somewhat more sophisticated system of microphone placement, which did not establish the exact identity between visual and auditory perspective employed by Cinerama and which, therefore, drew attention to the camera itself. Rather, they adapted standard Hollywood sound recording practice to the new medium of stereo and placed microphones in positions that matched "visible or desired implied [onscreen] action" instead of the position of the camera itself (Grignon, 376). In this way the microphones, like the camera itself, occupied quasi-objective, unmarked positions and functioned as omniscient onlookers rather than as a subjective presence identified with the position of the camera.

Sound recordists set up microphones in an attempt to capture the original "directionality" of the sound information. Sound effects, such as the footsteps of a character walking across the screen, would "travel" from speaker to speaker with the onscreen action. In *The Robe*, when Demetrius scours Jerusalem in search of Christ in an attempt to warn Him that He is about to be arrested, Demetrius hides behind a range of pillars from troops of Roman legions whose marching footsteps move with them (from speaker to speaker) from screen right to screen left. During the crucifixion scene, first thunder signalling an impending storm, and then sound of wind and rain, engulfed the theater, moving from one speaker to another. On occasion, even music would have a directional quality. At the end of *Demetrius and the Gladiators*, the romantic sacrifice of Messalina (Susan Hayward), who has repressed her desire for Demetrius (Victor Mature) in order to assume her place as the wife of Caesar, is underlined with a melodramatic violin solo which emanates from a single speaker located at the same position in the frame that she occupies, underscoring her individual emotion within a larger context of an impersonal public ceremony.

For a time, stereo recording actually dictated onscreen composition; actors would be positioned across the frame so that their voices would be picked up by different microphones, ensuring their separation upon playback in the theater. Zanuck insisted that "stereophonic sound is not effective when two people are face to face, unless of course they are in big closeups or a big 2-shot. The full value of stereophonic sound comes from the *distance* between the two people who are talking. If one person is planted at one end of the set and the other person is on the other side of the set then the sound has an opportunity to add to the illusion of depth."[23] As a result, even stationary performers spoke from screen right, left, or center, and the sound shifted from one theater speaker to another during conversations.

For the first time in film history, offscreen dialogue was literally off-screen, emanating from surround speakers on either side of the auditorium. In *The Robe*, when Marcellus bids farewell to Diana before his departure to Judea, fog-enshrouded shots of the couple are accompanied by offscreen calls warning him of his ship's immanent departure. From *Battle Cry* to *Spartacus*, stereo sound extended offscreen space further to the right and to the left than it had ever gone before, and provided a specificity of location which monaural films could only vaguely suggest. The effect was decidedly theatrical, duplicating the offstage voice which the theater had exploited for centuries, but which monaural cinema could only loosely approximate. Offscreen voices literally drew the audience's attention to offscreen space, spectacularizing the concept of voice off.[24]

Although a number of studios eventually adopted CinemaScope's 4-track stereo magnetic sound process, only Fox (and Todd-AO, which employed a somewhat different, 6-track stereo system) persisted in maintaining both "directional" and "traveling" dialogue. By the mid-1950s, M-G-M, Warners, Columbia, and Universal, for example, recorded and played back music in stereo but recorded original dialogue and sound effects in mono; they played dialogue back in mono through all the behind-the-screen speakers and played sound effects back in stereo.[25]

At Paramount, sound engineer Loren Ryder complained that "the movement of dialogue to follow picture action can be very annoying," though stereo playback could be quite effective for sound effects and music.[26] New York *Times* critic Bosley Crowther found travelling dialogue to be distracting and complained that "the business of switching from one to another outlet . . . as the character moves becomes an obvious mechanical contrivance that confuses the image on the screen" (Crowther). Though Crowther concurred with Ryder and others that stereo was ideal for "background music and disassociated sound effects," he concluded that voices and onscreen sound effects were "more uniform and plausible" when played back through a single, behind-the-screen horn (Crowther).

Crowther's reaction and that of the major studios, who refused to adopt completely both Fox's directionality of dialogue and sound effects and its practice of "travelling" dialogue, would seem to have been prompted in part by a sense that certain practices identified with stereo violated the accepted conventions of monaural sound playback. In other words, Crowther, Ryder, and others perceived stereo sound not as realistic but as artificial. This perception can be attributed, I think, to essential differences between stereo sound, with which audiences had little familiarity, and mono sound, which audiences had already experienced for a number of years. Stereo records and tapes were not mass marketed until 1957 and FM broadcasts in stereo were not licensed by the FCC until 1961; thus audiences could not draw upon these other media for an understanding of stereo's codes and conventions (Fornatale and Mills, 124). Mono, on the other hand, was a familiar fixture in mass entertainment, made accessible to audiences through both radio broadcasts and the "talkies." As a commonplace in these media, mono had come to be associated by audiences with realistic representation.

In the first days of the transition to sound period—in 1926 and early 1927—theater loudspeakers were placed to the side or below the screen. Early Vitaphone films even drew upon silent film conventions, playing back orchestral scores through speakers placed in the area of the former orchestra pit.[27] The development, in 1927, by Earl Sponable of a porous screen material facilitated the placing of loudspeakers behind the screen. This encouraged the illusion of the homogeneity of sound and image, which was achieved quite literally through their physical superimposition. Over the years, this location became a rigid convention—sound came from the center of the image. For over twenty-five years, dialogue had been played back to audiences from central speakers located behind the screen.

CinemaScope changed that, shifting actors' voices from speaker to speaker. Though the directionality of stereo sound does have a source in the world of theatrical performance, upon which CinemaScope, Todd-AO, and several other wide-screen formats consciously drew, theatrical codes did not translate smoothly into the cinema, particularly when those codes violated pre-existent cinematic codes. On the other hand, the playback of film music in stereo succeeded for somewhat similar reasons, relying upon codes established earlier to insure its reception as verisimilitudinous. The live orchestra which accompanied the first-run exhibition of silent films had established a precedent for the "stereo playback" of music; it is this tradition to which *Fantasia* appealed in 1940 with its depiction of Leopold Stokowski conducting the Philadelphia Orchestra and which *How to Marry a Millionaire* revived in 1953 with its filmed overture, "Street Scene," featuring Alfred Newman and the Twentieth Century-Fox Orchestra. Cognizant of this tradition, critics, industry personnel and audiences accepted stereo musical scoring, while rejecting directionality for dialogue.[28]

Stereo's perception as artifice can be attributed to technological factors as well. All multi-track stereo systems *channelled* the original sound into a finite number of theater speakers. Ideally, as stereo expert Harvey Fletcher pointed out, every square inch of the screen should have a separate speaker and track to reflect the nearly limitless number of potential sources for sound, while an infinite number of speakers and tracks would be needed to duplicate sounds emanating from offscreen space (Fletcher, 356). Stereo systems that established three, four, five, six, or even seven sound sources, rather than creating a more perfect illusion of depth on the screen, necessarily called attention to the arbitrariness of their choice of sources. The number of sound channels, however, did play a major role in the reception of stereo sound. While CinemaScope was critiqued for its noticeable channelling of sound, other multi-track systems with more channels fared better in their overall reception. For example, Todd-AO's 6-track sound enabled it to use five, rather than three, speakers behind the screen; this lessened somewhat the abruptness of shifts in travelling dialogue as it moved from speaker to speaker and proved less objectionable to critics.[29] Contemporary 70mm stereo magnetic formats similarly avoid the excessive channelling of CinemaScope by relying upon six tracks instead of four.

The identification of stereo magnetic sound with spectacle was the product not only of diachronic but of synchronic differentiation as well. As I have suggested, stereo marked a dramatic departure from earlier, mono sound styles. Audiences, at least in certain CinemaScope and Todd-AO films, were repeatedly "distracted" by the dialogue, which travelled from one position to another behind the screen, and were overwhelmed by sound effects on the fourth track (when it was used).[30] But stereo also attempted to define itself against the background of monaural film sound, with which it competed. Stereo entered an industry dominated by monaural sound and sought to distinguish itself as a marketable commodity from its predecessor. The myth inspiring its evolution may have been the quest for "greater realism," but that demand was already being satisfied, it would seem, by existing sound technologies—in particular, by monaural optical sound. Instead, it satisfied other demands—the need for spectacle and the desire for/fascination with technological display.

The film industry satisfied these differing needs in different ways. Inexpensive neighborhood theaters offered general audiences the traditional "realism" of monaural sound on a regular, day-to-day basis, while the more expensive, first-run theaters provided them with the occasional opportunity to experience the spectacle of stereo sound as a special entertainment event.

Stereo's association with genres of spectacle and with special presentation in first-run theaters confirmed its status in relation to mono: it was not only different but deviant. Mono remained the dominant form of sound reproduction in theaters around the country, functioning as a norm or "background set" against which stereo emerged as a violation of that norm. The conventions associated with mono had not only established its dominance but also its identification with realism as a representational form. For over twenty-five years, mono had served as the realistic form of sound reproduction par excellence. By contrast, stereo sound emerged in the early 1950s as "unrealistic." This distinction was only confirmed by the widespread perception of certain non-stereo (black-and-white) 1950s films, such as *On the Waterfront, High Noon,* and *Marty,* as more realistic than their wide-screen, stereo, and color counterparts, such as *The Robe, Brigadoon,* and *A Star is Born.* Unable to displace mono as the dominant, stereo could only retain its status as a variant. And, as a variant, it could only continue to attempt to exploit its spectacular characteristics.

If this study of the wide-screen revolution teaches us anything about the nature of technological change and its relation to realism, it demonstrates that, as Buscombe observed years ago, greater realism is not the only determinant governing the development of new technologies. But realism nonetheless does play a crucial role in the ultimate form those new technologies take. Though it was introduced as a single technological phenomenon, wide-screen cinema subsequently evolved in two radically different directions—towards greater realism and towards greater artifice. These different forms of wide-screen cinema satisfied the demands of a new motion picture marketplace, which served different groups of spectators, ranging from the mass audiences serviced by CinemaScope and other 35mm wide-screen systems to the "class" audiences courted by Todd-AO and other wide film formats.

Ironically, the "greater realism" which inspired the evolution of wide-screen led to a dismantling of the original technology (wide-screen and stereo sound) and the substitution of a supposedly "less realistic" form—monaural sound—for a supposedly "more realistic" form—stereo sound. The first stage of the wide-screen cinema's evolution towards "greater realism" lay in its adoption of monaural sound. The "failure" of stereo suggests that the combination of wide-screen images and multi-track stereo sound proved to be too much of a revolution in the mid-1950s. Wide-screen cinema and stereophonic sound, as idealistic phenomena, conceived by the film industry to provide a perfect illusion of reality, proved to offer an excess of spectacle that could survive only in the most artificially theatrical of venues—in high-priced, reserved-seat, first-run theaters which, like the legitimate theater they sought to emulate, adopted theatrical schedules, featuring matinees in the afternoon, one show in the evening, and three shows on weekends and holidays.

During the tumultuous transition period from narrow-screen to wide-screen cinema, monaural sound provided audiences with a stabilizing convention to help them navigate the bewildering spectacle of the widescreen revolution. The spectacle of widescreen was grounded in the everyday "reality" of monaural sound reproduction. In other words, the widescreen revolution needed to anchor itself in the conventions of the past in order for it to break with that past. It was not a complete overthrow of traditional cinema; it only went so far and then stopped. It was a frozen revolution.

Neglected Domains

Introduction: Sound's Dark Corners

Rick Altman

Critics will continue to argue over sound's role in audiovisual media. Is sound an integral part of the cinema experience? Does sound have independent ways of making meaning? Is sound simply an add-on to an already established visual medium? Whatever answers we may offer to questions like these, there is one claim on which we can all agree: the image has been theorized earlier, longer, and more fully than sound. Incapable of being stored until the last quarter of the nineteenth century, sound was not fully explored as a physical phenomenon, until this century. The science of acoustics flowered during the first quarter of the century, though the Acoustical Society of America was not founded until 1929. The basic sound research of Bell Laboratories was carried out primarily during the twenties and thirties. The theorizing of sound as an audiovisual medium did not really get underway until the cinema industry's conversion to sound. In short, sound's importance has been recognized only belatedly, thus tending to make sound theory and analysis tributary of image theory and analysis (even if sound itself is not dependent on the image).

The ramifications of sound's tardy entrance onto the critical stage are strongly evident in the topics typically chosen by sound critics. By far the majority of work on sound has addressed questions of what might be called technological history, usually in the context of the Hollywood industry. Articles on sound style have typically been organized around the work of key auteurs. Even the terminology with which we describe film sound is often built around image vocabulary. At every turn, we sense that sound critics are gleaning from a field already harvested by image critics, making it exceedingly difficult to work on sound without being corrupted, as it were, by a prior image-based Gestalt. Remember how hard it is to see the duck once you've been shown the rabbit?

As long as we remain in the familiar area illuminated by image critics, we will find it hard to give sound an unbiased hearing. Among the dark corners that call most urgently for investigation, I note the following.

Third World Cinema

Working with mainstream cinema industries artificially limits the varieties of sound which we confront. We are accustomed to languages and cultures where the term for voice is the same as the term for (democratic) vote, where amplification is cheap, where access to the media is reasonably easy. We have much to learn from contact with systems where the voice exists in another political configuration, where the simple fact of speaking is a political act, where access to amplification and the media are reserved for a reigning few. From exhibition practices to the mode of film's social and intellectual diffusion, from the otherness of unfamiliar languages to the novelty of differing cultural uses of sound, Third World film has much to teach us. As we see from Amy Lawrence's essay, it challenges us to ask new questions about our relationship to the space and time of an always already politicized world.

Local and Regional Productions

Radio's standardizing practices all but killed the variety of speech patterns that characterized this country and Europe during the first third of the century. National cinema industries, it might be argued, accomplished the same leveling with regard to aesthetic structures. Today, with the rapid spread of audiovisual technology, films are being made by smaller groups with more distinct identities than was formerly the case. Indian tribes, inner-city recreation programs, cable television access groups, women's cooperatives, prisons, retirement communities, athletic clubs, foreign-language classes, aspiring musical groups—these and many more are now making regular decisions about what their films should sound like. While these documents must be studied with some skepticism (about the level of liberty likely within the available technology and operative conventions), they deserve our attention precisely because of their ability to reintroduce a personal note into a world homogenized by radio, film, and television.

Documentary

For years, the field of documentary study has needed a basic essay on its approaches to sound. Jeff Ruoff's essay provides just that: a starting point for critics and filmmakers who want to think seriously about the sound of documentary films. In the past, many misleading claims have been made about documentary sound. "Direct" sound, for example, has been treated by people who should know better as an unmediated form of film sound recording, as if a preference for sync recording of location sound could possibly circumvent the mediation implicit in the choice of a particular microphone, location, or volume level.

One of the most common criticisms about documentaries is that they misuse voice-over sound, commonly slapping an omniscient voice-over with minimal spatial signature over images that receive the majority of the filmmaker's attention. While this critique was once all too apt, sound critics will profit from careful attention to a new generation of documentaries characterized by the complexity of their voice-over. *The Fayum Portraits*, for example, is a haunting presentation of Hellenistic Egyptian funerary portraits, produced in the context of the "Art on Film" program sponsored by the Metropolitan Museum of Art and the Getty Museum. Using varying reverb levels for different voices-over (many of which are recorded in carefully chosen locations rather than in a traditional studio), filmmakers Bob Rosen and Andrea Simon have given to this film a texture and a complexity that could not possibly have been achieved by the traditional "spaceless" voice-over. In choosing actors for voice-over recording, Simon reports that she regularly prefers a voice that destabilizes the meaning of the text: an older voice, a foreigner, an inner voice. From films like *The Fayum Portraits* we learn lessons about sound that Hollywood cannot possibly teach us.

Music in/on Film

For years, music has been one of the very few sound-oriented domains to receive systematic attention from critics. While the quality of work on film music made this attention something of a mixed blessing, it certainly did help maintain awareness of certain aspects of film sound. It also helped to foster the distribution of film sound track records. Yet nearly all this attention has been paid to the aesthetic side of film music, with little or no attempt to deal with the many interlocking aspects of the cinema and music industries: purchases of music publishers by film studios, the cultural impact of sheet music derived from film songs, copyright changes, Hollywood bankrolling of Broadway musicals, cinema's borrowings from the music industry, and many other topics. Today, with the increased visibility and influence of music videos, there is perhaps special cause for critics to pay close attention to the connection between the music and film industries, though critics with historical sensitivity will immediately note that cinema has never been without such close connections to the music industry. We are fortunate in this endeavor to have the aid of Russell

Sanjek's recent authoritative three-volume set on *American Popular Music and its Business*.

Animation

As Scott Curtis demonstrates in his article on the early Warners cartoons, the field of animation conceals a gold mine for sound theoreticians. Neglected by image and sound critics alike, cartoons question some of our most basic film terminology. Faced with a succession of drawings, we are hard put to draw a line between onscreen and offscreen sound, between diegetic and non-diegetic sound, or even between voice-on and voice-over. Indeed, as Curtis points out, there are other established categories as well that simply do not hold up to the animation test. Curtis also helps us to realize the importance of cartoons in the overall film/music commodity complex. While cartoons were benefitting from the trickle-down of music purchased or composed for feature films, they were actively developing many of the process methods that Hollywood would soon adopt for general use. With animation currently experiencing a renaissance, thanks to the wonders of electronic graphics, this seems like an appropriate time to reopen the animation dossier.

Short Forms

Of course, animation is not alone among short films in failing to attract consistent critical attention. In fact, nearly every short form has received all too little scrutiny from image and sound critics alike. Only recently have pre-1915 films become the object of academic interest. In spite of their cultural importance, silent newsreels have never attracted much attention; even Movietone News and other sound newsreels generally take a back seat to feature presentations. Perhaps the recent UCLA/MOMA project to restore and exhibit a large number of the early Vitaphone shorts will alert scholars to the importance of these short films for an understanding of evolving sound conventions. More recent short forms also deserve the attention of the sound critic: avant-garde films, industrial films, advertisements and public service announcements, trailers, and many other abbreviated genres, not to mention scores of short television spots. It is certainly no secret that the highest production values (particularly with regard to sound, so often slighted in the feature film world) are often to be found in the shortest films. If the industry's approach to sound should change, here is where the winds of change would first be felt.

Media shifts

One of the best ways to understand the specific investments of a particular medium is to compare the approaches that two different media take to the "same" material. Is a song mixed the same way for a 45 rpm release and as the theme song of a fifties film? How are the acoustics of a live event (theater, concert, public address) altered by film presentation? How are music and choreography transformed when a dance concert is televised? Does filmed opera differ from televised opera? As Mary Pat Klimek demonstrates in her incisive article on film adaptations of Shakespeare's plays, there is more than one way to think about these problems. Not surprisingly, Klimek's inquiry about Shakespeare on film poses further questions about the problems of spectatorship in general. How does hearing contribute to theatrical and filmic spectatorship? Are there two basic approaches, one theatrical and the other filmic, or does subject formation depend on entirely different parameters? It is hard to imagine a better crucible for analyzing the basic concerns of cinema as a medium, and of sound as one of its constitutive components.

Silent Cinema

Frankly, it is not surprising that the sound accompanying silent cinema should have been given such short shrift by critics. After all, careful analysis of silent film sound involves nothing less than the reconstruction of exhibition history in all its variety and ephemerality. But isn't this precisely what the current generation of silent film scholars has set about to accomplish—reconstituting exhibition history? Why is it that historians can tell you who the projectionist was, what projector was used, when the electrical system had been overhauled, how many ushers were in attendance, and what was offered in the rest of the program, but they either can't or simply don't provide any information on the music that accompanied the program. Personally, I find this situation scandalous. If you want information on silent film music, you are most likely to get it from collectors of automatic instruments, cinema organ clubs, and local historical societies. If it were not for the valorous efforts of the Vestal Press of Vestal, New York, there would almost literally be nothing in silent film sound currently in print in this country.

Yet, like so many other eccentric forms, silent film sound holds a special lesson for us. While the musical accompaniment of the twenties offers few surprises to fans of sound cinema, the early cinema's unexpected combinations of music, effects, lecturers, human voices behind the screen, sound-on-disk, and many other sound sources constitute a special challenge to the sound specialist. Silent film's formative period

(1905–15), which is in many ways the formative period of the cinema industry itself, offers a strange mixture of descriptive and prescriptive language drawn from any number of contributing discourses. If we want to understand how sound came to be defined by the film industry as it did, then we can do no better than consult the trade press of the end of this century's first decade and beginning of the second, when the very definition of cinema was at stake, along with its status, its artistic allegiances, and its narrative investments. The time has surely come to shed some light on this dark corner.

Idiosyncratic Auteurs

One of the prime methods of understanding sound, over the years, has been to look closely at the work of sound stylists, directors whose work reveals or indeed expands the possibilities of cinema sound: Rouben Mamoulian, Orson Welles, Jean-Luc Godard, and Robert Altman, to name but a few. Today, however, few names are being added to the list. The great classics were discovered long ago (which is not to say they wouldn't profit from renewed analysis); the rebels of the sixties and seventies are fast being tamed by success (or television, which for many is the same thing); the great sound achievements of the last decade or two tend to be made by teams (including developers of new technologies, teams of technicians, and independent sound designers). It is thus with great pleasure that I greet Andrea Truppin's work on Andrei Tarkovsky, one of the last, perhaps, of the great auteurs. As a consummate sound designer and technician, Tarkovsky continually challenges his audience to make meaning(s) out of sound. Like many of the recent generation of Australian filmmakers, Tarkovsky eschews traditional narrative sound mixing in favor of the bizarre, the numinous, and the sacred. Eventually, other writers with the sensitive hearing of an Andrea Truppin may reveal to us yet other auteurs, working undoubtedly on the fringes of the international cinema industry, who have Tarkovsky's power to make us listen and, perhaps, hear.

Technicians

In many ways, the heroes of this volume are the sound technicians— those who came from research laboratories, like Maxfield and Fletcher; those who rose to the top in their studios, like Dreher, Shearer and Stewart; those who continued to labor in the trenches, like Cass and Heman; the proponents of stereo, like Grignon and Offenhauser; and many, many others. In my own teaching, I have made increasing use of the writings of technicians, so convinced am I that the secret pathways of film sound start as tunnels from the trenches. All too often, the pathfinding discoveries of an auteur will eventually prove to be heavily influenced by an unsung technician. It took years for Gregg Toland to garner some of the attention regularly afforded to Welles for the deep-focus cinematography of *Citizen Kane*. Not surprisingly, it took even longer for Perry Ferguson to receive full credit for set design and for James G. Stewart to get his due for contribution to the sound track (Carringer). The time has come for film scholars to begin to pay careful attention to the sound style of individual studios and technicians.

There are undoubtedly other sound areas that have remained in the dark. Film scholars have paid far too little attention, for example, to the diverse media that have contributed to film sound—not just the obvious ones, like radio and television, but everything from illustrated songs and vaudeville to public address, recorded music, and theater sound reinforcement. If we want to understand the workings of film sound in its overall cultural context then we must broaden our scope and direct our attention to this enlarged corpus.

9

Women's Voices in Third World Cinema

Amy Lawrence

Recent feminist film theory has been concerned with the way women's voices have been constructed by mainstream cinema so as to reinforce certain ideological assumptions about the roles of women and men (Kaplan, Renov, Silverman). Most of this work, however, has centered on US and European production, whether classical or experimental. Trinh Minh-ha's 1989 film *Surname Viet, Given Name Nam* redefines the terms of the discussion by actively examining issues of voice, gender and language in a space located precisely between the US and the Third World. Issues of synchronization, central to the representation of women's voices in Hollywood films, are complicated by questions of language and made problematic by having actresses in California literally "give voice" to the transcribed and translated testimony of women still in Vietnam. By considering this film and its theoretical context, we can begin to reopen and redefine the relationship between the cinematic representation of women's images/voices on the one hand and the construction of a female subject on the other, and to unravel some of the issues tangled in the terms US/Third World, feminist, woman's voice/women's speech, synchronized sound, subjectivity, and "talking heads"—all of which come into play when a woman in a film speaks.

Feminist Theory and Sound

The term "voice" can be used in several ways: to refer to the physical voice reproduced in film through sound technology; to refer to the use of language; or to refer to the possession of an authorial voice. The relationship between the physical voice and language is usually collapsed under the term "speech," however the interaction between voice and language is particularly important in the film I will be focusing on later, so it is necessary to keep them distinct.

In traditional-style narrative film, the synchronization of image and voice is sacrosanct. Mary Ann Doane (1980a) argues that the primary purpose of flawless "invisible" sync is to obscure the medium's "material heterogeneity"—to mimic a unified and coherent text out of the mass of technology and technicians required to make a piece of sound film.

The ideal of a coherent, unified text mirrors the fantasy of a coherent, unified spectator, and in "The Voice in Cinema: The Articulation of Body and Space" (1980b) Doane expands her argument to focus on the goal behind classical sound film's sleights of hand. She argues that the conventions of sound reproduction, together with classical techniques of invisible editing and narrative transparency, work to create the illusion of a unified source of audio-visual information in the theater where the film is viewed. The body of the film itself becomes a "fantasmatic body," the text demonstrating a kind of self-sufficiency where images and sounds seem to be internally (even organically) generated by the fictional world of the film and not externally constructed. The spectator thus identifies body to "body," reading the "film body" as analogous to him- or herself along the flattering terms offered by bourgeois subjectivity.

> At the cinema, the sonorous envelope provided by the theatrical space together with techniques employed in the construction of the sound track works to sustain the narcissistic pleasure derived from the image of a certain *unity, cohesion, and hence, an identity* grounded by the spectator's fantasmatic relation to his/her own body. The aural illusion of position constructed by the approximation of sound perspective and by techniques which spatialize the voice and endow it with "presence" guarantees the singularity and stability of a point of audition, thus holding at bay the potential trauma of dispersal, dismemberment, difference. (Doane 1980b, 45, my emphasis)

For Doane, the purpose of classical cinema's construction of sound is to reassure the spectator that "he" is a stable and unified subject, a subjectivity forever indebted to and inseparable from the institution that creates it.

In *The Acoustic Mirror* Kaja Silverman addresses the questions raised by Doane eight years earlier by transforming the generic "spectator" into a *gendered* "spectator-position" constructed by the classical system and confronted with gendered voices. Silverman argues that camouflaging the work that goes into sound/image production masks the medium's material heterogeneity not simply in order to guarantee the cohesiveness of any subject but specifically to shore up male subjectivity. Classical cinema's "denial of its material heterogeneity" (the "effacement of work . . . [characteristic] of bourgeois ideology" [Doane 1980a, p. 47]) is for Silverman merely one of a series of displacements enacted by cinema to lessen the anxiety of the male subject, for whom the "potential trauma of dispersal, dismemberment, and difference" held at bay by the "invisible" sound editing techniques is castration. These "displacements follow a precise trajectory" from the original "loss of the object" (in the accession to language), "to the foreclosed site of production, to the representation of woman as lacking. These orchestrated displacements," she argues, "have as their final goal the articulation of a coherent male subject" (Silverman 1988, 10).

Feminist film theory has traditionally focused most of its attention on the last category—the representation of woman as lack. Silverman shows how this is communicated not only through the image of woman's body as fetishized object of the male gaze but through the construction of the woman's voice. While synchronization of the man's voice and image marks the traditional beginning of sound film with *The Jazz Singer* in 1927, Silverman shows how, when women's voices are linked to their bodies through synchronization of sound and image, women are threatened paradoxically with silence, that is, erasure of their subjectivity. Using a selection of films from the 1940s, Silverman shows how women's voices are narratively taken away from them, held within the diegesis and out of their control. In these films, female characters are no longer subjects but bodies that can only be made to signify through the masculine agency of doctors, lawyers, etc. The male characters wrench sounds out of women through techniques such as hypnosis, sodium pentathol, or torture, and then interpret or make meaning out of the sounds "they" have produced. Synchronization in such circumstances not only contains women within the diegesis of the film, barring them from the realm of enunciation "outside" the narrative (a position reserved for the male subject), but at its most chilling "[identifies] the female voice with an intractable materiality" and alienates the female subject from the meanings "produced" by her own voice (Silverman, 61).

For Silverman, the only way for the woman's voice to escape "that semiotics . . . [that] obliges the female voice to signify the female body, and the female body to signify lack" (168) is to be disembodied. Avantgarde feminist films such as Yvonne Rainer's *Film about A Woman Who . . .* (1974), Mulvey and Wollen's *Riddles of the Sphinx* (1976), and Bette Gordon's *Empty Suitcases* (1980) present a radical disjuncture of female voice and body. The woman's voice thus

> escapes that anatomical destiny to which classical cinema holds its female characters. . . . At the same time, it never assumes the privileged and transcendental qualities of a traditional voice-over, or even

the much more limited powers of a traditional voice-off. It is more
. . . a voice "apart," . . . a voice which asserts its independence from
the classic system. (Silverman, 130–131)

For instance, Rainer's *Film About a Woman Who* . . . "shows the alignment of sound and image to be an agency of entrapment, one of the means
by which the female subject can be made to emerge within a discourse
contrary to her desires, and to submit at least temporarily to a fixed
identity" (Silverman, 167).

For all its estimable sophistication, the danger of Silverman's argument
is its susceptibility to oversimplification: synchronization as automatically
bad and "asynchronization" or the disembodied voice as always potentially
good for women.

I would like to reopen the issue of sync by focusing on a film that
radically problematizes the synchronization of women's voices and images. In doing so, the film puts into question the "unity, coherence," and
"presence" assumed of a synchronized image and voice as well as the
unity, coherence, and presence of a stable viewing subject. I shall argue
that in Trinh Minh-ha's film the synchronized voice points not to a singular
cohesive female subject but to a more complicated conception of subjectivity as multiple, shifting, and communal—pointing not only to the psychological but to the social heterogeneity of a talking head. For this more
complex conception of subjectivity, it is important to keep in mind Teresa
de Lauretis's definition of subjectivity:

[A] woman, or a man, is not an undivided identity, a stable unity,
"consciousness," but the term of a shifting series of ideological positions. Put another way, the social being is constructed day by day as the
point of articulation of ideological formations, an always provisional
encounter of subject and codes at the historical (therefore changing)
intersection of social formations and her or his personal history.
(1980b, p. 187)

The question, then, is how can the synchronization of image and voice
render such a complex subject readable in a film text?

Western Feminism and the Third World

Before looking at the film's representation of Third World women in
translation and in transition, it is necessary to examine the ways contemporary Western feminism initially failed in its attempts to engage in a true
dialogue with the feminism(s), texts and people from other cultures.
Among the primary questions to be addressed are: How do we discuss

Third World film without defining a monolithic "other" and without imposing our own Western feminist agendas? And how do we discuss voice in
relation to language and gender in an other- or multi-cultural context? As
a Western academic feminist, how do I avoid defining (limiting the reading) of Trinh's film? I shall argue that *Surname Viet, Given Name Nam*
is already a text which examines issues of voice, gender, and language
from a space located precisely between the U.S. and the Third World.
Given its prominent use of direct address (which I shall discuss later), the
film is itself initiating a dialogue with its audience. It is our turn to respond.

Feminist writer Chandra Talpade Mohanty points out the ways American feminist attempts to promote an idea of "universal sisterhood" have
ended up romanticizing women of other cultures, obscuring differences,
and illustrating Western feminism's power to define (1984). "Woman,"
as Western feminism has pointed out, is not a universal term transcending
histories or cultures; it is socially constructed, and culturally and historically defined. By homogenizing and systematizing the oppression of
women in the Third World, Mohanty argues, Western feminism positions
"woman" and the "Third World Woman" as stable categories (1984, 334–
35). She states that "the production of the 'Third World Woman' as a
singular monolithic subject in . . . (Western) feminist texts" is an act
of discursive colonization, a "mode of appropriation and codification"
whereby the other is restricted to certain stereotypical roles which reaffirm
the Western feminist/colonizer as the sole possessor of political consciousness and knowledge (1984, 333).

Mohanty traces the way the "average" Third World woman is described
again and again in feminist works on the Third World as

> ignorant, poor, uneducated, tradition-bound, domestic, family-ori-
> ented, victimized, etc. This . . . is in contrast to the (implicit) self-
> representation of Western women as educated, modern, as having
> control of their own bodies and sexualities, and the freedom to make
> their own decisions. (1984, 337)

In this system, women of the Third World are defined "in terms of their
object status (the way in which they are affected or not affected by certain
institutions and systems)" (1984, 338), that is, as victims with needs or
problems but not choices—a discursive strategy that denies Third World
women both political consciousness and, more importantly, agency.

The term "Third World" was originally coined as a means of constructing a coalition among post-colonial states, unifying a disparate group
into a cohesive identity neither Soviet-block nor U.S. influenced.[1] The
Third World encompasses countries in Asia, Africa, the Middle East,
Central and South America, the Pacific, India—in other words, nearly all

the world. When using the term "Third World" one is always faced with the question "Who uses this term and for whom?" This is crucial because "Third World" has been appropriated by much of Western discourse to mean something quite different from the political and economic self-determination implicit in its origin. Instead it is used as synonymous with poverty, destabilized governments, and underdevelopment; "Third World" has become the multiply stigmatized Other to "our" unified subjectivity.

The primary danger of the concept of a "Third World Woman" is traditional Western humanism's tendency to project its own fears and desires onto an Other. But Mohanty recognizes more subtle risks inherent in the very desire for unity represented by the self-identification "Third World." In privileging sameness over difference, material differences between cultures can be suppressed. Mohanty reiterates the importance of Bernice Johnson Reagon's distinction between "coalition" and "home" (Reagon 1983). For Reagon, "home" is a "nurturing space" based on "sameness of experience, oppression, culture, etc." but which "ultimately provide[s] an illusion of community based on isolation and the freezing of difference" (Mohanty 1987, 38–9). Coalition, on the other hand, is founded on a strategic "cross-cultural commonality of struggles" where a community is formed as part of a political strategy. "*Survival*," according to Johnson, "rather than *shared oppression*" is the basis for working together (Mohanty 1987, 38). In "Feminist Politics: What has Home Got to do with It?", Mohanty and Biddy Martin note that

> The assumption of, or desire for, another safe place like "home" is challenged by the realization that "unity"—interpersonal as well as political—is itself necessarily fragmentary, . . . struggled for, chosen, and hence unstable by definition; it is not based on "sameness," and there is no perfect fit. But there is agency as opposed to passivity. (Martin and Mohanty, 208–209)

Speaking as a subject whose own unity or identity is necessarily "fragmentary, struggled for, chosen, and hence unstable," isn't easy. Mohanty describes how the speech of the stereotypical Third World Woman has been privileged in Western feminist works as that of "truth teller." In this conception women transcend history as well as cultural indoctrination and consequently possess "a privileged access to the 'real,' [and] the 'truth' " (both singular) (Mohanty 1987, 35). (Mohanty refers specifically to Robin Morgan 1984.) She finds in Reagon's work a potentially more helpful definition of a global women's community that does not deny difference(s) among women. Instead of positing a community of women who exist outside of a "man-made" history and who almost unconsciously and inevitably tell the Truth, this elected community "is forged on the basis of memories and counternarratives, not on an ahistorical universalism" (Reagon, 40). What women say is thus implicated in history and culture; what provides common ground are the positions women take discursively in relation to specific goals. This is an active and a conscious construction of community (and identity) through the use of language, the positioning of self and other, of community and resistance, as opposed to the passive ahistorical victim or "truth teller."

As we'll see, the positions available to Third World women in constructing themselves and possible communities through language differ from those available to Western feminists. In her concept of a "politics of location," Adrienne Rich states that "A place on the map is also a place in history" (212).[2] What you are is determined to an extent by "where" you are (in geography as much as history) and you cannot evade it.[3] But this location is not stable, monolithic, or beyond change. Feminism itself is an intervention in the Western humanist tradition. As members of a post-colonial society or as refugees from Vietnam living in the United States, the characters in Trinh Minh-ha's *Surname Viet, Given Name Nam* exist between cultures and between languages.[4] Mohanty avers that the "movement *between* cultures, languages, and complex configurations of meaning and power [has] always been the territory of the colonized" (1987, 42). For those fighting colonization, as for the refugee, community as well as identity becomes a matter of choice, alignment, a series of choices played out in the film in the relation between women's voices and women's speech. It is this relationship between cultures, languages, identity, and gender *as exemplified by the representation of the voice* that I wish to examine in Trinh's film.

Surname Viet, Given Name Nam

The first section of the film presents a series of Vietnamese women describing conditions in post-war Vietnam. As they do so, their words appear at times, written either before the image begins or directly over it. Interspersed with the carefully staged testimonies are segments of black and white archival footage from pre-war Vietnamese life with excerpts from Vietnamese folk songs on the soundtrack as well as voice-over commentary by the filmmaker. The second half of the film reveals that the women of the first section have been played by actresses selected from Vietnamese emigrées living in the United States. While the women's speech in the first section of the film is giving in halting, heavily accented English, the "real" women in the second part speak subtitled Vietnamese and are presented in a vérité cinematic style. It is the distances between image, voice, and language in the seemingly contradictory first and second halves of the film that I want to focus on here.

All the women in the film confront what it means to speak as a woman, an historical experience that is lived through the body and which is at the same time a culturally constructed position. Even within a traditional culture, however, woman's identity is not fixed but fluid. One maxim we hear on the sound track relates that before marriage a woman is a lady, during marriage she's a maid, and when old and husbandless, a monkey.

The narrator underscores how even within the most traditional patriarchal cultures there has always been a parallel history of resistance. Folk tales or popular novels such as *The Tale of Kieu* detail the suffering women have endured trying to fit the ideal roles prescribed for them. However, women's attempts to speak from a position of authority have been appropriated as metaphors for national struggle and women's authorship of important literary works denied, especially when they address topics deemed unacceptable for a woman, such as sexuality or war. Trinh comments, "Each government has its own interpretation of Kieu. Each has its peculiar way of using and appropriating women's images."

Women's relations to their voices are constructed by culture as well. Of the "four virtues . . . required of women" in Vietnamese tradition, the third, *Ngon*, applies to voice and speech. A woman, we're told, is required "to speak properly and softly and never raise [her] voice—particularly in front of the husband or his relatives." Women's speech can be countenanced only for certain purposes and to the husband's advantage. As Linda Peckham notes, "the very act of speech is self-effacement" (1989, 32).

In the first half of the film, the Vietnamese women who directly address the camera speak English. Many post-colonial films and books raise the sensitive issue of language and decolonization. For instance in Ousmane Sembene's *La Noire . . . (Black Girl,* 1966) the title character Diouana seems restricted to a life as a domestic because of her inability to speak the fluent French of her employers; however, a more psychologically devastating trap is that of colonial thinking that privileges the European over the African, epitomized by Diouana's thinking in French. Sembene has since begun to make films in Wolof. However, replacing the language of the colonizer with an original "native" language does not automatically eradicate colonized thought, nor is an "original" language always easy to locate. In countries like India, where many different languages exist over a large area, the language of the colonizer may serve as a universal second language enabling the speaker to avoid the political conflicts involved in privileging the language of one indigenous group over another. In countries whose histories include more than one colonizer—for instance the Dutch and the British in South Africa, or France and the United States in

Vietnam, one of the foreign languages may be chosen as a tool of resistance—especially if the other is the language of the state.

A possible reason the women do not speak Vietnamese is because for them (as for the film) there is no "Vietnam." There is a traditional culture founded on Confucian and Chinese influence, colonized by France ("French Indo-China"), engulfed in civil war fanned by the United States ("North Vietnam, South Vietnam"), and restructured as a single nation by a Communist government. Each stage had its own internal resistances, contradictions, and ruptures. Under the Communist government, silence becomes these women's strategy of resistance. When some of the women are officially commanded to speak against themselves in reeducation camps, they distance themselves from language through the mechanical repetition of writing. One relates how, when ordered "to produce and periodically update 'a resume of [her] past life,' . . . she simply recopied it verbatim each time she was required to submit it" (Peckham, 32).

The use of English in the film emerges as multiply determined. It suggests first a conscious address to an English-speaking audience; resistance to the official government line epitomized by the government's language; a consciously political alienation from their "own" country and culture. This last gap between subject and language in particular breaks any simple equivalence between women of the Third World and "home" or their so-called "native" lands—that women of the Third World are automatically and unproblematically representative of their cultures. For survival, these women consciously select/construct a highly negotiated identity both "at home" and as speakers addressing a non-Third World audience.

As each woman speaks, her accent foregrounds the *effort* of speech, separating the speaker from the language she speaks. Grammatical mistakes and unfamiliar cadences underscore the constructedness of this address, as when ex-party member Thu Van says, "I am deeply rebelled." The extreme close-up of the right half of her face as the camera bisects her makes us aware of the effort and artifice of this self-conscious construction of words, and of the fact that the film's representation of Thu Van must always be incomplete. Silverman argues that accents (in Hollywood films) limit the speech of a female character by calling attention to the grain of the voice and the body (thus containing her firmly within the diegesis and making her subject to the control of male characters) (1988, 49). Here I would argue that accents locate women in history, in "the politics of location."[5] What an accent deprives its speaker of is the unlocatable timeless universality of Man in the humanist sense, such a concept of subjectivity encouraging an illusion of unproblematic wholeness and domain to which these women make no claims.

In her writing as well as in her film work, Trinh insists that subjectivity is never homogeneous but "multiple and shifting" (Gordon, 2), a conception of identity similar to the politics of location but one where the location sits on shifting ground. In *Woman Native Other* she describes writing as "a practice located at the intersection of subject and history" (1989, 6). For the writer/filmmaker who is Third World-identified and who considers herself a "multiply organized, unstable, and historically discontinuous" subject, (de Lauretis 1988, 141) "I is not unitary, [just as] culture has never been monolithic" (Trinh 1988, 76).

One of the techniques Trinh uses to foreground the distance between the women and English is to print their words across the frame like a barrier in scenes throughout the first half of the film. This is done in different ways. The first time we see it, parts of the women's speech are printed against black before the women appear. As they speak, we wait to hear them say the words we've read. In later scenes, the entire screen is filled with words so that the viewer's relationship to the film becomes fragmented between image, graphics, and sound track. We can choose to listen, to read quickly and then listen, to read as we hear, or to use the written words as a backup when the spoken words become difficult to understand. As we do so, we discover that the transcription is almost always at variance with some part of the spoken text. The position of native English speakers, I would argue, is one of acute self-consciousness—the insider confronted, distanced from "our" "own" language. The use of titles also calls attention to the fact that the women could speak Vietnamese and simply be subtitled. The double presentation of English however insists on the difference between spoken language and written—which is precisely the voice, rhythms, and accents of speech versus the declamatory authority of the printed word. The message written on the screen is one thing; the slow and difficult delivery of it exists in time, insisting on history, person, and geography, establishing the women as conscious, active, *and* Other.

In *Surname Viet* language is spoken, transcribed, and translated, yet the narrator states that translation betrays the spirit, the letter, and the aesthetics of what was said. With the best of intentions, the speaker's act of speech when translated has been taken over, tamed, colonized. A more interesting issue though, is that of self-translation. Speaking, for an exile, is a matter of constant self-translation, "the transcription of a new culture onto one's very being while still speaking the language of the original" (Peckham, 35). For Trinh translation "graft[s] several languages, cultures and realities onto a single body," the body becoming the site for multiple identities.[6] Seen the first way, the self-translated speaker would be colluding in her own colonization. However, as heterogeneous and shifting subjects, the women cannot be accused of betraying a more authentic "inner self" in their struggle to speak English over Vietnamese.

Linda Peckham points out how in the traditional "talking heads" documentary "interviews are conducted and reconstructed according to this sense of articulation [as] . . . reflecting and embodying 'truth' value" (33). This kind of documentary privileges language over image and makes simplistic and reductive assumptions about subjectivity and its relation to cinema that have important ramifications when the speaking subject is a Third World woman. Once again the Third World Woman becomes truth teller, without self-consciousness or the ability to shape her story.

> The assumption that an individual is a passive receptor, a static reflection of experience is the same as the assumption that documentary can restore to the present that experience as unmediated testimony. (Peckham, 33)

Peckham finds that the constructedness of the film's image precisely mediates between testimony and any conception of presence. Visually the women are fragmented by the camera through close-ups of hands, body parts, or seen in long shots and long takes (one as long as twelve minutes) that fix them in static compositions of dramatic symmetry. Absence, she argues, is built into the "artifice of style and form," its exaggeration "a disturbing demarcation of an abyss between the camera and the woman, the viewer and the experience" (Peckham, 33). The use of the long take charts the passage of time and implicitly of space between the woman "here" before us and the events in Vietnam.

Equally important is the mediation between language and voice.

> It is when we recall that the speaker is an actress, a substitute, a 'fake,' that the interview style becomes . . . subversive—for the artificial subject points to the absence of the 'real' speaker, an absence that suggests internment, censorship and death, as well as the survival of a witness, a record—a history. (Peckham, 33)

The use of actresses to read the translated testimony of the "real" Vietnamese women is the most radical choice of the film, blurring traditional boundaries between documentary and fiction, and more importantly the association of synchronized speech and subjectivity. Halfway through the film Trinh reveals that the women of the first half have been actresses reading scripted roles. *Surname Viet* is not a "talking heads" documentary but an acted adaptation of another author's book of interviews with women in Vietnam, published in French (Thu Van, 1983). On the soundtrack, Trinh tells how she then interviewed 150 women to find the five who act in the film. These women are then seen in California discussing the "roles" they played. The act of translation on which the entire first half of the film is based, then, is Trinh's translating the Vietnamese women's testimony from French into English, which the actresses then play out as they illustrate (realize) the first essential of exile existence which is self-translation—into another language, another culture, even—as a woman—another body.

The use of actresses—literally putting one person's words into another body—seemingly undermines the traditional documentary's construction of speech-as-subjectivity where sync "proves" an essential link between image/sound track/being. In doing so, *Surname Viet* would seem to complicate the relation between language and referent: these women are mouthing someone else's words, words that have already been translated by a third party. Given all these mediations, how can one locate what we're being told? Where is the truth value? I would argue that *Surname Viet* does not devolve into a simple deconstructionism (and actually resists being positioned as such a text by Western audiences) because of the moral claims invoked by the women's self-presentation as witnesses. The relation between language and a referent cannot be dismissed, given the political context of testimony and the women's claims to linguistic agency (seen in their attempts to communicate the "truth" of a political reality as well as the truth of personal experience).

The use of actresses does not undermine this project; on the contrary, as Peckham says, the "artifices of [the film's construction] are used [paradoxically] to *augment* the reality of a woman's story" (33, my italics). What it does is construct a new way of thinking about women's synchronized speech. The actresses choose to contribute their voices and images to embody the words of other women with whom they share a cultural and political history. Unlike women in Hollywood films (also actresses), whose voices are appropriated for patriarchal ends and who in effect are made to speak against themselves, these actresses take on the words of others as their own in an act of community, the refugee women living in San Francisco and Berkeley electing to carry the words of sisters in struggle to an American audience.

In the film's second half, the women who played the "characters" in the first half speak "as themselves"—in Vietnamese. Each of the women, none of whom is a professional actress, mentions how she accepted a role in the film despite her community's disapproval of singers and cinema actresses. The use of Vietnamese notwithstanding, the traditional beliefs are no longer internalized. "Home," as Bernice Johnson Reagon says, is simply something they've outgrown.

The use of a cinema vérité style, coming after the highly posed scenes of the first half, cannot be read as a simple relapse into documentary realism. As narrator, Trinh states that "By choosing the most direct and spontaneous form of voicing and documenting, I find myself closer to fiction"—fiction being the illusion of an unproblematic and unfragmented cohesiveness.

However, if the film does have a problem it is in its reticence about confronting the issue of speaking Vietnamese in California, of the presence of the Third World within the United States. On the one hand, Trinh's stance toward the Vietnamese women in America avoids the tragic or melodramatic overtones of "exile." On the other, an American audience can comfortably situate the film along a traditional Cold War axis with "the commies" as the bad guys and America the land of the free. There are no racist incidents directed against Vietnamese immigrants, no poverty or unemployment. All of the women have nice jobs—the teenage daughter of one woman is a particularly forceful example of becoming American without tears.[7]

Modern Western ideology has been defined as "valorizing . . . the individual as an autonomous moral being" while neglect[ing] or subordinat[ing] the social whole" (Ong). What Trinh does in her construction of the women's voices in *Surname Viet* is disrupt our perception of the "individual as autonomous moral being" in order to refocus our attention on the women as part of a wider social context. When one woman speaks, there are three superimposed: the witness, the translator, the actress. When the actresses speak "as themselves," we "see" them through/in relation to the women they've played, the country they've come from, and the country they're in. No woman speaks from a single place, including Trinh. Each woman is plural, in transition, in process even (to use Kristeva's term—Moi, 13, 88–123). They transform their bodies into the site from which the other can speak—not in a mystical, transcendental sense, but historically and politically.[8]

Trinh problematizes the classically transparent link between voice and language, image and speech, in order to undermine film's presentation of the Third World woman as "witness to Reality." This does not mean that the women in the film cannot speak the truth or take a political stand. The truth value of their testimony rests not on Third World woman as truth teller, nor on cinema vérité's "myth of an essential core, of spontaneity and depth as inner vision" (Trinh 1988, 77), nor on bourgeois conceptions of personal experience as proof of a cohesive subjectivity, but on faith in women as politically conscious social agents forming coalitions with other women in shifting communities of resistance.

10

The Sound of the Early Warner Bros. Cartoons[1]

Scott Curtis

Film scholarship is notoriously "feature-centric" in that much of its energies go to discussions of feature-length motion pictures. Standard film histories might acknowledge the variety of texts and practices that make up our experiences of cinema (that is, newsreels, animation, trailers and other promotional material, and so on) but they rarely devote significant time and space to that diversity. Given the economic dominance of feature films in the filmmaking industry, this bias is quite understandable. But an unfortunate side effect of this lopsided view of film history is its influence on film theory. Theory tends to echo history in its choice of examples; consequently, theorists' categories and assumptions are based generally on viewings of live-action, dramatic features films. However, close viewings of other types of cinematic texts, such as animation, reveal that the categories are not as readily applicable.

This is certainly true of recent work on film sound. Claudia Gorbman, for instance, outlines a set of "rules" for film music composition, mixing, and editing in her book *Unheard Melodies*. While she makes it clear that these rules apply only to dramatic, feature-length fiction films of the thirties and forties, and that they are by no means invariant, films that would systematically violate those rules (comedies and reflexively modernist films) are labelled "exceptions that prove the rule" (Gorbman, 70ff). But exceptions don't "prove" rules, they disprove them, challenging us to rework our assumptions about film sound.

Hollywood studio animation presents such a challenge. A history of the use of sound in these cartoons would be particularly interesting in that it could show how an ostensibly marginalized set of texts can stand at the very intersection of economics, technology, and art. The Warner Bros. cartoons of the early thirties are by no means unique in this respect, but they do provide a strikingly clear example of the interrelatedness of these three terms, especially how economics and technology influenced the specific character of cartoon sound. But they provide us with more than mere illustration; a closer examination of the use of sound in these cartoons might encourage us to rethink our conceptions of how sound works in feature films, or at least rethink the categories we persistently use to classify sound. Our vocabulary for describing sound in film becomes increasingly inappropriate when confronted with certain aspects of these cartoons. The terminology does not quite fit the phenomena. Three common schemata—the image/sound hierarchy, the separation of the sound track into dialogue/music/effects, and the "diegetic/non-diegetic" distinction—are particularly unwieldy when dealing with animation, suggesting that we should reconceptualize our descriptions of film sound to include other types of film texts besides live-action features. This essay provides the beginning of such a project by pointing to the deficiencies in the current terminology and offering some alternatives, while exploring the economic and technological influences on the sound of the Warner Bros. cartoons.

The Warner brothers were relatively slow to establish an animation branch to their studio. It wasn't until Disney's success with *Steamboat Willie* in 1928 that they began to consider the possibility. Indeed, most of the original Warner Bros. animation staff—Hugh Harman, Rudolf Ising, Isadore "Friz" Freleng, Carmen "Max" Maxwell, Norm Blackburn, Paul Smith, and Rollin "Ham" Hamilton—learned their trade with Disney. Harman, Ising, and Freleng were with Uncle Walt as far back as 1922, when Disney was still in Kansas City. In 1928, just before the premiere of *Steamboat Willie*, an entrepreneur named George Winkler lured away much of Disney's staff (a practice many rival studios adopted when they were short of personnel) with his plan to form a new studio in order to make "Oswald the Rabbit" cartoons. But when that fell through, Harman, Ising and the others were left without a job.

Later that year, Harman, Ising, and Freleng located a recording studio and made a pilot cartoon featuring "Bosko," a rubbery kid in blackface. They had trouble finding a distributor, but Leon Schlesinger, then head of Pacific Art and Title, expressed interest. Having been a backer of *The Jazz Singer*, Schlesinger was in a position to propose the series to Warner Bros. The success of the Disney sound cartoon encouraged them as did the prospect of reusing the popular songs from their music catalog. Warner Bros. began distributing the "Bosko" cartoons and set Schlesinger up as producer. The first of the series, christened "Looney Tunes," was recorded in March 1930 and released in September 1930. Harman and Ising supervised, Freleng animated, and Frank Marsales directed the music. One cartoon was released every month for a year, at the end of which the contract was renewed to include the "Merrie Melodies," specifically designed to feature songs from the Warner collection (Maltin, 224).

Indeed, the importance of the economic incentive to use material from the Warner-owned music publishers cannot be overlooked. In August 1929, anticipating the continued success of its talkies, Warner Bros. invested $8.5 million to buy up a number of publishers affiliated with Harms Music, Inc. Only months previously, the studio had spent $1 million in cash to acquire Witmark and Sons, "perhaps the oldest established popular music house" (*Variety*, August 21, 1929; 5). Such acquisitions meant considerable savings in royalties and taxes (by holding the copyrights to the songs used), and they also could be used as a bargaining chip for booking films in the theaters of rival studios.

Having acquired the rights to any given song, producers were eager to get as much mileage out of the tune as possible. The four featured songs from Mervyn LeRoy's hit musical *42nd Street* (1933), for example, were included in at least six cartoons of the same year. Two of the songs had their own Merrie Melodies: *Young and Healthy* and *Shuffle Off to Buffalo*, but both of these songs were also included in *The Dish Ran Away with the Spoon* and *Bosko's Knight-Mare*. *Bosko's Knight-Mare* also featured the tune "42nd Street" as did *The Organ Grinder*, while "You're Getting to Be a Habit with Me" found its way into *Honeymoon Hotel*, which took its title and theme song from another Warner Bros. feature, *Footlight Parade* (1933). The success of these musicals certainly played a role in the choice of music for the cartoons, but the practice was not limited to box office winners. Songs from obscure musicals such as *Oh! Sailor Behave!* (1930) and *Manhattan Parade* (1932) also spawned a number of early cartoons.[2]

The musical director of the cartoons was heavily encouraged to use compositions owned by the studio. By and large, Marsales adhered to these restraints by drawing from either the public domain or the largest of the publishers (Harms, Witmark, or DeSylva, Brown and Henderson) for his compositions. A typical cartoon of the early thirties would have anywhere from five to fifteen separate compositions (mostly partial usage, of course) requiring "application for domestic license"[3] from as many as five different companies. In the first year of production, however, at least one of those companies (per cartoon) was "outside"—not one of the Warner Bros. acquisitions—much to the dismay of the studio accountants. An inter-office memo dated January 30, 1931 gives a hint of the type of pressure exerted on the musical director:

> My dear Mr. Murphy,
>   Enclosed please find cue sheets [lists of the compositions used and companies owning the copyright] for Looney Tunes #9 [*Dumb Patrol*,

recorded January 22, 1931, released May 1931]. Also note that I have almost got them around to our way of thinking. Out of nine numbers—one outside number.

Hastily,
Arthur Frankl[4]

Economics, then, had a clear influence on the musical director's "way of thinking," so to speak, and on the choice of music for the cartoons.

Economics might also have some influence on *our* way of thinking about sound in cartoons. For instance, why was it necessary to have two separate series? The usual explanation holds that the split was a compromise between image and sound. In this respect, the functions of the two Warner Bros. series duplicated that of Disney's Mickey Mouse and Silly Symphony series, in which, supposedly, music followed action in the first and action followed music in the second. Legend has it that the split between the two series at Disney studios came about due to disagreements between Disney and his first musical director, Carl Stalling. Disney animator Wilfred Jackson tells the story this way:

> Walt and Carl would time the pictures in Walt's office. Timing them consisted of working out what the music would be and what the action would be. A lot of times Walt would want more time or less time for the action than could fit the musical phrase. So, there would be a pretty good argument going on in there. . . . But, finally, Walt worked out a thing with Carl. He said, "Look, let's work it out this way. We'll make two series. On the Mickey Mouse pictures you make your music fit my action the very best you can. But we'll make another series, and they'll be musical shorts. And in them music will take precedence and we'll adjust our action the best we can to what you think is the right music." (Barrier, 22)

Here the struggle between image and sound is played out as explicitly as any in classical Hollywood cinema. The image/sound hierarchy—in which sound is assumed to be motivated by the image and thus supplemental—has an almost allegorical status in the two series, where it holds true in one and is simply reversed in the other. But as an explanation and description of the split between the Warner Bros. series, the concept is not as tidy as it may seem. The economic considerations already mentioned hint at an alternative explanation, while examination of the actual production practices put the hierarchy in doubt.

Ostensibly, the Warner Bros. series split worked on the same principle as Disney's, that is, action taking precedence in the Looney Tunes and music guiding action in the Merrie Melodies. But the actual scoring of the cartoons (and close listening) blurs the distinction between them. With regard to the Looney Tunes, for example, while most music was actually recorded after completion of the images, Harman and Ising would begin a film by deciding first on a beat with their music director, then timing the cartoons on sheets of written music, indicating so many frames for each action.[5] This action was coordinated with the bars of music and the timing was then transferred from the music sheets to exposure sheets, from which animators drew and exposed the requisite number of pictures. Very often, the music directors would work from these exposure sheets, too, prerecording the music even before the drawings were committed to celluloid (Barrier, 24). To ensure precise synchronization, the music director would create a "click track" for his musicians. Invented by Carl Stalling (not Max Steiner) during his first years at Disney (1926–1933), the "click track" was a prerecorded rhythmic beat (sort of an electronic metronome) timed to the tempo of the images. The first click tracks were recorded on disk, but later holes were punched into black leader that would be read by an optical reproducer (Barrier 23, Handzo 410). The musicians would listen to these beats through headphones as they played the written music, and the finished product would be closely synchronized.

Song and dance numbers in all the cartoons, particularly important to the Merrie Melodies series, were treated a bit differently because of the need to synchronize voice and mouth. The vocals would be recorded beforehand without accompaniment; the artist would sing in time with the click track. The words and timing would then be read off onto exposure sheets, from which the music director would write the accompanying score (Barrier, 26).

These production methods—standard procedures for Warner Bros. cartoons—show that the image/sound hierarchy does not justify the existence of two separate series. If there were only slight production differences between them, the reason for the split remains unresolved. This division of output was not unusual for major animation studios, and given the success of Disney it is certainly reasonable to assume that their split would have been accepted as an industry norm. But there were also further compelling financial reasons. At Warner Bros., "in-house" music was used for all cartoons, not just the Merrie Melodies. It seems clear that the best way to showcase these songs would be to follow a successful formula: stage the numbers in song and dance routines. Indeed, most of the songs for the cartoons had been already featured in this way, either through Broadway shows or early Warner Bros. musicals, such as *Gold Diggers of 1933, 42nd Street,* or *Footlight Parade. Lady, Play your Mandolin,* for instance, a Merrie Melody released September 1931, features a stage show in a canteen. *Three's a Crowd* (1933) is the usual toys-at-midnight romp with the songs performed on an impromptu stage. *You Don't Know What You're Doin'!* (1931) also features a mock vaudeville show. This setting became standard for many Merrie Melodies: *Hamateur Night* (1939), *Rhapsody Rabbit* (1946), and *What's Up, Doc?* (1950) are just a few of the later examples. While bona fide stage settings are not typical of the early Bosko Looney Tunes, musical performance is still an important part of the action. In many of the Looney Tunes, such as *Sinkin' in the Bathtub* (1930), Bosko takes time out to serenade his girlfriend Honey with a version of a well-known contemporary melody. There are any number of reasons for the high incidence of musical performance in these early cartoons, including the close formal and economic ties to the musical genre and the desire to highlight synchronized sound. Perhaps the most immediate generic precedent was set by the Warner Bros. Vitaphone shorts of the late twenties and early thirties. The conventions established by these films for recording vaudeville acts were carried on in many of the cartoons. In the Vitaphone short *Elsie Janis in "Behind the Lines"* (1926) vaudeville entertainer Janis sings to a chorus of soldiers, who function as a surrogate audience in the space of the film. The same pattern occurs in many vaudevillelike Merrie Melodies.[6] These narrative resemblances certainly had economic motivations: if Sam Warner hoped the Vitaphone system would be a substitute for expensive musicians at the theaters (Koszarski, 16), then the cartoons themselves, along with other live-action shorts, could have been seen as a substitute for vaudeville performances before films.

Yet to stage numbers exclusively in song and dance routines would have violated successful protagonist-centered narrative formulas. The cartoon series based on a single hero is an established convention of late silent cartoons. The Warner Bros. Bosko series followed a pattern established by such successful characters of the twenties as Max Fleischer's Koko the Clown or John Randolph Bray's Col. Heeza Liar. To showcase the songs themselves, as Warner Bros. was probably eager to do, required a narrative framework that did not emphasize plot and action, but rather privileged a play of movement without narrative urgency that is more at home in filmed musicals or musical theater. It would have been difficult to reconcile the two narrative patterns, and there were strong economic reasons not to try.

Economic and narrative influences can account for the choice of music, but not its particular character. For that, we must look to the technology of sound recording at the time. But again, a look at the contemporary practices shows that another common schema—the dialogue/music/effects trio—does not adequately describe the sound tracks. It becomes harder and harder to decide what is "dialogue," what is "music," and what are "effects."

Warner Bros. initially recorded sound for their motion pictures with their sound-on-disk system, but by mid-1930 they began using a sound-on-film process that recorded sound optically. During the transition from disk to film, both processes were used and exhibitors equipped with disk technology could buy special attachments to read optical sound tracks. By the beginning of 1932, all the recording was done with the sound-on-film process. The first Warner Bros. cartoons were made during the transition period, and recorded on both disk and film.[7] However, the Vitaphone recording system in use until 1933 required that all elements of the sound track be recorded at once. In the Warner Bros. live-action shorts, these elements are usually separated for each film; Will Hays gives his speech without accompanying music (which certainly would have been appropriate), the New York Philharmonic plays "Tannhäuser" without spoken introduction. When orchestration of different sound elements was required but proved to be too unwieldy, the "playback" system was used: prerecorded music was played on a phonograph while the dialogue was recorded (Altman 1980b, 46).

The Vitaphone system's sound recording practices directly influenced the specific character of the music written for the cartoons. For instance, there are no classical pieces in these cartoons; unlike the live-action shorts, they contain only jazzy popular tunes such as "Smile, Darn Ya, Smile," and "You Don't Know What You're Doin'!" This difference could be attributed to a high/low distinction; many of the live-action shorts sought to be labelled "culture" (such as *Giovanni Martinelli [in] the Temple Scene from "Aida"* [1930]), while the animated shorts sought to be nothing more than "entertainment," especially if they were to take the place of vaudeville acts in theater programs. But why jazz? Obviously, if Warners wanted to highlight their popular songs, they would naturally pick a popular style. Yet this is not necessarily so, considering that by 1937 Carl Stalling was drawing from the Warner Bros. stock using his famous neo-classical style. To be sure, if fast-paced action had become the convention for animated cartoons, almost to the point of becoming movement for its own sake, then the accompanying music also required a quick tempo. Nevertheless, this convention does not fully explain the particular orchestration and arrangement we find in these early examples. It must be attributed to a coincidence of musical structure, technological limitations, and generic demands.

Rick Altman neatly sums up the relevant limitations of the microphones used for Vitaphone technology:

> Simply put, the problem lay in the difficulties of producing a high quality and complex sound track (including dialogue, music, effects) with an unselective microphone at a time when the technology of sound mixing practically forbade postmixing of multiple tracks without audible loss of quality. In fact, until approximately 1933 it was ex-

tremely rare for music and dialogue to appear simultaneously on the sound track unless they were recorded simultaneously. The latter solution of course presents other difficulties. The amount of reverberation generally required for dialogue varies greatly from that which is appropriate for music . . . similarly, dialogue and music require different amplification and thus are difficult to record with the same microphone(s). (Altman 1980b)

A good example of the problems inherent in this setup occurs in *Hold Anything* (1930). The theme music plays at a constant level, but Bosko's shouts to Honey are barely audible. The playback system, the usual solution to these problems, was unacceptable for the cartoons because the music was a central attraction and could not withstand the loss of sound quality. If dialogue and effects were going to be included without competing volume levels, the answer had to lie in the arrangement of the music itself. The abrupt starts and stops of these early arrangements made it possible to orchestrate the different sound elements without competing volume levels and still maintain a fairly constant musical background. More specifically, the arrangement of these early cartoons was defined and symmetrically constructed into eight-bar phrases. This highly ordered system allowed cartoonists to place significant action on the cadential accent at the end of every eighth measure. It also gives the orchestra an opportunity to pause for a second or two while dialogue is spoken or some other effect is sounded (Dahl, quoted in Prendergast, 171).

In another example from one of the very first Merrie Melodies, *Smile, Darn Ya, Smile* (1931), Foxy (a Mickey Mouse look-alike with long ears and a bushy tail) helps a large hippo onto his trolley. The volume levels for the music in this cartoon are constant, so while the singing is closely miked and compatible with the level of the instrumental music, the dialogue from secondary characters (presumably further from the microphone, or perhaps using the one calibrated for the orchestra) is often drowned out. The arrangement remedies the problem: the music plays gaily along as Foxy pushes, the beat stops at the end of a phrase, the hippo complains, and it resumes when her line is over.

This same pattern occurs very often with what we might call "sound effects." Significant action (usually a blow to the head or some other sort of bodily harm) is accompanied by a sound effect. In the early cartoons, this effect is provided by the percussion section of the orchestra: a knock on wood, a cymbal crash, or a variable-pitch whistle. Produced by musical instruments, they become part of the music, entering at rhythmic breaks at a compatible pitch and volume. At the beginning of *You Don't Know What You're Doin'!* (1931), after an eight-bar intro over the credits, the singing begins to ¾ time, allowing a two-measure break at the end of the sixth bar for a character to slap out a rhythm on another character's behind. After another six-bar section, the second character echoes the first by tapping out the same rhythm at the break. Eight bars later, the hero of the story, Piggy, is riding his motor scooter down the street to the club; the clippity-clop of his engine is perfectly timed to the rhythm of the new refrain. As it arrives at its destination, the scooter backfires to the tune of "shave and a haircut, two bits."

It's clear that this particular arrangement is not unique to cartoons, but comes directly from silent film scoring practices. In fact, this "residual" practice certainly had a strong influence on the character of the music in these early cartoons. Mike Barrier quotes Carl Stalling, a former silent film accompanist, on this very topic: "I just imagined myself playing for a cartoon in the theater, improvising, and it came easier" (Barrier, 26). But we cannot attribute the features of early cartoon sound to either silent scoring practices or technology alone; they are due, of course, to both. The regular rhythm of the popular music and the conventions of silent film scoring made it easier to "orchestrate" the music, dialogue, and effects for the existing technology. What we have here, however, is an interesting paradox: the technology and the arrangement of the music work together to separate the various elements of the sound track; music, dialogue, and effects tend not to overlap. Yet the same technological limitations and the instrumentation of the orchestra also work together to blur the distinctions between the sound elements by using music as a sound effect and orchestrating all the elements into a continuous musical track, a practice that will become standard and emblematic of animated cartoons. Just as an examination of the actual practices upsets the strict division between the series, an investigation of the technological practices shows that the boundaries between sound elements are not that clear.

As the technology changes, however, so does the arrangement and character of the sound. By 1933, it was possible to separately record various tracks, mixing and synchronizing them after editing. This allowed easier handling of multiple tracks and volume levels (Salt, 43). The most notable change in the sound of these cartoons after this period is the continuous music. In earlier cartoons there were a number of rhythmic breaks in the music, but in *Petting in the Park* (1934), for instance, the same sort of jazzy music is played continuously and the volume levels are lowered to make room for other sound elements. The ability to record the effects on a separate track at least partially relieved the orchestra of the task of providing the effects. While the musical instruments would still match the action and even serve as effects, others would be added separately. In this cartoon, two lovebirds sing along to the theme tune and then embrace, the sound of their kiss coming through loud and clear, even though the volume of the music has not lowered. The trend toward continuous background music would continue through the Carl Stalling period (1936–1956) as silent scoring methods were left behind.

Even as the music of the Warner Bros. cartoons took on a different style under Stalling's musical direction, certain conventions of cartoon sound were set, such as the use of music as a sound effect. It is difficult to make strict divisions between the different elements of the sound track and this difficulty extends to the sound/image relationships as well. It is not too surprising that the close marriage of music and image results in certain formal patterns on the image track. Given that the tempo of the music has already been decided upon in any given cartoon, the "mise-en-scène" enacts that tempo in a variety of ways. The characters sing and dance, of course, but buildings also sway, the horizon line rocks, and nearly every object "comes alive" to the beat of the music. This reversal of the image/sound hierarchy is also common in musicals; indeed, Rick Altman argues that it is one of the defining features of that genre (Altman 1987, 62–73).

Most conspicuous in animation, though, is the way in which images are repeated in order to fit the music. Repetition is one of the hallmarks of studio animation, both in terms of representation and actual construction. Thousands of drawings—the same effects repeated again and again—are required for a single cartoon. In the cartoons themselves, backgrounds are repeated as characters chase one another, even in finite spaces: the inside of a house may be elongated to fit the duration of the chase. Characters repeat actions over and over again: the motif of the assembly line is especially exemplary. "Assembly lines" of all sorts show up throughout the history of Hollywood studio animation. In *Hold Anything*, a group of mice work together in assembly line fashion while helping Bosko lay bricks. In *Baby Bottleneck* (1946), for instance, Daffy and Porky Pig work on an elaborate assembly line designed to create, well, babies. In *Buddy the Woodsman* (1934), the lumberjacks come in for dinner, but not before passing through, one by one over and over again, an elaborate face washer and dryer. The theme of mechanization and repetition metaphorically reminds us of the routine of image generation in an animation studio. The assembly line motif echoes the rhythm of the work image generation, but it is also a more particular instance of the larger patterns of repetition in a cartoon. This repetition, occurring at discrete intervals and in distinguishable units, is the visual equivalent of the repeated patterns of the music. The actions, mise-en-scène, and motifs of the animated cartoon's image track duplicate and are determined by the sound track.

But how do we think about the relationship between sound and image when the entire shape of a cartoon is complemented and determined by the music? The relationship certainly points to the inadequacy of the "diegetic/nondiegetic" distinction that functions so centrally in most discussions of film sound. The term "diegetic" refers to that which is accessible to the characters of a film, and yet buildings in cartoons sway to music that has no source in the diegesis. Even when there is a source, animators play with the notion of diegesis and the audiences' acceptance of the convention. In *Red-Headed Baby* (1931) the characters are dancing in time with the music, but it is only after a couple of minutes have passed that the protagonist turns on the radio from which the music supposedly emanates. That a diegetic orchestra will occasionally provide sound effects for diegetic action further complicates this issue. The "diegetic/non-diegetic" distinction does not even apply to the image track of the cartoon if we consider that elongated space and time in chase scenes are more closely related to musical rhythm than to a fictionally unified space. Thus, the traditional "diegetic/non-diegetic" categorization, when applied to even the most ordinary cartoon, is rendered practically useless. The relationship between music and image in animated cartoons can be better described by distinguishing between what might be called *isomorphic* and *iconic* uses of sound.

An "isomorphic" use of sound occurs when the sound and image have the same "shape." Over the years, this convention has become familiar to everyone: a character's wide-eyed blinks are accompanied by a couple of light, sprightly notes, buildings sway to the music, characters dance to the tempo, or a glissando accompanies a "pan" across an animated landscape. For example, in *Big Man from the North* (1930) Bosko rides his dogsled over a series of steep mountains and a variable-pitch whistle sounds with each descent into a valley. As Bosko's sled descends, its speed matches the rate at which the whistle's pitch varies. Throughout the cartoon, the tempo of the music and the image match, as when bass strings are plucked or wood blocks are tapped with each step. "Isomorphic," then, refers to the close matching of image and sound—that is, a relationship based on *rhythm* in both the action and the music. The term "isomorphic" recognizes not only specific features of the sound, but also the inseparability and equality of sound/image relationships. Thus, sound is not reduced to its role in the space of the fiction.

The practice of synchronizing music and image to a very precise degree is traditionally referred to as "mickey-mousing," so named because it was used in Disney's cartoons (although silent film music also used it to a great extent). But mickey-mousing seems to carry a pejorative meaning, both because of the lower status animated cartoons have traditionally held in film studies and because of the implication that exact illustration is a rather tedious and silly way to relate music and image. The term is also imprecise. It tells us nothing about the rhythmic relations between sound and image. Indeed, it implies, like "diegetic/non-diegetic," an image/sound hierarchy that is simply untenable. And there are other instances of synchronized action and music that are not normally considered mickey-mousing. For instance, when one character slaps another on the head and we hear a cymbal crash. This would normally be called a "sound effect" even though an instrument from the orchestra created the sound.

Moments such as these, when the orchestra provides the (diegetic?) "sound effects," might be called "iconic." In *Big Man from the North* the villain pounds his fist on the bar and we hear a cymbal crash and a blare of horns. Or, considering Bosko's dogsled again, the "highness" or "lowness" of the variable-pitch whistle matches the peaks and valleys of the mountains. After C. S. Peirce, it could be argued that, with respect to the sound and the image in this case, "there is no sensuous resemblance between it and the object, but only an analogy between the relations of the parts of each" (105). The relationship between the sound effect and its visual representation is not one of fidelity, but of analogy. Short, violent, and surprising, the pounding fist and the cymbal crash have certain matching, yet not necessary, components. The advantage of the terms "isomorphic/iconic" is that they are not mutually exclusive, as are "diegetic/non-diegetic," and they can describe multiple sound variables. In another, completely different example, Oskar Fischinger's *Motion Painting No. 1*, the bass line of Bach's Brandenburg Concerto broadens as the circles in the image broaden and deepen in hue. This seems to be isomorphic in that the rhythm of bass and the movement of the circles coincide, but it is also iconic in that the change of colors matches the deepening pitch. If isomorphic relations refer to those governed by rhythm and movement, then iconic relations pertain to analogous relationships between visual events and the timbre, volume, pitch, and tone of the accompanying sound.

Synchronous speech in live-action film illustrates an *indexical* sound/image relationship. An index is "a sign which refers to the Object that it denotes by virtue of being really affected by that Object" (Peirce 102). A footprint is the sign of a person who left it, as a film is a photographic record of the action it records. Through live-action sync speech, the actors leave their indexical mark on the sound track; there is a necessary connection between sound and image that is missing from cartoons. This fact might answer a question we have all asked at one time or another: why do cartoon characters always have funny voices? Certainly, it is because they have funny bodies: following the pattern of indexical relationships in live-action film, the voice matches the body. But given that indexicality is impossible in a cartoon, no match between sound and image is required except by analogy, that is, iconically. Iconic relations obtain in cartoons especially with regard to voice and body: the "distorted" voices of cartoon characters are analogous to their "distorted" and "elastic" bodies.

Of course, isomorphic and iconic sound/image relationships are not limited to cartoons. Even a casual look and listen to any Three Stooges short will confirm this. Dramatic films also exhibit these uses of sound: a fight scene from a fifties *noir* might be accompanied by blaring horns and excited drums. Indeed, the point is not that cartoons are different— it is exactly that they should not be treated as an entirely separate category of cinema. Separating cartoons and other shorts or "untypical" cinematic texts from mainstream film histories does a disservice to those histories, especially when it becomes apparent that cartoons can be exemplary. The way in which economics and technology influenced narrative and stylistic conventions is indicative of Hollywood studio animation's "typicality" with respect to classical Hollywood cinema. But more importantly, close study of cartoons allows us to reconsider what is "typical" in classical Hollywood cinema. The dividing lines between types of texts and practices are too easily set in film studies. Serious attention to animation may lead to a reexamination of these cinematic boundaries: between the different elements of the soundtrack, between the sound and image, between features and shorts, or between comedy and drama. The first step is a history that will lead to further theoretical considerations.

11

Imagining the Sound(s) of Shakespeare: Film Sound and Adaptation

Mary Pat Klimek

Imagine one of Shakespeare's plays as a film. This isn't difficult; many filmmakers have brought Shakespeare to the screen. Now, imagine in particular the sound of your film. What do you hear? Your answer will depend on whether you imagine Shakespeare as a playwright or a poet. Such an opposition may seem absurd, since Shakespeare's brilliance lies precisely in his melding of poetic language with dramatic action. Our encounters with Shakespeare, however, vary widely. Sometimes we have front row seats at Stratford; more often, we quietly page through a dog-eared text, rereading favorite passages to ourselves. These varied experiences stimulate our imaginations in quite different ways. When adapting Shakespeare, a filmmaker must represent not only the play's actions, but also its sounds. Decisions regarding recording strategies (number of mikes, mike placement, sync or post-sync, amount of sound manipulation) reveal the filmmaker's conception of how the audience will imagine the play.

First, let's consider the Shakespeare-as-playwright model. When André Bazin critiques adaptations of Shakespeare and other playwrights, he focuses on the theatrical qualities of the performed play. He argues:

> The true solution, revealed at last, consists in realizing that it is not a matter of transferring to the screen the dramatic element—an element interchangeable between one art and another—of a theatrical work, but inversely the theatrical quality of the drama. The subject of the adaptation is not that of the play, it is the play precisely in its scenic essence. (1967a, 115)

If one remains faithful to the text, the outcome is predetermined: "The text determines the mode and style of the production; it is already potentially the theater" (84–85). Bazin argues further that Shakespeare and other great playwrights wrote with the theatrical mode of reception firmly in mind: "the handling of the action and the style of the dialogue were conceived as echoing through the architecture of the auditorium" (106). Although Bazin acknowledges that the action of the plays can easily be adapted to "the realism of the screen," he maintains that the "verbal form which aesthetic contingencies or cultural prejudices oblige us to respect . . . refuses to let itself be captured in the window of the screen" (107).

The way to coax theatrical language to cooperate in the adaptive process, Bazin suggests, is through the proper choice of décor:

> The theater stage is a closed centripetal universe spiraling towards its own center, like a seashell. The movie screen is a centrifugal surface, a photographer's mask set up before the limitless universe of nature. The language of the theater is designed to resound within a closed space; in a natural setting it dissolves and disperses irretrievably. In passing from the stage to the screen a play must find a new theatrical locale which will satisfy the two contradictory qualities inherent in cinematographic and theatrical space. (1974, 338)

Bazin praises Orson Welles for the settings of *Othello*. Using natural elements from Venice and the castle at Mogador, Welles recreates an imaginary dramatic architecture through careful use of camera angles and swift editing. "Thus," remarks Bazin, "*Othello* unfolds in the open, but not at all, however, in nature. Like mirrors, those walls, arches and corridors echo, reflect and multiply the eloquence of tragic speech" (1978, 114).

It takes more than appropriate sets, however, to recreate a theatrical experience. One must record sounds with attention to their propagation through space.[1] J. P. Maxfield, a pioneer in movie sound at Bell Laboratories and Electric Research Products, Inc., advocated a miking system which meets the needs pinpointed by Bazin. Maxfield proposes that "the microphone be placed in the same general direction from the scene as is the camera so that when an actor recedes from or approaches the camera, he also recedes from or approaches the microphone" (1930a, 91). Such a placement would approximate the experience of a theatrical audience: as an actor moves towards the back of the stage, his voice reaches the seats with more reverberation, indicating he is further away. Clearly, a theatre patron cannot change seats from moment to moment, as can the spectator of a film, whose position moves from shot to shot. Nevertheless, Maxfield's proposal ensures that at least within a given shot, the spectator's position remains fixed relative to the sound source. He emphasizes that "the use of more than one microphone in a set at one time tends to destroy the proper depth illusion. . . . The use of only one microphone for each camera condition cannot be too strongly stressed" (1930a, 88). Thus, in a given shot, "the character of the reverberations present should be that which one would expect to find were he actually placed in the scene being shown" (1930a, 88).

The careful listener realizes that we rarely hear Maxfield's techniques put into practice. As Hollywood sound evolved, technicians instead placed emphasis on intelligibility of dialogue. Thus, in a typical Hollywood scene, shot scales may vary dramatically, but the sound remains at a consistent level of volume and reverb throughout. In two British Shakespearean adaptations, however, the sound strategies remain remarkably faithful to Maxfield's aims. Significantly, Laurence Olivier, a renowned Shakespearean actor, produced and directed both films. By listening to Olivier's films, we can explore the intersection of Bazin's and Maxfield's notions of correct film sound.

In *Richard III*, examples abound of single-microphone setups. In one scene, Richard (Olivier) moves forward and back in an empty hard-walled throne room while the camera remains in a fixed position. When he is close to the camera, directly addressing it, his voice is very direct; we can tell he is in a large room, but the reverb is minimal, as it would be were he directly facing us as we stood in the camera's place. (For simplicity's sake, I am assuming the photographer did not use special lenses; the effect throughout *Richard III*, whether or not they were employed, is of camera and microphone occupying the same place, as will be demonstrated.) As Richard moves away from the camera, and us, the reverb of his voice increases, while its volume decreases (except when he raises his voice for emotional impact). There are no cuts, so we can hear the slow increase in reverb as Richard moves through space.

In several scenes, Richard walks along a corridor at balcony level, above the throne room which is visible through open windows. Richard is in medium shot; we see the characters in the throne room in long shot behind him. Richard's voice reaches us directly, while the voices of the characters in the background are less distinct, at much lower volume, and full of reverb.

Some simple examples indicate the care given to create a sound which places us "in the scene." When Richard moves from an open grassy area to a covered stone walkway surrounding it, the reverb of his voice increases accordingly. As the Duke of Clarence leans his head on another man's shoulder, his voice is muffled, but as he raises his head up, his voice becomes much more distinct.

Putting us "in the scene" takes on more complex variations in *Henry V*. In an early series of shots, the camera pans around the interior of the Globe Theatre, passing nearly every possible seating position (groundlings, balcony, on the stage itself). Thus, as the play commences and the film begins to cut from one camera setup to another, we can imagine ourselves in a new seat within the theatre with each cut. The system does "cheat," in that it makes us into particularly tall spectators; we rarely have to look around other people's heads to get a good view. Eventually, too, the film adds reverse angles of the audience and also reveals actors bustling backstage, expanding our potential viewpoint beyond theatre seats.

Within individual shots, the reverb characteristics remain true to our assumed position (again, camera and microphone seem to be together). Thus, when the chorus character approaches the camera, his voice is indirect, but as he backs up within the same shot, the reverberation increases. We observe Olivier (as Henry) from backstage as he prepares to make his first entrance. After he walks onto the stage and begins his lines, his voice sounds as if he is far from us and facing slightly away (as indeed he is).[2] Even when the scene shifts from the Globe Theatre to "real" space, Maxfield's rules are still employed. Thus, when Henry addresses his men in a small canyon, as the camera pulls back, his voice reverberates increasingly within the confines of the canyon.

More interesting than examples of simple obedience to Maxfield's rules, however, are situations where the camera and microphone seem to be wise, knowing when a particular dramatic situation is coming up and positioning themselves (and us) in such a manner as to catch the full impact of the power of the spoken word. (Thus, anticipatory *microphone* placement is tied to anticipatory camera placement.) Time and again, the camera and microphone pull back just as a character begins to speak more loudly (to yell, to speak with passion, to make a vital speech). By pulling back, the camera allows us to savor the richness of the spoken word as it resounds through a space; our experience of the language in these moments approximates that of a theatrical audience. A prime example of this technique is Olivier's famous St. Crispin's day speech in *Henry V*. The camera holds Olivier in a relatively close shot while he quietly begins his speech. As he adds more and more emphasis to his words, and increases his volume, the camera pulls back and allows his voice to reverberate triumphantly over his loyal men. Similarly, in the throne room scene in *Richard III*, discussed previously, the camera wisely stays put when Richard moves away and angrily begins to speak more and more loudly; we sense some of this anger precisely because his voice is reverberating throughout the room.

At other times, the camera chooses to pan or track along with a character as he or she moves through a space. In these instances, the character is usually not declaiming in any particular manner, but rather, speaking in a normal tone of voice and conveying information to other characters or to us. In such cases, the turning or moving camera and microphone ensure that we catch the dialogue without difficulty. (Maxfield's rules do not take panning and tracking cameras into account. These shots, however, fit his guidelines in that the camera and the microphone stay together.) Thus, as the Archbishop of Canterbury criss-crosses the Globe stage in *Henry V*, the microphone and camera move with him so we can attend to every silly pronouncement he makes. Later, the camera moves in a similar manner with the French king as he wanders through his throne room.

Beyond wisely using Maxfield's rules for dramatic effect or adapting them to the panning or tracking camera to ensure intelligibility, there are some instances where sound strategies in these films simply break his rules. In most cases, the discrepancy results from a tension between cinematic and theatrical concerns, the very tension underlined by Bazin.

In a scene in *Richard III*, two monks chant throughout several shots of varying scale in the throne room. No matter whether the monks are in two-shot or deep in the background, their chant is audible at a constant level of volume and reverb. This sound technique is the typical Hollywood approach, but Olivier incorporates it here to serve his dramatic purpose. In the scene, we see Richard's shadow looming over the king's, then view Richard whispering inaudible words to the king. The steady volume of the chant covers the words we are not meant to hear. It also serves as something of an ironic commentary: while the monks chant religiously, Richard schemes. Shifts in sound over cuts might have been needlessly jarring; we're supposed to concentrate on the menace of Richard's shadow and the suggestion of treachery in his face. The sequence compromises between theatrical sound and cinematic visuals: our ears stay in one place, as they would in a theatre seat, while our eyes can change positions across cuts.

In another scene, we see a man in medium shot as he speaks. In the middle of a sentence, the camera cuts to a medium-long shot from behind the man's back, yet his voice quality remains unchanged. In this case, intelligibility wins out over fidelity to space. It's important to have the cut, so we can see the reaction of another character, but we'd struggle to understand the end of the line were the reverb and directness suddenly shifted to be true to the new sound space.

Characters with their backs to us are unusual in the theatre—generally, the reverb is unacceptable. Cinema allows for this blocking because the microphone can be placed so as to maintain intelligibility. Usually, the two films under consideration avoid such blocking, but as noted above, sometimes they cheat. In *Henry V* we have no difficulty understanding the Dolphin's messenger, even though he speaks with his back to us. Such cheats permit more variety in blocking without loss of intelligibility. It's important to note, however, that whenever a character turns his back to us while declaiming (as opposed to merely providing information), the microphone stays put, ensuring that we experience theatrical reverberation and directional cues.

Battlefield scenes put Maxfield's rules most sorely to the test. In long shots, according to his rules, it should be just about impossible to hear anyone speaking distinctly. Even someone shouting would be difficult to understand. The two films come up with two distinct solutions for this problem. *Henry V* avoids the issue by including scarcely any dialogue at all in the battle sequences. The montage-style scenes include generic battle noises, with only a couple of brief insert shots of characters speaking. These shots either aren't lengthy enough for us to judge whether the sound fits the general pattern of the film, or place characters in medium shot so it's reasonable, according to the rules, that we can hear them. In *Richard III*, the sound cheats in favor of intelligibility on the battlefield. In a long shot of Richard exhorting the men to fight, the volume and reverb of his voice are almost identical to a prior medium shot of the beginning of his speech. In some brief sequences, however, matching shot/sound scale is maintained, but always when the characters are moving about in a relatively limited space (that is, no extreme long shots). Convincing battlefield scenes are, of course, extremely difficult to present on the stage. In the long shots of battlefields in *Richard III*, cinema's capacity to depict such events overrides the imperative to remain true to theatrical visual and aural space.

Bazin would not be happy with the opening out of space in the battlefield sequences. He remarks that the problem "that faces the filmmaker is to give his decor a dramatic opaqueness while at the same time reflecting its natural realism" (1967a, 111). By "opaqueness" Bazin means that the dramatic space must maintain the feeling of being a "resonance box" for the voice. Ultimately, the "realism" that the cinematic adaptation must adhere to is the reality of the stage experience, in the process "rejecting the resources of the cinema" (1967a, 111–112).

Pushed to the extreme, such a stance would force the camera and microphone to remain in one position (one seat) throughout the entire film; this is an unacceptable solution which Bazin recognizes as "a childish error" (1967a, 114). As an alternative, Olivier's *Henry V* and *Richard III* indicate that cinema can convey a strong sense of the theatrical sound experience while at the same time using peculiarly cinematic potentials to enhance that experience. The wise camera and microphone allow us to experience the drama of an actor filling a space with the sound of his voice during a crucial speech. These same instruments, however, also save us the frustration of straining our ears to hear an actor as he wanders around a stage speaking in a less insistent tone. The various "cheats" with respect to the Maxfield system allow the cinema to expand beyond the limitations of the stage: Olivier's cinema can show wide-scale outdoor scenes, get around the frontality of stage blocking, and occasionally use sound to tie together shots. Rather than presenting the "reality" of the theatrical space in these instances, one could say that cinema improves on it. Essentially, the sound strategies in these two films allow us to enjoy the core of the theatrical experience, while enabling us to become moving spectators, who may view and hear scenes from the best possible location. In this system, every seat is a good seat.

Up to this point we've explored how Maxfield's rules can blend with Bazin's concerns to create a workable strategy for bringing Shakespeare to the screen. Like every model, however, this dramatic model has its limitations. We can begin to discover these limitations by returning once more to Bazin. So enamoured is he of his theory, he suggests that the student who labors over reading Shakespeare late at night is experiencing a sort of proto-theatre: " 'Armchair theater,' having only imagination to rely on, is lacking as theater, but it is nevertheless still theater" (1967a, 82).

In using the phrase "only imagination," Bazin reveals the chink in his theoretical armor. Why must armchair reading be linked to theatre, rather than to its own distinct imaginative realm? Freed of the *a priori* precedence of theatre, a reader's imagination loses its secondary status.

A couple of seemingly minor points indicate the affinity of many film adaptations of Shakespeare to the written text, and, by extension, the imagined soundscape of the reader. None of the films I listened to used overlapping dialogue, just as the reader always must complete one line before moving to the next. Although I'm sure all the films cut dialogue for time and thematic considerations (just as most stage plays do), if a line is left in, we hear all of it. Even when the camera cuts away from a comedic dialogue in Zeffirelli's *Taming of the Shrew*, we catch the end of the line over the beginning of the next shot.

Bazin trips up on a more basic level, undermining his own argument, when he applauds the solution to the problem of décor in Welles' *Macbeth*, where the setting is "artificial in every particular, a world closed in on its own incompleteness, like a grotto" (1978, 114). Bazin assumes that the appropriate dramatic setting inevitably leads to a correct resonance chamber for theatrical speech. But did he actually listen to *Macbeth*? Welles's sound is obviously post-synced, mismatched, manipulated, and patently artificial—anything but Maxfieldian in technique.

Why didn't Bazin notice this? His blind—or rather, deaf—spot urges a reexamination of the usefulness of his model for adaptations. It may fit some adaptations, but certainly not all of them. Are all the others simply "wrong"? This hardly seems an acceptable answer. Perhaps Welles employs a different model, Shakespeare-as-poet, for which consideration of Maxfield's spatial signature is largely irrelevant. The armchair reader, after all, is less likely to experience a theatrical "voice in space" than an internalized "voice as poetry." He or she dwells on the richness of the language, but does not necessarily imagine it reverberating within a specific space.

James Agee applies such a model in his review of Olivier's *Henry V*. Continually referring to *Henry* as a poem, he comments on the "brilliance, vigor, and absoluteness" (333) of Shakespeare's language, then continues:

> The one great glory of the film is this language. The greatest credit I can assign to those who made the film is that they have loved and served the language so well. I don't feel that much of the delivery is inspired; it is merely so good, so right, that the words set loose in the graciously designed world of the screen, like so many uncaged birds, fully enjoy and take care of themselves. (333–334)

Agee emphasizes pronunciation, enunciation, the sound of words themselves, as opposed to the sounds of words propagated within a specific space. He is pleased that the text is neither "read in that human, down-to-earth, poetry-is-only-hopped-up-prose manner" (334) nor "intoned in the nobler manner, as if by a spoiled deacon celebrating the Black Mass down a section of sewer pipe. Most of it is merely spoken by people who know and love poetry as poetry and have spent a lifetime learning how to speak it accordingly" (334). With the exception of the joking reference to the sewer pipe, Agree makes no reference to spatial signature.

Unlike Bazin, Agee does not privilege the theatre. Indeed, he says that in his experience, most stage productions of Shakespeare are, in comparison to Olivier's *Henry V*, "just so many slightly tired cultural summer salads . . . whereas this, down to the last fleeting bit of first-rate poetry in a minor character's mouth, was close to solid gold, almost every word given its own and its largest contextual value" (334). He sees certain advantages to cinema that don't fit into Bazin's argument. For instance, close-miking makes it possible "to get all the considerable excellence there is out of an aging player like Nicholas Hannen, who seemed weak in most scenes when, on the stage, he had to try to fill and dilate the whole Century Theater with unhappy majesty . . ." (334). For Bazin, the point of theatre, and of film adaptations, is precisely this "dilation."

Agee is interested in more than simple Hollywood-style intelligibility. Beyond merely ensuring understanding of the spoken word, effective sound recording can allow us to appreciate its richness, its rhythm, and tone. Manipulation of dialogue in postproduction can bring out the unique qualities of each spoken word, emphasizing the poetic nature of the text. Such manipulation depends on our imagining Shakespeare not only as theatre, but also as poetry.

Welles' sound manipulation in the opening scenes of *Macbeth* asserts his control over the soundtrack. The microphone is not slave to the spatial environment of the image, as it generally is in Maxfield's system. We hear the voices of the witches in direct, close-up sound no matter what the shot scale. Unlike theatrical models, which emphasize the matching of voice to moving lips so we may revel in the actor's skill, we rarely see the witches' faces; in the one instance where we do, their lips are not moving, though their voices still sound direct. When the witches hail Macbeth, their voices are manipulated to sound like yowling cats. A close shot of Macbeth speaking is followed by a longer shot where Macbeth's voice is unexpectedly louder. We get the sense that Macbeth is in some sort of specific sound environment, but the misty scene frustrates our efforts to pin it down. At other points, "natural" sound effects enhance the dialogue: when Macbeth says, with surprise, "I am . . . Thane of Cawdor," thunder immediately booms, as if to punctuate his statement. The remarkable timing of the thunder underlines the sound designer's complete command.

Rick Altman has commented that *Macbeth* may sound "bad" to some, but proposes that Welles is not looking for proper matches (1990). Rather, Welles wants particular qualities which can only be achieved in post-sync. Using these methods, Altman claims, Welles draws attention to sound as such. To draw out this idea a bit, I'd argue that Welles highlights poetic language by making it difficult for us to "space out." I use this term in two senses. In Welles' world, sound and space are not linked. We can't confidently expect sound signature to function as a spatial indicator. Reverberation no longer necessarily signals "space-out-there." Because the rules have changed, we cannot so easily "space out" in the popular sense of the term, either: the unexpected uses of sound constantly demand our attention.[3]

Lady Macbeth's voice exhibits strange qualities. In comparison to Macbeth's deep and somber tones, her voice is high and curiously lilting. This lilting quality is not youthful and melodic, but rather, takes on a sinister tone due to its non-rhythmic cadences. In a film which in many places seems "badly" synced, her voice is particularly off. It reminds us of the witches, whose high-pitched voices are entirely disconnected from their bodies. The (a)sync for Lady Macbeth is not that extreme, but it does suggest an affinity with the cunning and crafty witches. To add to the disturbing nature of her voice, it is frequently excessively closely miked in comparison to the image. For example, her voice announces, in an extremely closely miked voice-over, the arrival of King Duncan, who is shown in long shot. Even if her voice were meant to be from the point-of-audition of Macbeth, who stands beside her, it is still too closely miked.

Quietly spoken words, "King Duncan" overwhelm all the activity shown in the long shot.

Maxfield's system leads us to expect that the voices of characters at a distance will have a fair amount of reverb. At first, Welles' characters seem to have this quality, but upon a closer listening, one notices how processed the voices are. Instead of sounding like voices miked from a distance, these voices sound as if they were miked closely, with a reverb effect added later. This lends them an ethereal and mysterious quality. We can understand them perfectly; we don't have to fight the reverb at all.

In the scene when Macbeth bids an ironic farewell to Banquo, Banquo's voice has the above-mentioned curious quality. This seems almost ordinary, however, in comparison to Macbeth's oddly shifting vocal qualities. With each new shot, Macbeth's intensity and tone change. It's not possible to explain the shifts in terms of image/sound scale matches. Instead, Welles seems to be exploring every possible variation of vocal inflection within a few short shots. Even in mid-sentence, across a cut, Macbeth's voice alters from loud and reverberant to soft and timorous, though the loud voice from the first shot seems as if it would perfectly match the image of the second.

We can't even get comfortable with such a simple thing as accent. Various characters, Macbeth in particular, slip in and out of American, Scots, and English accents throughout the film. Welles draws attention to all the possible permutations—the poetry—of the spoken word. He accomplishes this primarily by divorcing a sound's spatial signature from the image. Frequently, the dialogue comes from nowhere; the sounds are muffled, betraying no specific spatial signature. At other times, we notice a distinct spatial signature, but it doesn't match the image. Instead of being "realistic," the signature calls attention to the pitch, accent, or rhythm of the words being spoken.

Welles' *Falstaff/Chimes at Midnight* draws attention to the voice in an entirely different, though equally manipulated manner. We might recall that we sometimes encounter Shakespeare in the form of a Readers' Theatre, most often in the classroom, when students take on various roles and read them aloud. The readers may be able to indicate intense emotional variations, but they cannot shift the sound space as the scenes change. We still hear everything in the same classroom. At most, vocal qualities suggest that characters are further apart or closer via louder or quieter tones. In *Falstaff*, quality of voice takes precedence over sound/image match even more so than in *Macbeth*. All the voices have a somewhat reverberant quality, which fills them out and gives them richness. Each is closely miked. Depth cues are generic, not related to the scene we see.

Instead, it seems that the actor reading the role in post-sync might simply have stepped away from the mike to indicate a distance. A rare instance of sound/space fidelity (in Maxfield's terms) is saved for the climactic moment when Falstaff yells to the now-king Henry V in the midst of the royal procession. Falstaff's voice echoes off the high stone walls, contrasting dramatically with Henry's silent, cold reception of him. Only such an echo could convey the futility of Falstaff's dreams.

In discussing the dramatic model for Shakespearean adaptations, I suggested that when Olivier deviates from Maxfield's model, it is usually in the service of intelligibility, a concern of many Hollywood and Hollywood-influenced filmmakers. This begs the question, however, of why Hollywood technicians imagined dialogue intelligibility to be of the utmost importance.

Cinematic sound was influenced by sound techniques and codes of reality in preexistent technologies and practices. People's familiarity with public address systems, telephones, phonographs, radio, theatre, and silent cinema all had a bearing on how they expected cinema to sound. Before any of these technologies existed, however, our primary way to communicate language at a distance was via the written word. Over the centuries, we have developed complex narrative and receptive skills to broaden the range of writing's storytelling efficacy. Our familiarity with how this system "translates" sound (the spoken word) to text (written word) may have more bearing on our reception of cinematic sound than our familiarity with more recent sound-carrying technologies. For instance, when we read a written story, we can visualize the events described in our mind's eye; similarly, all the dialogue is perfectly intelligible in our mind's ear. We don't have to strain to hear sounds; we can imagine them in all their richness and complexity. The stress on intelligibility in cinema, particularly in adaptations of literature, may derive from an attempt to remain true to our imaginative ability to "hear" dialogue perfectly when we read.

When reading Shakespeare's plays, we primarily concentrate on the written dialogue. Once we become familiar with Elizabethan English, we are able to differentiate voices of characters within our minds. We read the stage directions regarding other sound sources (party frivolity, battle clamor, and so on), but within our minds, the background sounds never interfere with the dialogue, except when key sounds introduce new elements to the plot—a trumpet announcing the arrival of a king, for example. Adaptations which initially seem simple examples of intelligibility generally represent in their sound techniques the inner workings of the reader's imagination.

In Roman Polanski's version of *Macbeth*, when a character has an interior monologue (spoken in voice-over), the external sounds which have heretofore accompanied his or her speech drastically diminish in level, only to regain intensity when the character completes his or her thoughts or is interrupted in mid-thought. When Macbeth sees Banquo's ghost, his agitation is so intense that the background banquet sounds disappear entirely. Such manipulations parallel our imagined scenes: we hear voices, but we rarely construct complex aural backgrounds to accompany them, particularly when reading extended monologues. Instead, we concentrate on the words. Thus, when Polanski's Macbeth and Lady plot evil deeds while in the midst of a crowded party, the "realistic" cocktail party effect is not functioning; they don't have to yell at each other to be heard, nor do we have to strain to hear them.

The Capulet party in Franco Zeffirelli's *Romeo and Juliet* also exemplifies how sound techniques may parallel our interior hearing patterns. Initially, we notice the diegetic music playing in the background (as if the script had mentioned it in describing the setting), but once Romeo begins a monologue, the music drops under. Later, when a boy sings, all the room noise disappears. In each instance, the sound parallels the text we would read. The relative intensity of cinematic sound shifts remarkably "in sync" with how a reader's attention functions. When Romeo and Juliet sneak off to an isolated area of the party room for a tête-à-tête, the boy's song disappears and non-diegetic music replaces it. Logically, given the layout of the set, we should still be able to hear the diegetic song, but just as a reader forgets all about a suggestion of diegetic music in a script and substitutes his/her own "mental violins" during a passionate scene, the film drops the diegetic music in favor of non-diegetic accompaniment.

Seemingly illogical shifts in reverb or volume may also be explained by comparison to readers' imaginations of events. Another scene in Zeffirelli's *Romeo and Juliet* demonstrates this point. Juliet is on a balcony while Romeo is down below in the trees. Shifts in the volume of their voices make no sense in terms of their distance from each other. The variations from whisper to passionate declamation fit their emotional states—effects the reader would add to the dialogue—not the space separating them. In the real world, Juliet's whispers might be too quiet for Romeo to hear, but in the imagined world, such concerns are unimportant.

Whenever Shakespeare is adapted for the screen, the question of how to handle the language inevitably arises. As we have discovered, however, it's important to consider which aspect of the language is emphasized. Is that language theatrical or poetic? Does it suggest an auditor who actually hears spoken words in a space or who simply imagines them in the mind's ear? We've always known that great literature sparks the imagination; the sounds of Shakespearean adaptations depend upon which imaginative ear is listening.[4]

Film Credits

Falstaff/Chimes at Midnight 1966. Dir.: Orson Welles. Sound Editor: Peter Parasheles.

Henry V 1945. Dir.: Laurence Olivier. Sound: John Dennis and Desmond Dew.

Macbeth 1971. Dir.: Roman Polanski. Dubbing Editor: Jonathan Bates. Dubbing Mixer: Nolan Roberts. Sound Mixer: Simon Kaye.

Macbeth 1948. Dir.: Orson Welles. Sound: John Stransky, Jr. and Garry Harris.

Richard III 1955. Dir.: Laurence Olivier. Sound: George Stephenson and Red Law.

Romeo and Juliet 1968. Dir.: Franco Zeffirelli. Dubbing Editor: Michael Hopkins. Assistant Dubbing Editor: Pat Poster. Sound Mixer: Sash Fisher MIEE.

Taming of the Shrew 1967. Dir.: Franco Zeffirelli. Sound credits not legible on film credits.

12

Conventions of Sound in Documentary

Jeffrey K. Ruoff

This essay draws comparisons between various examples of sound practices and narration in the documentary tradition, focusing primarily on synchronous sound observational films from the 1960s and 1970s, in particular the 1973 PBS series *An American Family*. While documentary sound tracks may include voice-over, dialogue, music, and effects, the hierarchy and distribution of these sounds differ in important ways from classical Hollywood conventions. In fact, Hollywood's increasing reliance on multi-track postproduction techniques contrasts significantly with documentaries that use only location-recorded sound. In a series of articles, Rick Altman has described the conventions of sound in classical Hollywood cinema as an interplay between intelligibility and fidelity, a system in which fidelity is sacrificed in favor of the more narratively central dimension of intelligibility (Altman 1984, 1985a, 1985b, 1986).

Similarly, Noel Carroll has argued that the hallmark of Hollywood movie narration is clarity and comprehensibility. Popular movies offer experiences of places, events, characters, and drama more clearly delineated than in our ordinary lives. In Carroll's words, "The flow of action approaches an ideal of uncluttered clarity. This clarity contrasts vividly with the quality of fragments of actions and events we typically observe in everyday life" (Carroll, 180). Hollywood filmmakers use cinematic techniques of image and sound to focus the attention of the spectator on the salient elements that further the narrative action. Carroll suggests that it is not the purported realism of the cinematic apparatus that millions of viewers find compelling, but rather the heightened intelligibility that is the hallmark of Hollywood cinema. If audiences were truly interested in greater fidelity to the real world, then presumably documentary films would form a larger part of the corpus that has made motion pictures a very popular art form in the 20th century.

While documentary films often use narrative forms, they rarely demonstrate the degree of clarity that these writers see as the standard of classical Hollywood cinema. Location sound work in documentary films occasionally makes discrimination among sounds difficult, if not impossible. Although works like Pare Lorentz's *The Plow That Broke the Plains* (1936) and Ken Burns' *The Civil War* (1990) are perfectly comprehensible, the intelligibility of documentary only rarely approaches that of popular movies; characters lack clear motivations, speech may be inaudible in parts, lighting haphazard and variable, camera movements follow actions with difficulty, sound spaces differ radically between scenes, microphones accidentally appear in the image, jump cuts disrupt continuity, and questions remain unanswered.

History of Observational Cinema

In the late 1950s, innovators in television journalism worked to apply different principles of storytelling to the documentary format, in an attempt to move away from illustrated lectures. Following the tradition of the photojournalism of *Life* magazine, producers like Robert Drew wanted to give the impression of lived experience by being there on location as events happened. During a Nieman Fellowship at Harvard University in 1954, Drew studied the narrative structure of the 19th-century realist short story, a form he wanted to apply to documentary (O'Connell, 88). Returning to New York with funding from Time-Life to create a new kind of actuality film, Drew assembled a team of talented young filmmakers to form Drew Associates—Richard Leacock, D. A. Pennebaker, Albert and David Maysles, Hope Ryden, James Lipscomb, and others. New portable 16mm equipment, developed during World War II for use by the military and expanded by the needs of television in the post-war era, made observational synchronous sound filmmaking a possibility for the first time in the late 1950s.

Observational filmmakers were not to intrude on the lives of their subjects, not to ask questions, conduct interviews or otherwise direct, stage, or influence the events for the camera; they were to be as flies on the wall. These filmmakers wanted to eliminate overt narrational devices like voice-over in favor of stories that begin *in medias res* and unfold seemingly without a narrator. Drew Associates opted for stories that had inherent drama and were structured around crisis events with clear beginnings, middles, and ends (Mamber, 115–38). Similar experiments at the National Film Board of Canada by Tom Daly, Colin Low, Michel Brault, Roman Kroiter, Terence Macartney-Filgate, and Wolf Koenig were broadcast on the series "Candid-Eye" that ran from 1958–61 on Canadian television. The Canadian filmmakers were directly influenced by the street photography of Henri Cartier-Bresson, which mixed formal composition and spontaneity (Jones). Early observational films focused heavily on biography for their narrative unity, with titles such as *David* (1961), *Eddie* (1961), *Lonely Boy* (1962), *Nehru* (1962), *Jane* (1962), and *Susan Starr* (1962). As Robert Allen and Douglas Gomery point out in their case study of Drew Associates in *Film History: Theory and Practice*, these innovations in television journalism were never fully adopted by the networks and probably had more influence on fiction film, especially on the work of Jean-Luc Godard and John Cassavetes, than on commercial television (Allen and Gomery, 239).

Modernist variations on the theme of observational cinema quickly emerged. The Maysles brothers constructed open-ended episodic narratives in films like *Showman* (1962) and *What's Happening! The Beatles in the U.S.A.* (1964), while Andy Warhol moved towards minimalist experiments in *Sleep* (1963) and *Empire* (1964). Jim McBride and L. M. Kit Carson parodied the search for truth in the mock-autobiography *David Holtzman's Diary* (1967), while Allan King looked at private life in *A Married Couple* (1970). Frederick Wiseman, eschewing the earlier concentration on celebrities as subjects, introduced a multiple-focus narrative structure for his series of films on everyday life in American social institutions—*Titicut Follies* (1967), *High School* (1968), *Law and Order* (1969), *Hospital* (1970)—claiming in each case that the institution itself is the star. During this period, Craig Gilbert made celebrity portraits like *Margaret Mead's New Guinea Journal* (1968) and *The Triumph of Christy Brown* (1970), mixing observational footage with reenactments, archival footage, and voice-over narration.

Documentary filmmakers in the 1970s turned increasingly to more private subject matter in autobiographical forms. Joyce Chopra's *Joyce at 34* (1972), Amalie Rothschild's *Nana, Mom, and Me* (1974), and Jill Godmilow's *Antonia: Portrait of a Woman* (1974) explored personal issues in the growing women's movement. As Craig Gilbert commenced work on *An American Family*, filmmaker Ed Pincus embarked on the autobiographical *Diaries, 1971–76* (1981), adopting a loose chronological first-person narrative style, based on chance and the everyday, in which the filmmaker appears as the main character. *An American Family* represents a mixture of these different tendencies.

Produced by veteran National Educational Television director Craig Gilbert, *An American Family*, a twelve-hour series on the Loud family of Santa Barbara, California, captured the imagination of the American viewing public in the spring of 1973. Under Gilbert's supervision, filmmakers Susan and Alan Raymond filmed the everyday lives of Pat and

William Loud, and their children Lance, Kevin, Grant, Delilah, and Michelle for seven months. The extensive filming gave the crew and family ample time to get to know one another, so that the family members could perform their everyday lives in the presence of a camera crew and the filmmakers could become temporary members of the family. Gilbert deliberately chose an upper-middle-class white family whose standard of living approximated that of the suburban families shown living the American dream in television situation comedies such as *Father Knows Best, Leave It To Beaver, Make Room For Daddy, The Adventures of Ozzie and Harriet, The Dick Van Dyke Show*, and *The Brady Bunch*.

The series focused on the small details of the everyday lives of the seven family members, while relying on the overall crisis structure of the Loud's divorce to organize the story. The concentration on individual biography was mediated by the ability to shift the narrative focus from one family member to another. Gilbert initially considered organizing *An American Family* around episodes devoted to individual members of the family before eventually choosing a chronological multiple-focus narrative framework for the series. A major innovation of the WNET series was that the film unfolded in twelve separate episodes over the course of twelve consecutive weeks, allowing for ongoing viewer involvement in the lives of the characters. Critics responded to the series format and subject matter by referring to *An American Family* as "real-life soap opera." Although unusual in documentary, serial structure was, of course, standard practice with situation comedies and soaps well before the 1970s. While Gilbert worked as a documentary producer for television in New York throughout the 1960s, he acknowledged that he was never really part of the vanguard independent community gathered around Drew Associates, although he knew their films well. Significantly, *An American Family* was made for public television and never received theatrical distribution. Although this style of observational filmmaking was standard in the world of independent film by the 1970s, never had it attained such a wide audience. To this day, *An American Family* remains the most widely seen and debated example of observational cinema in the United States.

Although observational filmmakers in the 1960s justified their new narrative style through references to Gustave Flaubert and claims of fidelity to the real world, the classical Hollywood cinema, whose roots may also be found in 19th-century realism, provided the clearest example for the new documentary. However, documentary filmmakers who argued that they were brushing up against the truth could hardly cite the classical Hollywood cinema as their model; this was a period when many documentary filmmakers defined Hollywood as their enemy. In 1983, Robert Drew admitted that "You don't need Dan Rather in the middle of a fiction motion picture to tell you what's going on" (Hindman, 47). Similarly, David

MacDougall stated, "Many of us who began applying an observational approach to ethnographic filmmaking found ourselves taking as our model not the documentary film as we had come to know it since Grierson, but the dramatic fiction film, in all its incarnations from Tokyo to Hollywood" (MacDougall, 112). These observational filmmakers abandoned the established Griersonian tradition of direct address in favor of a style which used techniques of storytelling and continuity editing conventionally associated with fiction films, although documentary pioneers like Robert Flaherty had also worked in this narrative tradition.

Location Sound in Documentary

One of the major stylistic characteristics of documentaries that use sounds recorded on location is the lack of clarity of the sound track. Ambient sounds compete with dialogue in ways commonly deemed unacceptable in conventional Hollywood practice. A low signal-to-noise ratio demands greater attention from the viewer to decipher spoken words. Slight differences in room tone between shots make smooth sound transitions difficult. Indeed, listening to many of the scenes of observational films without watching the screen can be a dizzying experience. Without recognizable sources in the image to anchor the sounds, we hear a virtual cacophony of clanging, snippets of dialogue and music, and various unidentifiable sounds, almost an experiment in concrete music. Freed of their associations to objects, the sounds resurface in their phenomenological materiality. Because scenes in observational films are not usually shot under optimal conditions, such as those found in a Hollywood studio, the sound track lacks the clarity and directness signifying that the sound was created for the listener. While Hollywood sound tracks are typically easier to understand than sounds in everyday life, documentary sound tracks are potentially more difficult to follow than such sounds.

The history of industry practices indicates that film production in the United States moved inside studios around 1908 to avoid the kinds of uncertainties encountered in actuality and location filmmaking (Izod, 13). Mass-production techniques and a precise division of labor ensure the maximum efficiency and technical quality of Hollywood productions. Repeated takes are done until satisfactory sound has been recorded; if necessary, dialogue will be postproduced through dubbing techniques to ensure clarity. Hollywood directors shoot individual shots one at a time under optimal conditions, while documentary filmmakers often shoot entire scenes in one long take in unpredictable situations. In Hollywood films, the degree of direct sound, as opposed to reflected sound, indicates the level of control exercised over all aspects of production. The brilliance of sound practice in the classical Hollywood cinema derives from a combination of direct sound, closely miked in order to reduce reverberation and increase clarity, with an overall system of impersonal narration.

The clarity of sound in documentary usually depends on the degree of control that the filmmaker has over the profilmic events. Voice-over narration allows for maximum control over sound quality, and it has long been one of the stylistic signatures of documentary sound. Recent documentaries like Jill Godmilow's *Far From Poland* (1985), Ross McElwee's *Sherman's March* (1985), Tony Buba's *Lightning Over Braddock* (1988), Lise Yasui's *A Family Gathering* (1988), and Michael Moore's *Roger and Me* (1989), have rediscovered the possibilities of voice-over narration, using personal, ironic, and interpretive commentary to counterpoint the synchronous images and sounds. In these documentaries, voiceover narration is more than just a necessary concession to the needs of storytelling. In Hollywood cinema, voice-over is still considered "the last resort of the incompetent," as Sarah Kozloff points out in *Invisible Storytellers: Voice-over Narration in American Fiction Film*, a view shared by many observational documentary filmmakers (Kozloff, 21). When Leacock and Pincus taught documentary filmmaking at the Massachusetts Institute of Technology in the 1970s, voice-over was not considered an acceptable technique (Ruoff 1988). When voice-over narration appears in fiction films, it often serves as a marker of documentary realism, as in the "News on the March" sequence in Orson Welles' *Citizen Kane* (1941) and in John Ford's *How Green Was My Valley* (1941), Anthony Mann's *The T-Men* (1947), and Jules Dassin's *The Naked City* (1948).

Speech in Documentary

Characters in documentary films typically demonstrate a wider variety of accents, dialects, and speech patterns than those found in fiction films. In their discussion of the films of Frederick Wiseman, Thomas Benson and Carolyn Anderson see this breadth as a marker of truth to reality, "No other filmmaker has more to say to us about the American language than Frederick Wiseman. In film after film he has shown us the structure and uses of the American idiom, inviting us to listen, at length, to conversational passages that most other filmmakers would have left on the cutting-room floor" (Benson and Anderson, 31). While this breadth promotes a rich diversity, it presents obstacles for the viewer's understanding. Regional accents, slang, and idiosyncratic syntax make documentary representations of speech more difficult to understand than their fictional counterparts. In order to assure comprehension, Pincus had to subtitle the conversations of some of the children who appear in *Black Natchez* (1967), his film about civil rights struggles in Mississippi in the mid-1960s. However, subtitling may imply deviance from an assumed linguistic norm.

Observational films often do not succeed outside their national boundaries because of the difficulties presented for viewers who are not native speakers of the language. Part of the delight comes from hearing the material texture and richness of unrehearsed speech, the grain of the voice (Marcorelles, 63).

Speakers in everyday life typically fill in the gaps of their phrases with various exclamations and sounds that maintain the flow of verbal communication. In conversation, we interrupt one another, digress, ask questions, hem and haw. Telephone conversations exemplify these characteristics of spoken language. The absence of non-verbal cues necessitates a constant use of verbal signals to indicate that the listener is in fact awake and listening. Much of verbal communication consists of what sociolinguist Dell Hymes calls the phatic function of speech, the banal chit-chat that signifies sociability, "talk for the sake of something being said" (Hymes, 40). Anyone who has ever transcribed interview tapes recognizes the differences between the conventions of spoken and written language. Characters in Hollywood films typically speak scripted versions of spoken language and are careful not to interrupt one another's lines. In addition, from one take to another, actors must be capable of maintaining virtually identical volume, pitch, tone, and inflection in the delivery of their lines for continuity purposes, a talent for which they are handsomely paid. Dialogue in observational documentaries overlaps considerably as characters interrupt one another, speak at the same time, and affirm their listening stances. As Michel Marie remarks of synchronous sound recording techniques, "Direct is really a manifestation of a new modality of voice recording in film" (Marie, 39). Interview films attempt to circumvent the fullness of ordinary speech in various ways. Staged to be filmed, interviews may be miked for maximum intelligibility of speech.

Documentary makers learn how to stage interviews so that the interviewee will appear to speak directly to the viewer. Michael Rabiger instructs in *Directing the Documentary*, "During the interview, you should maintain eye contact with your subject, and give visual (NOT verbal!) feedback while the interview goes on. Nodding, smiling, looking puzzled, signifying agreement or doubt are all forms of feedback that can be relayed through your expression" (Rabiger, 59–60). In an article in the *New Yorker*, Errol Morris, director of *The Thin Blue Line* (1988), describes the importance of providing these non-verbal cues: " 'Listening to what people were saying wasn't even important,' he says. 'But it was important to *look* as if you were listening to what people were saying. Actually, listening to what people are saying, to me, interferes with looking as if you were listening to what people were saying' " (Singer, 48). Interview films increase the clarity and directness of speech through editing techniques and shooting conventions.

Roger Silverstone makes note of this process in the shooting of a BBC documentary, in which the director instructs the interviewee to answer in full sentences so that the questions may be left out of the sound track:

M: Say that again because you spoke while I was speaking.
L: Stability is the key word in terms of what he is, would be, receptive to. . . .
M: So he's a tougher judge than scientific colleagues almost?
L: Exactly.
M: Say that again from the start.
L: What, about the . . .?
M: Yes, as a sentence (Silverstone, 69).

Interview films permit a *mise-en-scène* of speech, a trimming of the materiality of conversational speech in favor of clarity and comprehensibility.

In the 1970s and 1980s, independent documentary filmmakers returned to the direct address style of interview films in part because they allowed for greater control over what was happening in front of the camera. Films like Julia Reichert and Jim Klein's *Union Maids* (1976) and *Seeing Red* (1984), Peter Adair's *Word is Out* (1976), Connie Field's *The Life and Times of Rosie the Riveter* (1980), and Noel Buckner's *The Good Fight* (1984) allowed for more thorough preparation during the preproduction phases of fundraising and writing. Connie Field describes this process for *Rosie the Riveter*: "We did extensive preinterviews—seven hundred women were interviewed over the phone, two hundred in person on audio tape, thirty-five were videotaped; and we filmed five" (Zheutlin, 237). This passage also suggests the importance of casting in documentary. The use of a string of interviews permits a stronger sense of textual voice, not unlike that of a voice-over dispersed across multiple characters (Nichols 1983). While voice-over narration and interviews allow for more direct sound in documentary, they remain marginal techniques in observational cinema. "Interviews" that appear in observational cinema are carried out by characters who appear in the films, such as the psychiatrists in Wiseman's *Titicut Follies* who interview the incoming patients about their medical histories, thereby introducing us to the characters and the institutional procedures in the film.

Location sound recording in observational documentaries does not clearly differentiate foreground and background spaces; rather, all sounds compete together in the middleground. The lack of clarity of the sound undermines the communicative intent of these films. Shotgun microphones are frequently used in documentary productions precisely because they allow for a choice of narrative information and raise the ratio of direct to reflected sound, thus isolating sounds in the environment. Directional microphones enable recordists to place certain sounds in the foreground while relegating other sounds to the background. Instructions for location sound recordists include standing as close as possible to the speaker without appearing in the frame. Observational cinematographers prefer viewfinders which allow them to see beyond the frame of the film; the perfect space for the roving microphone. In this way, the cinematographer has a constant view of the microphone and the location of the soundperson, while the viewer never sees them. In Alan Raymond's words, "The camera/sound team must develop a kind of choreography where both parties are aware of each other all the time. The cameraman must listen to the dialogue and the sound recordist must watch what the cameraman is shooting" (Raymond, 594). The development of microphone technology has been guided by demands for clarity as well as fidelity. Wireless lavalier microphones fulfill similar stylistic requirements. Extremely small and unobtrusive, they are designed to be worn on the chest of individual speakers, reproducing the human voice with great fidelity at the expense of the ambient sound environment.

Occasionally in observational films, poorly recorded scenes are included because of their central importance to the story. In *An American Family*, a conversation between the Loud couple at a crowded restaurant is virtually inaudible due to the presence of competing ambient sounds. A determined viewer may overcome the marginal quality of the sound track to catch snippets of the Loud's argument, an important indication of the downturn of their marriage. Pat's comments are the harshest heard throughout the series: "I think that the things that you do are shitty. And perhaps you think that the things I do are shitty, that's your problem. But I think that you're a goddamn asshole." Narrative considerations necessitated the use of less than technically satisfactory footage. Although the sound is muddled, the point is clear. Anything that contributes to our understanding of the drama of the divorce finds its way into the narrative. The filmmaking team admitted that such technically difficult, and ethically sensitive, scenes would have been impossible to film without unobtrusive wireless lavalier microphones (Raymond, 605).

Observational shooting and editing techniques conform to continuity conventions established in the film industry during the silent era. Hollywood studios developed elaborate means of maintaining continuity through supervision of scripts, props, lighting, performance, and shooting style, means typically unavailable to documentary filmmakers. David Hanser, series editor of *An American Family*, describes how continuity conventions dictate the shape of the material, "If somebody says what they're going to do that night or the next weekend, maybe that's useful, knowing what else you have. Then you try to make sure that you include that in the editing, because we're trying to tell the story without any narration" (Ruoff 1989b, A7). Continuity conventions make it difficult to edit together actuality material shot at different times, because characters will likely be wearing different clothing or they may change their appearance from one day to another. For these reasons, observational films usually follow the chronological order in which they were shot. Observational filmmakers do not necessarily believe that chronology best represents actual experience, but a particular system of narrative causality and continuity leads them to tell stories in chronological order. Reflecting on the difficulty of maintaining continuity in *An American Family*, the coordinating producer exclaimed, "The problem with public television is there are no commercials" (Ruoff 1989b, A14). As this comment suggests, commercials provide a convenient way to make transitions between scenes.

Music in Documentary

Music plays an important part in the soundscape of documentary films. Many of the classic documentaries of the 1930s, like Harry Watt's *Night Mail* (1936) and Lorentz' *The River* (1937), were scored by famous composers such as Benjamin Britten and Virgil Thomson. Highlighting the importance of sound in their titles, Dziga Vertov's *Three Songs of Lenin* (1934), Basil Wright's *Song of Ceylon* (1935) and Humphrey Jennings' *Listen to Britain* (1942) make extensive use of music. Stephen Mamber suggests that documentary filmmakers in the 1960s moved away from these techniques: "In line with this commitment [to an observational ethic], some of the standard devices of fiction film and traditional documentaries fall by the wayside, especially music and [voice-over] narration" (Mamber, 4). While the rhetoric of observational cinema demanded the exclusive use of synchronous sound, the new conventions did not preclude the use of music in documentary. On the contrary, music was fine as long as it was diegetic, and throughout the 1960s, there was plenty of music in observational films. In fact, in this period, the documentary musical emerged as a distinct subgenre, focusing primarily on the sounds of the new youth counterculture of rock music.

Just as the coming of sound fostered the growth of the Hollywood musical in the 1930s as a genre of spectacle and pleasure, innovations in location sound recording technology led to the rock documentary in the 1960s. The rock documentary brings together the documentary cinema's traditional focus on actuality and the fictional cinema's emphasis on stars and spectacle. The Maysles' *What's Happening! The Beatles in the U.S.A.* and *Gimme Shelter* (1970), Leacock's *A Stravinsky Portrait* (1964), Pennebaker's *Don't Look Back* (1966) and *Monterey Pop* (1968), and Michael

Wadleigh's *Woodstock* (1970) offer views of performers which incorporate music into the structure of the films. Wiseman's *Titicut Follies* uses a musical revue performed by mental patients as a framing device, a grotesque inversion and parody of the music documentary, in which the patients sing, "Have You Ever Been Lonely," "I Want to Go to Chicago Town," and "So Long For Now." Still today, music documentaries are among the most popular of nonfiction forms, with commercially successful works such as Martin Scorsese's *The Last Waltz* (1979), Michelle Parkinson's *Gotta Make This Journey: Sweet Honey in the Rock* (1985), George Nierenberg's *Say Amen, Somebody* (1985), Jonathan Demme's *Stop Making Sense* (1985), Stevenson Palfi's *Piano Players Rarely Ever Play Together* (1985), Susan and Alan Raymond's *Elvis '56* (1986), Bruce Weber's *Let's Get Lost* (1988), Charlotte Zwerin's *Straight: No Chaser* (1990), and Les Blank's *The Blues According to Lightning Hopkins* (1990) and *French Dance Tonight* (1990). The canonization of music documentaries is only more apparent through successful generic parodies like Rob Reiner's *This Is Spinal Tap* (1984).

Recorded music appears frequently in observational documentaries. As in the early days of sound film, a shot of a radio or record player often signals the diegetic source of recorded music. While the filmmakers want to indicate that the music was found on location, this practice is also the result of legal and financial concerns. Filmmakers believe that if they can prove that they are using a musical segment as a social document, they will not be obliged to pay users' fees to the copyright owners. In a recent appearance at the Ohio Film Conference in Athens, Wiseman argued that his extensive use of location-recorded popular music by bands like the B-52s in *Model* (1980), for which no fees were paid, would be defensible in court. Negotiating for the rights to use contemporary music in film is a notoriously difficult and expensive process, forcing some filmmakers to avoid such scenes altogether. Tony Buba addresses this issue in an amusing scene in *Lightning Over Braddock* in which a song by the Rolling Stones is *not* heard on the soundtrack. As we watch a mock performance of the song by local teenagers in a bar in Braddock, Pennsylvania, Buba tells us in voice-over that the rights to the song, which was played on the jukebox, would have cost $10,000. He remarks that if he paid such an extravagant amount of money, for a low-budget film about the economic downturn in the rust belt during the Reagan years, St. Peter wouldn't allow him into Heaven.

In *An American Family*, after Pat Loud has instructed her husband to move out of the house, we see her languishing by the poolside. On the soundtrack we hear the strains of Carole King's "Will You Still Love Me Tomorrow?," which Delilah is listening to in the adjoining bedroom. The bitterness of the breakup after twenty years of marriage is not lost on the viewer. This scene neatly echoes that of Bill and his new lover dancing on New Year's Eve as a piano man croons King's "You've Got a Friend," from the same album, "Tapestry." Although documentary filmmakers often imply in interviews that such incidents simply happen and are just happy coincidences, their use clearly demonstrates an intention on the part of the makers, a sense of aesthetic and thematic unity, and an implicit point of view. The music comments on the action, providing an editorial perspective for interpreting the images, as Claudia Gorbman has noted of the function of narrative film music in general.

While the conventions of observational film require that music be recorded on location, the function of music in the narrative structure of these films appears quite similar to that of music in classical Hollywood cinema. Music provides continuity, covers up edits, facilitates changes of scenes, provides mood, offers entertaining spectacle, allows for narrative interludes and montage sequences, and comments on the action. Eleven of the episodes of *An American Family* open with musical passages, while ten episodes end with music over the credits; these musical passages bracket the programs. Wiseman begins *High School* with a car radio playing Otis Redding's "Sitting on the Dock of the Bay" and the chorus about "wasting time" quickly comes to stand for the experience of the students at Northeast High. For the most part, Wiseman avoids such commentative uses of music in his later films. The virtual absence of music in *Hospital* no doubt contributes to its oppressive atmosphere of suffering and pain. The young man who overdoses on mescaline in that film begs his attendants to "play some music or sing" to relieve his anxiety. By and large, documentary filmmakers have become as rigorous as their Hollywood counterparts in finding musical passages that contribute to the narrative and thematic concerns of their films. Barbara Kopple's *Harlan County U.S.A.* (1976) profits from a rich and moving sample of folk songs that shows music to be a repository of community and memory in the miners' struggle for their civil rights.

The new conventions of observational documentary in the 1960s required that filmmakers find their musical selections in the original scenes that they filmed. Not surprisingly, the ordinary people who populate observational documentaries often happen to play music themselves. In Marc Obenhaus' *The Pasciaks of Chicago* (1976) from the television series *Six American Families*, the son's dedication to rock music creates tensions within his Polish working-class family; his mother wants him to play traditional polkas on the accordion and his interest in contemporary rock music reflects his attempt to assimilate into the mainstream of American popular culture. The characters in Nick Broomfield and Joan Churchill's *Soldier Girls* (1981) perform a lively rap tune in the barracks during a break in their basic training sessions in Georgia.

In *An American Family*, young Grant diligently plucks away on his guitar and sings in a budding garage band. During the course of the twelve-hour series, we hear the band perform the Rolling Stones' "Jumping Jack Flash" and "Brown Sugar," and the Who's "I Can See For Miles" and "Summertime Blues." These regular appearances culminate in an amusing parody of rock concerts staged by Grant's band at a pep rally at Santa Barbara High School. With his friends cheering in mock hysteria, Grant arrives on a motorcycle wearing black leotards, a skin tight black shirt and a cape, to sing "I'm Gonna Get You In My Tent," a song of his own composition.

This sequence shows how thoroughly Grant, Kevin, and their friends had absorbed the ecstatic performance style of Mick Jagger, canonized in the Maysles brothers' portrait of the Rolling Stones, *Gimme Shelter*. The sequence of Grant's band also suggests that the value of music as entertainment and spectacle was recognized by the Raymonds, Gilbert, and the editors of *An American Family*. Later, Grant serenades his mother in the living room with acoustic versions of the Kinks' "Ape Man" and the Beatles' "Mother Nature's Son," joking self-consciously, "It's entertainment time at the Loud house. Will you get situated, please." After the series was broadcast, in a turn of events in which life may be seen imitating art, the Loud children performed several songs as a group in a televised fundraising event for PBS. Meanwhile, Lance attempted to capitalize on his newfound celebrity by forming the Mumps, a punk rock group that played original music in clubs in New York throughout the 1970s. In the Raymonds' remake *An American Family Revisited: The Louds Ten Years Later* (1983), Grant pursues a career as a lounge singer in night clubs in southern California.

Conventions of Observational Film

While *An American Family* may be the most famous example of the observational cinema, it deviates significantly from the proscriptive rules of that style. These stylistic ruptures shed light on the conventions of documentary sound in broadcast television and independent film. At the outset of each episode, a split-screen montage sequence and a musical theme song introduce the family members one by one. Gilbert commissioned Elinor Bunin to make this one-minute series title film. The sequence ends with the title shattering like glass, a suggestion of the break-up of the family that forms the basis and narrative unity of the whole series. The series title film indicates to the viewers that they are entering the frame of a narrative, the world of a story. The musical introduction was not recorded during the shooting, an important violation of the observational aesthetic. In this passage, Gilbert can be seen conforming to the standards and conventions of broadcast television, rather than independent film, a balancing act that becomes more apparent over the course of the series.

The opening episode uses on-camera narration as well as recorded images and sounds to introduce the characters, the time and place of the setting, and the dramatic tension. *An American Family* opens with a shot of producer/director Gilbert standing on a hillside above the city. He speaks directly to the audience, "During the next hour, you will see the first in a series of programs entitled *An American Family*. The series is about the William C. Loud family, of Santa Barbara, California." Gilbert's opening monologue, in which he attempts to frame audience expectations and deflect possible criticisms, is a central deviation from the observational model. He apparently believed that the novelty of the form and subject matter necessitated this introduction. He denies that the Loud family is either average or typical, thereby contradicting the thrust of the series title. Viewers nevertheless understood the significance of the title; still today it is commonly referred to as *"The American Family."* Gilbert also admits that the filmmaking inevitably influenced the Louds, although no evidence of this may be seen in the series. Furthermore, he asserts that the series was a cooperative venture between the family and the film crew "in every sense of the word," although few traces of this interaction appear. In this way, the tensions of the textual system are displaced onto the opening monologue, a displacement which also occurs in John Huston's *The Battle of San Pietro* (1945), in which an introductory statement from a representative of the army attempts to deflect the main point of view of the film (Nichols). Similarly, the on-camera narrator who introduces Jennings' *Listen to Britain*, on the 16mm print in distribution in North America, deliberately calls attention to "the first sure notes of the march of victory, as you and I listen to Britain."

Gilbert continues his description of the setting of *An American Family*, "The population of Santa Barbara is somewhere around 73,000. Located on a slope of the Santa Ynez Mountains, Santa Barbara faces south on the Pacific Ocean, ninety miles north of Los Angeles—driving time an hour and a half, flying time twenty minutes. The average daytime temperature is 78 degrees in summer and 65 degrees in winter." Throughout this introduction, Gilbert sounds curiously like the Stage Manager in Thornton Wilder's *Our Town*, who sets the stage for a reenactment of family life both particular and universal. Like the Stage Manager, Gilbert remains somewhat detached from the everyday affairs of ordinary mortals. After introducing the characters and the setting for the series, he disappears. Indeed, *Our Town* presents a model for understanding *An American Family* as social commentary; both make appeals to family, community, and nation. The camera and tape recorder serve as witnesses to the events, an internal audience like the Stage Manager or Emily who, after her death, returns to observe her family going about their everyday lives. In Emily's eyes, they are painfully unaware of their singularity and existential importance. Many of the reviewers of *An American Family*, in the subsequent controversy generated by the series, echoed Emily's angst in their critiques of the family and the film.

In both *Our Town* and *An American Family*, viewers are invited to see everyday events with their ordinary significance heightened. Gilbert's voice-over narration gives away the drama of the series within the first thirty minutes, so that the viewer is primed to read all of the events of the Loud's unfolding lives as telltale signs of the inevitable decline of Pat and Bill's marriage, "This New Year's will be unlike any other that has been celebrated at 35 Woodale Lane. For the first time the family will not be spending it together. Pat Loud and her husband, Bill, separated four months ago after twenty years of marriage." As in Greek drama and popular film genres, we know the ending already and the suspense lies more in the telling than in the tale. Here, Gilbert embodies the voice of God, knowing the end and the beginning.

At another point in the film, Gilbert presents new story information in the voice-over narration, a trade-off, as the coordinating producer Jacqueline Donnet described it, between the comprehensibility of the narrative and the conventions of observational film, "There's [a scene] in the show where she is telling her brother that she's going to divorce [Bill] and she wants to separate and get a divorce. That was the other time that we wrenched the convention of not telling you, by telling you up front that she was driving down to speak to her brother about the divorce. The reason for that was the sound track is so garbled; it's very, very hard to hear. You miss half of it and all of a sudden realize what she's saying and you haven't heard the front half." (Ruoff 1989a, B7). Voice-over presents essential story information and restores a potentially incomprehensible scene. Throughout the rest of the twelve-hour series, Gilbert's voice-over occasionally resurfaces to provide details about the time and place of the action.

Gilbert, however, is not the only one to speak in voice-over. Both Pat and Bill Loud narrate voice-over passages. In her voice-over narration, Pat speaks her words haltingly, as if reading from a script or answering offscreen questions. Her voice lacks any specific spatial signature and the sound is uncharacteristically clear. She is literally not speaking in her own voice; a photograph published in *Studies in Visual Communication* shows Pat Loud and Craig Gilbert composing the narration for this sequence, a stopwatch and film projector within view (Gilbert, 49). The rehearsed style of her speech contrasts vividly with the spontaneity of her voice in the observational scenes of her daily life; her inexperience as a voice-over narrator becomes a touching signifier of the authenticity of her routine appearances in front of the camera. In this scene, Gilbert at once undermines and reinstates the claims of observational filmmakers to observe human behavior without unduly influencing it. Later in the series, Bill reads in voice-over a letter that he wrote to his son Lance shortly after the parents' separation; his delivery shares many of the same qualities of awkward direct address as Pat's voice-over. There is no ambient sound at all in this scene as we see Lance bicycling through his home town.

When Lance travels to Paris, we hear the sound of accordion music; the clarity of the music and the complete lack of spatial signature suggest that it was recorded not on location where he was vacationing, but rather came directly off a record. Needless to say, accordion music provides the most conventional associations with France, a convenient way of announcing the setting. Gilbert also uses canned music with the home movies which Pat Loud describes in voice-over. The scenes from childhood are accompanied by the sounds of a toy music box. Another sequence of home movies, originally shot in Brazil where Pat lived as a young girl, unfolds with generic samba music in the background. Again Gilbert fulfills conventional expectations about the narrative television soundscape, which apparently cannot tolerate silence. The use of home movies and family photographs also represents an important deviation from the observational focus on images and sounds recorded in the present. One of the criticisms of observational film is that it fails to deal adequately with the past, an important limitation which Gilbert simply ignores in favor of other means of expression—interviews, voice-over narration, canned music, family photographs and home movies.

Interview material also occasionally appears in the series. When we see Lance for the first time, he delivers a long monologue about his family, entirely in voice-over, as we see him sorting his clothes "alone" in his room at the Chelsea hotel. Lance describes his family in ways that sound like a series of answers to questions not heard on the soundtrack, "I have two brothers and two sisters; Kevin, Grant, Delilah, and Michelle. I don't know any of their ages or any of their birthdays or anything like that. I can never remember anything of those private things of anybody, except my own." Lance goes on to comment that Michelle is really "selfish and snotty" and that Grant is "unfortunately" the one most likely to succeed. Lance's witty descriptions and criticism help to introduce the personalities of his siblings, while underlining his own marginal status in the family. This uncharacteristic voice-over technique suggests that the film endorses Lance's point of view. In another instance, Lance recreated his half of a long-distance telephone conversation with his mother, "When they were editing the show, they took me in the recording studio, and they had me do overdubs. . . . They would just give me rough outlines of areas they wanted me to talk about" (Ruoff 1990, A4).

Although I have spoken little of sound effects in *An American Family*, one anecdote provides some illuminating information about them. After escorting his mother to a taxi, Lance returns to his room at the Chelsea hotel. Following him in a virtuoso long take, the camera climbs up four flights of stairs and enters his room, where Lance flips on the television in time to catch the beginning of Abbott and Costello's *Buck Privates Come Home*. The mood of this scene is melancholy, conveyed in some measure by the weary sounds of footsteps fading away in the empty hallways, appropriate enough for the life of a boy from Santa Barbara living alone in New York. Unfortunately, no synchronous sound was recorded to accompany this scene. Editor David Hanser returned to the hotel some time later and recreated the cavernous sound of footsteps by walking up the stairs, carrying a Nagra recorder, at exactly the same pace as Lance had done. For the sound of the television show, Jacqueline Donnet stated, "we knew exactly the day and the time it was shot and went to the *New York Times* and found out what film it really was, rented the film—and that was the exact same print that they had on the air—and just added it" (Ruoff 1989, AA11). No viewer ever noticed this betrayal of the conventions of synchronous sound recording. This supports Michel Chion's contention that we have virtually no way of knowing for sure, short of confessions from the filmmakers, whether sound effects in documentary were actually recorded at the time of shooting (Chion 1985). Donnet admitted that she "wouldn't trust anyone with audio in terms of saying that was really on the track or that wasn't on the track" (Ruoff 1989a, AA11).

Throughout this essay, I have attempted to characterize some of the conventions of documentary sound and narration, concentrating in particular on the style of observational filmmaking and *An American Family*. In both fiction and documentary, clarity of sound and image derives from the degree of control that filmmakers have over pro-filmic events. Interviews and voice-over narration in documentary provide exceptionally clear and direct sound, although observational filmmakers try to avoid these techniques. Observational documentaries still make extensive use of music, even if non-diegetic music falls by the wayside. Synchronous sound observational documentaries borrow conventions of storytelling and continuity editing from fiction films, without, however, offering the exceptional clarity of image, sound, and story that are the hallmarks of classical Hollywood cinema. Close analysis of *An American Family* indicates that conventions of observational cinema were circumvented in numerous ways in order to make the narrative more comprehensible, suggesting the director's commitment to other forms of documentary address. Forms of direct address occur in on-camera narration, voice-over narration, canned music, and interviews. This twelve-part PBS series represents a unique mixture of conventions of broadcast television and independent documentary film. The ruptures in the sound track suggest not that strictures for making documentaries were violated, or that audiences were necessarily deceived, but rather that all films are constructions, meaningful assertions about the world made by directors and by those with whom they collaborate.

13

And Then There Was Sound:
The Films of Andrei Tarkovsky

Andrea Truppin

"There is no such thing as facts here. It is all someone's devilish invention."

Stalker

In his later films, Andrei Tarkovsky develops a compelling language based on sound's potential for ambiguity and abstraction. He probes sound's ability to function both literally—attached to an object—and abstractly—independent of any recognizable source. In these films, sound moves beyond its traditional role as a secondary support for the image, at times surpassing the visual in its ability to convey certain types of meaning. In Tarkovsky's use of sound, meaning is produced as much through the synergism of narrative and formal elements, both aural and visual, as through the audience's efforts to establish coherence among these elements. These efforts by the audience represent internal struggles akin to those experienced by the films' characters.

The Mirror (1974) is a journey through the psyche in which memory, dream and fantasy are represented with the materiality of conventional reality. The film's conception of the mind is reminiscent of one of Freud's, who tentatively likened it to the city of Rome, in which layer upon layer of past experience constitute the same small patch of ground (Freud, 17–19), although in the mind the various realms of consciousness are interwoven in a constantly shifting pattern. Tarkovsky's use of ambiguous sound dissolves borders that typically separate these realms. In his last three films, *Stalker* (1979), *Nostalgia* (1983), and *Sacrifice* (1986), Tarkovsky's philosophical concerns turn to the viability of faith in the modern world. In these films, the use of ambiguous sound plunges the audience into a never fully resolved struggle to believe in the diegesis, much as the films' characters struggle with their own ability to have faith. Tarkovsky uses sound to embody this internal process by drawing a parallel between two "leaps of faith": that of accepting that a sound proves the existence of an unseen object and that of believing in the existence of an invisible spiritual world. Because we posit a source for every offscreen diegetic sound, we believe in the existence of this source even when we cannot produce a viable mental image of it. We believe, although we cannot explain or prove. This paradox is one of the bases of religious faith.

To understand how sound works in Tarkovsky's films, it is useful to examine how the "sound hermeneutic," as described by Rick Altman, functions in cinema. "The sound asks the question *where?* and the image [or the source of the sound] responds *here!*" (Altman, 1980c, 74). This powerful sound hermeneutic provides a sense of closure that allows perception of the depicted world as coherent. In film, as Michel Chion has noted in his article "Les trois frontières," sound does not actually emanate from the objects seen on the screen, but from a speaker, placed most commonly behind or above the screen. The spectator's imagination allows the objects seen on the screen to appear to produce the sounds, and one object's sound is not often confused with that of another. In addition, the viewer imagines that the sounds are actually coming from different places on the screen, while in fact, all the sounds, in the case of a single speaker, are emanating from exactly the same point. "If one sees a character go to the right, one will therefore *hear* the sound move to the right . . . It is on this that the "realism" of sound cinema rests, and without it, it would be impossible to believe in these sounds and these voices which do not move within the width of the screen, while the objects and the characters that produce them move about constantly" (Chion, 1985, 29, my translation). We are required to make a "leap of faith" in order to construct and believe this fiction of sound cinema.

In the case of offscreen sound, our tendency to attach a sound to an emitting source in the interest of coherence allows us to accept the existence of that which we cannot see. While the picture of the sound source may not be available, the imagination steps in to provide a mental image of this sound source which, if a confident one, retains all the properties of closure and coherence of a concretely observed sound source. In this way, offscreen sound enlarges the film space beyond the borders of the screen. We imagine not only the reality of the world seen on the screen, but that of a larger world stretching on indefinitely beyond it.

This persuasive quality allows sound to function, for Tarkovsky, as material with which to represent a numinous realm. The spiritual is mysterious, inaccessible to sensual experience. It becomes perceivable only through phenomenological representation. By extension, the Christian notion of a world peopled by signs of the spiritual realm, available only to those who have faith, and in which the universe is assumed to have some unknown but abiding purpose, is embodied in the constructed world of film. All filmic elements can be seen as "signs" of the film's purpose or meaning. Bearing their own significance, rather than redundantly supporting the image, Tarkovsky's sounds assume a great richness of meaning. Dialogue, while complex, loses its centrality. Tarkovsky's filmic worlds exude many voices, the human being only one of them. All sounds of the world can have meaning; all sounds can be signs. By extension, learning to hear the world is akin to coming into contact with the spiritual realm.

Tarkovsky's films present believable worlds that seem to function much of the time according to the logic of our own world, so that his ambiguous sounds call out for explanation that is often withheld. His sounds destabilize; they make the coherent and comfortable seem suddenly strange and disorienting. Convinced that to hear and see anew leads to new understanding, Tarkovsky disconcerts the viewer. Through the use of ambiguous sound, Tarkovsky engages us in a process that the characters in the diegesis must negotiate: cynicism, incredulity, search for explanation and finally, perhaps, acceptance of that which we cannot explain.

Sound, Source and Revelation

Key to Tarkovsky's creation of this type of sound is the treatment of sound sources, including the selective revelation of sources, purposeful misleading as to a source's identity, and withholding of resolution by refusing to reveal a sound source, strategies that correspond to the films' image treatment. Tarkovsky's films are notable for their use of long takes, deep focus, exaggerated chiaroscuro, and long tracking shots, both lateral and in depth, whose movement may be almost imperceptible. A tracking shot may take several minutes to finally reveal the "subject" of the shot— a person, an action, an object—the journey as vital to the mood and meaning as the destination. Similarly, a sound will fade in very gradually, often remaining at the border of audibility for so long that, as we begin to perceive it, we first question if we have in fact heard anything and then wonder how long we have been hearing it. Sounds often initially resemble something other than what they later prove to be. Instead of abrupt sound cuts, sound bridges straddle image cuts to new scenes.

In these films, several layers of aural representation of unseen objects occur. Most simply, an object may be represented by an audible sound, identifiable or not. Alternatively this sound may be represented by sound waves (vibration) at frequencies inaudible to the human ear. These inaudible sound waves are themselves represented visually by objects onscreen which shake, fall over, and shatter. The vibration may also be represented by audible sounds made by moving onscreen or offscreen objects. Finally, the sound source, the original object, can become visible, the ultimate resolution of this multi-layered sound hermeneutic. It is no longer simply a representation of the "true" sound source, however, but one that approximates or contradicts the previously imagined object.

The manipulation of these sound relationships is crucial to Tarkovsky's construction of ambiguous sound. These clues, revealed one by one, force us to embark on a backward journey through a series of representations, each seemingly closer to the original, with the hope of ultimately identifying the sound source. Yet we are often left with neither a glimpse of the sound source nor confidence in our mental identification of it. Allowing a sound source to remain a figment of our imagination, mystifying rather than orienting, subverts sound's traditional role in film.

Revealing a sound source may give a sense of coherence to our perception of the material world, but mystery, or the undeniable existence of a sound phenomenon for which there is no plausible explanation, is, in the world of these films, proof of God's existence and is linked to the Christian notion of Revelation. Throughout *Nostalgia,* a sound like that of an electric saw fades in and out, with no seeming connection to the action. It first occurs when Andrei enters Domenico's partially ruined house. As the sound of the saw begins, the camera dollies into the barnlike interior strewn with hay and puddles of water that reflect light from a window opening onto the distant hills. As the camera moves forward, the floor scale seems to enlarge and begins to resemble a hilly landscape with a winding river, seen in miniature from a bird's-eye perspective. Sounds of birds fade in and increase in volume as this landscape approaches. The camera moves closer until the miniature landscape blends inexplicably but seamlessly into the view through the window of the "real" hills beyond.

The Christian symbolism in Andrei's visit to Domenico becomes clear in the next scene: Domenico offers Andrei wine and bread, plays him a recording of the chorale finale from Beethoven's Ninth Symphony, and asks him to carry a candle across the pool of St. Catherine, an act that Domenico believes will save the world. The previous scene, then, brings to mind the Christian notion of seeing, as Blake put it, "a world in a grain of sand, and a heaven in a wild flower" (Blake, 174), or evidence of God's design on earth; one begins to associate the sawing sound symbolically with Christ the carpenter. The sound recurs in dream sequences, in the town of Bagno Vignoni, even briefly in a street in Rome, giving it an omnipresence akin to God's immanence in the universe. Use of the sound of an electric saw, rather than that of a hand saw that one might more readily associate with Christ's era, provides the sound with an immediacy and tangibility that influence the associations it engenders, notably the question of the viability of faith in the modern world.

The subtle transformation of a recurring sound throughout a film can promise to resolve open questions, although the source will again remain unverifiable. In *Sacrifice,* we are troubled by an eerie female voice that appears periodically. At the film's end, however, in the context of a sunny day, in which, according to the story, nuclear holocaust has been averted by the protagonist's vow of self-sacrifice to God, the sound seems to have metamorphosed into the simple calls of a goosegirl to her flock. Although recognizable as the original sound, the calling has become less abstract and melodic, more structured, with discernible patterns more akin to speech. This very quotidian sound leads us to examine our prior assumptions about the diegesis. We wonder if the earlier image of a naked girl chasing her geese down a hallway of Alexander's house was simply a banal visual concretization in his dream of the goosegirl's calls, the eerie cries their aural transformation. We suspect, then, that Alexander's nighttime visit to Maria and the nuclear holocaust were part of the dream. However, since we heard the original eerie calling when Alexander was clearly awake and before the cataclysm was reported on the TV news, it is impossible to interpret the sound with certainty. Ambiguity in sound stems not only from the inability to ascertain a sound's source, but also from uncertainty as to who, if anyone, in the diegesis is hearing the sound and in what state of mind.

When a concrete sound source is in fact revealed, it often contradicts what we have been led to expect. In *Sacrifice,* we see the maid drying a wine glass. Suddenly we become aware, as she appears to, of a tinkling of crystal. She looks up towards what we assume is the location of the sound source, probably a chandelier. Surprisingly, in a subversion of the shot/reverse shot convention, in which the shot following the glance reveals the object of the gaze, the next shot is not of a chandelier above her head, but of a tray of crystal wine glasses on a table at her waist, knocking together from the force of some vibration, perhaps an earthquake. As we hear a low rumble that grows into a deafening roar, we realize that this sound represents bombers overflying the house, although we never actually see them, and that the maid has not been looking at a chandelier, but looked up because she sensed the vibration to come from the sky, even before she heard the planes. However, the early vibration, manifested in the rattling glasses, which will not allow us to locate the source of the sound accurately, and the subversion of the shot/reverse shot convention suggest a force coming from the ground. This makes our eventual identification of the bombers in the sky all the more jarring.

In *Stalker,* image and sound collude to suggest an offscreen sound source that proves to be false. The camera moves towards a burned-out truck lying in a field, right after we have seen the three travellers set off on their trip through the Zone. The dolly-in suggests the movement of walking conventionally associated with a character's point-of-view. We hear close footsteps in the dry grass that coincide in rhythm and sound characteristics with the movement of the camera and the particularities of the terrain: we glimpse bits of metal on the ground that correspond to a slight ringing of a footstep, and we see the movement of successive tufts of grass at the bottom of the frame as if the feet of the character were crushing them. As the camera approaches the truck, we glimpse what appears to be a dead body, but before we have time to identify this image for certain, we are disconcerted more strongly by the continuing forward movement of the camera through the truck and out its far window. Suddenly, the camera seems no longer to represent a character's vision, but floats inexplicably through space on its own. Heightening our confusion, we glimpse all three characters entering the frame from the left, having obviously followed a different trajectory from that of the camera. We hear their footsteps in the dry grass, and realize that they sound much farther away than the ones we just heard. The blend of a plausible sound/image relationship, associated with the camera's tracking movement and the apparent point-of-view of a character, with an illogical narrative match—the characters' actual route—is an effective means of transforming a rather ordinary landscape into a forbidding environment.

The revelation of the source of an offscreen sound, such as a disembodied voice, can suggest different ways of seeing in terms of access to the spiritual realm. In *Nostalgia,* we hear several offscreen voices talking together at the baths of St. Catherine. The voices are characterized by two different spatial signatures, so that they can be placed in a near/far relationship to the camera and to one another. The conversation between Eugenia, the near voice, and the townspeople, the far voices, continues through several questions and long explanations without our seeing any of the interlocutors. We see, instead, Domenico and Andrei approaching down a long arcade that rims the bath, silhouetted so that they "resemble" one another. It is only when Domenico passes by Eugenia that we begin to "see" the source of her voice. Domenico, the faithful, is a bringer of vision. It is his arrival that allows us to see these floating voices, several of which we then realize, as the camera slowly tracks over the steaming water of the bath, are actually coming from people floating in the water.

The manner in which sound sources are revealed can imply very different kinds of offscreen space. In Tarkovsky, some sounds come full blown into existence as a function of the camera's seeing their source. In one sense, this can be considered an exaggeration of a sound convention of classical Hollywood cinema, in which the microphone records only a narrow range of sound delineated by the camera's visual field and very little offscreen sound is picked up from beyond the boundaries of this field. As the moving camera comes close to revealing an object, the object's sound becomes audible. In this convention, space does not exist until the camera "creates" it.

In *Stalker,* the use of offscreen sound is so strongly established that we do not receive this practice of limited offscreen sound range as a convention, but as a powerful indicator of meaning. When used, it appears as if not only the sound, but the object revealed by the camera, has appeared magically out of nowhere, reinforcing the narrative conceit that the Zone is a supernatural, inexplicable place. The rumble of a large river comes in only towards the middle of the tracking shot that reveals the river. Prodigious waterfalls adjacent to the locus of recent action are revealed by the camera at the same time as their loud roar. Inexplicably, in a later sequence in the same location, no rushing water is heard as the Writer and the Stalker reappear, amazed to discover themselves exactly where they started from. "It's a trap," says the Stalker. Like the cynical Writer, we struggle to provide rational explanations, and, like him, we want to consider the Stalker crazy when we fail.

The subversion of sound/image synchronization conventions also produces ambiguity in *Stalker*. The camera tracks past the waterfalls, revealing, one by one, a series of lamps hanging from metal cords. Although each lamp remains motionless as it comes into frame, we hear the creaking sound the lamp might make if it were moving. The camera's slow, relentless lateral movement is such that we expect it to reveal the "true" source of the creaking. Instead, it seems that the source of the sound is the immobile object itself, whose latent voice is revealed by the camera's gaze. The sequence suggests that sound is immanent in an animate, sentient world that is not what it seems. Like other sequences characterized by the unnerving rather than the blatantly strange, this scene makes us begin to believe the premise of the Zone's strange powers.

Sound and Space

The manipulation of spatial signature is another means by which Tarkovsky produces ambiguous sound. Spatial signature can be defined as a sound's auditory fingerprint that is never absolute, but subject to the sound's placement in a particular physical environment. These markers include reverb level, volume, frequency, and timbre that allow auditors to interpret the sound's identity in terms of distance or the type of space in which it has been produced and/or is being heard. The sounds in these films, albeit inexplicable and mysterious, are read as diegetic because they bear such highly specific spatial signatures. However, the signature may not coincide with the space from which the sound is apparently emanating. Seemingly "correct" spatial signature is used to provoke the reading of unrealistic scenes as realistic and exaggerated spatial signature is used to make apparently "normal" places seem strange and eerie. This is especially true of *Stalker,* in which sounds hover between the believable and the exaggerated, heightening our awareness of them. Feet stumbling against glass, the drip or rush of water, the breathing of the travellers, the whine of a dog, the hoot of an owl are often too loud, too present, too highly reverbed for the space in which they are apparently located.

However, Tarkovsky continually alters spatial signature to keep predictability at bay and to prevent the conventionalizing of the sounds' peculiar characteristics. Since not every sound functions in the same way within a scene, we are forced to interpret each individually. On the journey to the mysterious Room, the cynical Writer must pass through a tunnel that, according to the Stalker, is dangerous. At first, the Writer's voice is flat as he speaks facing into the tunnel's entrance. Logically, the large, hollow metal tunnel would be an excellent echo chamber. Paradoxically, his voice becomes more reverberant when he speaks facing away from the tunnel's entrance. Fear overcoming his bravura, the Writer seems to begin to doubt his mockery of the Zone's alleged powers. This time, as he enters the tunnel, his now reverberant voice echoes clearly. The change in spatial signature seems to imply that the Writer himself is changing. On the other hand, the highly reverberant sound of a stone hitting the water at the bottom of a well is not interpreted as exaggerated. Rather, the stone's spatial signature is used here as a pragmatic gauge of the well's extraordinary depth—a realistic measuring process used to convey an odd narrative fact. While this inconsistency of spatial signature keeps sound potent, it also allows sound to function symbolically. The shifting spatial signature gives credence to the idea promulgated by the Stalker that the Zone is a constantly shifting, dangerous place. "There is no such thing as facts here," comments the Stalker in despair. "It is all someone's devilish invention."

In *The Mirror,* voice-off is used to create the character of Aleksei, who remains invisible throughout the film. Present only through his voice, he is visible, and by implication fully alive, only in representations of his memories and dreams of himself as a child. In the film's second scene, Aleksei speaks to his mother on the telephone. Their disembodied voices float through space as the camera tracks through the empty apartment. The spatial signature of Aleksei's voice suggests at first that he occupies the depicted space, as opposed to his mother's voice which bears the small and filtered frequency range of the intervening telephone line. But because the quality of Aleksei's voice never changes and we cannot place him visually as the camera successively reveals the empty rooms we do not sense that he truly occupies his large apartment. We cannot place his voice any more than hers, as if the nowhereness of a voice on the telephone corresponded to the nowhereness of his own voice, whose inconsequential spatial signature reveals its lack of connection to the world. The strained conversation ends when Aleksei's mother hangs up on him. Aleksei has just dreamt about her as a young woman, and we feel that this present reality of the phone conversation is less real than the dream/memory he has just experienced.

Parallel Sound

Tarkovsky's use of sound permits his films to travel smoothly through multiple and equally weighted layers of experience. These layers flow simultaneously through one another without the rigid hierarchy that separates most filmic worlds into "reality" and "fantasy". Even in films that experiment with unconventional relationships of time and space, such as Bergman's *Wild Strawberries* and Resnais' *Hiroshima mon amour,* we are given very clear clues that allow us to differentiate among memory, dream, fantasy and the here-and-now. In *Wild Strawberries,* it is clear when Isak is dreaming and when he has awakened. In addition, in the dream/memory sequences, he appears as a ghost, hovering as an old man among the still young family members of his youth. In Tarkovsky's films, the entry into memory is total. In *Hiroshima mon amour,* the boundary between present reality and memory is clearly delineated. Although we see the woman as a young girl in Nevers, the non-diegetic music and the voice-over spoken in the cafe in Hiroshima make them clearly parenthetical to the present-day reality of her stay in Japan. Returns to reality from subjective sound are abrupt, such as when she gets carried away by her memories. Only her voice is heard in the café until her lover slaps her and the diegetic sounds of the café flood back in. For Tarkovsky, the separating of these realms is less meaningful and authentic than their interweaving.

Spatial signature is also used in what I will call a system of parallel sound to convey a sense of heterogeneous worlds existing simultaneously, but not necessarily interacting. If parallel action is used to denote simultaneous events in the material world, parallel sound represents both the relationship between the material and the spiritual realms and among the various realms of the psyche—the constantly shifting hierarchy of dream, memory, fantasy and the present. Tarkovsky's deep space cinematography corresponds to the deep space sound that characterizes parallel sound.[1] In his films, careful sound construction and mixing, with attention to volume and reverb levels, frequency and rhythm, retain the clarity and audibility of each voice, assuring the interpretive viability of densely layered parallel sound.

Parallel sound represents a subversion of a normal property of sound: its ability to travel through space and physical barriers and be perceived far from its point of origin. Whereas in normal deep space sound the many sounds heard simultaneously on the sound track are believably present at one time in a single space, in parallel sound Tarkovsky associates sounds that could not logically coexist in one space. The distinct spatial signatures of the sounds determine this impossibility, and suggest that the sounds are affected only by the diverse spaces in which they were produced, not by the space in which they are heard. In *Sacrifice,* in the sequence that starts with Alexander's nighttime visit to Maria's house and ends with his awakening in his own home to a bright normal morning, simultaneous sound layers include belllike tones of rattling crystal, the voices of Alexander, Maria, and Alexander's wife (who is presumably not in the same space as Alexander and Maria), a far-off female singing voice, Shakuhachi flute music and the footsteps of a crowd of running people.

The reverb characteristics of these sounds alter subtly throughout the scene and where they occur elsewhere in the film, yet this traditionally orienting aspect of spatial signature serves more here to confuse than to identify sound space or source for the auditor. The whispering voice of Maria, formerly with little reverb in accordance with the sound space of her bedroom, seems to take on the characteristic reverb of a much larger, open space when the singing voice fades in. In a sense, Maria's voice borrows from the reverb of the second voice, connecting her with this voice on some plane that is not spatial. Simultaneous with the increase of reverb in Maria's voice, the image shows her bed, where she and Alexander embrace, rising and revolving. The voluminous folds of the trailing white sheets are reminiscent of Renaissance depictions of Christ on his bier. The image here symbolizes resurrection, and the movement of Maria's voice from one spatial signature to another through an increase in reverb suggests movement from one realm of experience to another. Of course, exaggerated reverb has traditionally been used to label the voice of God or to connote the spiritual realm in the Bible movie genre, but Maria's whispering voice alters only subtly and retains its modest place as only one of several voices.

In addition to the manipulation of spatial signature, parallel sound is produced by sound bridges that join heterogeneous worlds, subverting our expectations of conventional depictions of reality that the films initially seem to follow. Sound bridges are used to join the real with the unreal, making each more like the other. At the start of a dream sequence in *Nostalgia,* the camera cuts from Andrei's face in the hotel in Italy to his sleeping wife in her bedroom in Russia as we hear his voice say her name: "Maria!" She starts up, seemingly at the sound of her name, as if she, the dreamed, had heard the dreamer's voice. She is clearly conscious and in her own space, her bed creaking, her confusion and fear visible as she gets up and goes to open the curtains to let in light, looking backwards towards the camera, to the point where she seems to have located the sound. At the same time, sounds of Andrei's space are still audible. The dislocation or transferral of point-of-view, from Andrei to his wife, makes this scene seem more like a parallel action cut to another real space inhabited by a conscious person, than the typical dream sequence which is from the dreamer's point-of-view alone.

In some sound bridges, spatial signature at first seems to coincide with the suggested space, but is then revealed to contradict both the first part of the shot and the established spatial signature. In a scene, perhaps a dream sequence, in *Nostalgia* which is parenthetical to the main action, Andrei opens a cupboard door in a Roman street. Simultaneous with the sound of wood, perhaps a chair, being pulled on a stone floor, Andrei quickly closes the cupboard door. The strong reverberation and long decay of the resulting creak and bang seem in accordance with this narrow alleylike street bordered with high stone buildings. As the camera cuts to a travelling shot of the interior of a stone cathedral, however, the still reverberating sound seems to belong as much to this space as to the previous one. Perhaps it was produced by a door closing nearby. We begin to hear the highly reverberant voices of invisible women praying somewhere within the cathedral. The scene is reminiscent of one of the film's first scenes, which takes place in a church in the Italian countryside. We think that we have exited a dream sequence and entered reality. However, as the camera travels laterally out of the side aisle of the cathedral and into the nave, we see that the building is in ruins; it has no roof, its windows no glass. Clearly, it could not contain such reverberant sounds as those we are hearing. Suddenly, our sense of orientation is shaken. Tarkovsky is able to create such a suggestive world precisely because of our strong attachment to what we consider normal image/sound relationships, and to conventions for announcing the appearance of symbolic sound. Tarkovsky subverts our expectations by refusing to announce the manner in which a sound should be read.

In *Sacrifice,* during Alexander's nighttime visit to Maria, we see a brief sequence of apparently panicked crowds fleeing through an alleyway. We hear, from that space, only the percussive sound of many blended footsteps and the occasional hollow ring of kicked metal. Other diegetic sounds, from Maria's house and Alexander's house, carry over inexplicably into this scene in the alleyway, whose location in actual space and time we can only guess at. These sounds seem to bear no more obvious relationship to the alleyway and its human throng than they did to Maria's bedroom in the previous sequence when they were also heard. Since we expect to hear other sounds from the people, such as their crying or yelling voices, they appear unnaturally mute. The footsteps are read as an asynchronous overlay, and the scene takes on an eerie, dreamlike quality, which the slightly slowed movement of the people augments. However, partway through the shot, it appears that some of the footsteps are, in fact, in sync, or at least have been matched rhythmically and in terms of distance from the camera, to the sound track. Further, the reverberance of the sound matches the hard-surfaced, high-walled alleyway. These details clue us in to the "reality" of this scene, but we still cannot logically locate it either temporally or spatially. The question then becomes, whose reality is this? Who is seeing this, hearing this? Is it a privileged moment for the spectator, let into another diegesis? Is it a parallel action sequence, a far-off city where the bomb has hit and people are fleeing? Or, since we begin to hear the sounds of a spoon clinking in a glass and Alexander's stuttering voice, we wonder if it is Alexander's hallucination or daydream. Sound is used simultaneously to disorient, to usher us into another realm of experience, and to narrate symbolically: the absence of "expected" sound can also be read as an allusion to the unnatural silence described by witnesses to the aftermath of the bombing of Hiroshima, in which people stumbled through the city, shocked beyond the ability to utter sounds. In the world of this film, defined and dynamized by sound, perhaps the most deadly sound of all is silence.

Specificity and Realism

While the incompatibility of the various spatial signatures in a single scene produces a sense of unreality, the specificity of spatial signature, like a fingerprint, individualizes the sounds and implies real space, giving them an undeniable and unsettling realism. The very loud, highly reverberant water drips that permeate Tarkovsky's films often make sense because we see water in the image, but their spatial signature is often incompatible with the scene. In *Nostalgia* the drip is heard in scenes at the baths, which is essentially an open, outdoor space, and in flooded ruins of buildings. In *Stalker,* it is heard not only when the travellers are within flooded buildings and metal pipes, but also when they are outside, in the open air.

This type of sound serves to give a sense of some transcendent, unlocatable space. As in parallel sound, the highlighting of insignificant noises hints at the existence of unseen worlds. The water drip is typically a sound that is not noticed in the bustle of daily life. When the world becomes unusually quiet, such as late at night, the sound suddenly surges up into our consciousness, relentless, calm, insistent, reminding us that it has been there all along, while we went about our lives unaware. Refusing to reveal its intentionality, it comments surreptitiously on the action of the film. In Tarkovsky, a sound effect's attachment to a place in the real world makes it seem pregnant with mysterious significance for the narrative of which the characters remain ignorant.

Small, unexplained noises are heard once or twice and never again, like the sound of a small metal object dropping and rolling along the floor in *Sacrifice,* or the sound of something knocked over by the dog who lies down next to Andrei's hotel bed in *Nostalgia*. The camera remains on glass bottles ringing with rain in a ruined house or a cup that falls from the table when children run outside, often dollying-in as if to reveal something more. The sound track insists on the gentle rattling, ringing or knocking that is occurring far from the characters' perception. The sounds' apparent inconsequentiality and lack of clear meaning, and the characters' seeming obliviousness to them, contradict our assumption that in this constructed world every sound that stands out is significant, and we wait in vain for explanations. This sound practice augments our uncertainty as to the significance to accord other sounds.

Like the use of specific spatial signature, the simple materiality of these straightforward sounds provides realism. There is nothing strange about them except their identity and their reason for being. They resemble aleatory sounds that occur throughout the day in real life. In the films, these small sounds give palpable texture to the scene. We are certain of the corporeal presence of the strange dog who appears out of nowhere because we hear him knock something over. The floor seems tangible and appropriately hard when we hear something drop and roll along it.

These sounds embody the idea that it is important to notice small things because small things change the world. Watering the dead tree in *Sacrifice,* carrying the candle across the pool in *Nostalgia,* will redeem the individual and the world. The decentering quality of this type of sound reinforces the theme that human beings are not the central focus of the world; it has a life of its own. The consequence of the hubris of the human race is suggested through recurring images of apocalypse: the detritus of modern society lies obscenely jumbled and rotting under water in streams, in pools, in mud, juxtaposed with objects that represent man's fall from grace—the statute of an angel, a reproduction of an icon of St. John the Baptist. These images comment on the finiteness of human life and civilization.

The Power of Sound

If, in the world of these films, sound can suggest unseen powerful realms, sound is itself an invisible power that literally moves the material world and, as such, lends itself well to the representation of the duelling forces of spirituality and the destructive tendencies of modern materialist society. While the unseen train in *Stalker* may shake the objects of this world, and the invisible planes in *Sacrifice* make objects fall and shatter, the Stalker's little daughter, who cannot walk, has telekinetic powers. In the last scene of *Stalker,* she quietly and steadily moves glasses on a table with her gaze. One of the glasses falls. The sound of its rolling on the floor blends with the warning rattle of a window that heralds an approaching train. As the little girl sits quietly at the table, it begins to shake.

The train roars by, obscenely blaring strains of orchestral music and filling the previously tranquil room with violence. The train noise dies away and the picture fades to black, but a soft rattling of windows remains as a reminder of the aural cataclysm that has just swept through. If the train's roar and its distorted music represent the destructive forces of Western civilization, the power of spirituality is represented by the small child, who calmly and gently moves the world, an embodiment of the Christian concept that "the meek shall inherit the earth."

The power of sound is also related to the power of speech, or the ability to express oneself authentically. In *The Mirror,* the protagonist seems depressed and bored, his urbane cynicism little protection from the guilt, regret and memory that torment him. He seems paralyzed by the paradox of the inextricable ties of family, child to parent to grandparent. Because of his inability to communicate with his mother, his wife and his son, he cannot act in an authentic way. He lives through the memory of his childhood, refusing his adult state. In the prologue that precedes the titles in *The Mirror,* his son watches a television program in which a doctor successfully hypnotizes a teenage boy to cure his stuttering. She says, "Concentrate . . . on your heart's desire. . . . You will speak loudly and clearly all your life." This scene metaphorically equates strong and clear speech with power and self-control and is a condition for entry into manhood.

Authentic speech is also equated with prayer and is opposed to the futility of empty words; sound is powerful and sacred because it reveals the word of God. In *Sacrifice,* Alexander says that he is tired of words; by the end, he has learned to pray. His vow to remain mute if God will hear his prayer is a promise to relinquish the material world, to communicate only with the spiritual. Alexander's coming to hear sounds he was oblivious to earlier symbolizes the power he has gained from learning this new form of speech. For Tarkovsky, entering manhood also means finding faith.

Sound, as a phenomenon that can bypass reason to communicate on a more immediate, more intuitive level, is a primary means of meaningful communication in Tarkovsky's films. At the start of *Sacrifice,* Alexander says to his small son, who is recovering from a throat operation and must not speak, " 'In the beginning was the Word', but you are as mute as a fish." At the end of *Sacrifice,* the little boy, now alone, looks up at the "Japanese" tree, symbol of faith that he planted with his father, and utters his first words, and the last words of the film: " 'In the beginning was the Word.' Papa, why is that?" For Tarkovsky, it is perhaps because sound, in its ability to exist independently of its source, free of a concrete, visually perceivable object firmly attached to this world, can transcend the material towards otherwise inaccessible realms of experience.

Afterword: A Baker's Dozen Terms for Sound Analysis

Rick Altman

Many factors contribute to the development of a field. The contributors to this volume have been able to renew the study of film sound for a number of reasons:

1) They are convinced that film sound carries meaning in more ways than simply by accompanying a visible object or person.

2) They have broadened the previous field of research on sound (through attention to trade papers, popular magazines, technical journals, archived collections, corporate records, and the like).

3) They have taken their interest in sound to new objects of study (recently remastered Vitaphone films, cartoons, documentaries, theatrical adaptations, Third World films, television).

4) They have often based their analyses on a new vocabulary, more attuned to the way in which film sound makes, rather than merely possesses, meaning.

I note with particular pleasure the extent to which sound-oriented vocabulary developed during courses at the University of Iowa has contributed to a number of essays in this volume. While much of the terminology related to sound has now become standardized, it will perhaps be helpful to mention here some of the additional terms that I have found useful in my teaching and writing, but that have not yet become standard vocabulary. Included in this list are also a number of terms defined elsewhere in this volume, along with the locations where each term is first mentioned.

attack: Hetero 5

auditory perspective: Sound Space 5

cocktail party effect: Hetero 22

compression: Hetero 3

compression/rarefaction cycles: Hetero 4

decay: Hetero 6

deep space sound: Truppin 20

directional characteristics: Hetero 18

direct sound: Hetero 9

emanation speech: Chion 2

establishing sound: Sound that establishes, from the very beginning of a scene, the general character of the surroundings. During the late twenties and thirties, Hollywood typically used onscreen establishing sound (for example, traffic sounds accompanying a shot of Times Square), but regularly turned to offscreen establishing sound during the forties (for example, traffic sounds accompanying a shot of a bedroom with the shades pulled down). Establishing sound is usually removed or radically reduced in volume during dialogue, but may return in the form of reestablishing sound (sometimes, but not systematically, accompanied by a reestablishing shot).

for-me-ness: The quality of sound with a high ratio of direct to reflected sound, like speech that is directed straight toward me from relatively close up. This quality characterizes most Hollywood sound, recognizing the auditor's presence while refusing to acknowledge the presence of a spectator, thus lending a discursive "feel" to images that seem to deny discursivity.

functional near-equivalence: Sound/History 15

fundamental: Hetero 4

generic sound: Sound that clearly represents a specific, easily recognizable type of sound event, but without salient particularities. Usually used *semi-sync* with a generic long-shot image, (for instance, of a crowd, a street scene, a race, or a battle), generic sound is often chosen from a sound library and arranged as a *sound loop*. Note that live crowd sound is often used generically in televised sports events.

harmonics: Hetero 4

historical fallacy: Four/half 1

Hz: Hetero 4

iconic sound: Curtis 18

identity redefinition: Sound/History 14

indexicality: four/half 11, Curtis 19

isomorphic sound: Curtis 17

jurisdictional struggle: Sound Space 24, Sound/History 16

location sound: Ruoff 7

loudness: Hetero 1

medium: Hetero 3

nominalist fallacy: Four/half 9

ontological fallacy: Four/half 3

overtones: Hetero 4

pitch: Hetero 1

point-of-audition sound: Sound identified by its physical characteristics (principally reduced volume and increased reverb) as it might be heard by a character within the film. Regularly used both to join spaces whose relationship cannot easily be presented in a single establishing shot, and to promote identification between the audience and carefully selected characters. Unlike the point-of-view sequence, which often moves from the viewer to the object or character viewed, the point-of-audition sequence typically begins with a shot of the sound source, introducing point-of-audition sound only when we cut to a shot of the auditor.

pressure changes: Hetero 3

rarefaction: Hetero 4

ratio of direct to reflected sound: Hetero 11

reflected sound: Hetero 9

refracted sound: Hetero note 2

reproductive fallacy: Four/half 7

reverberation: Hetero 9

scale matching: The matching of image scale and *sound scale*.

semi-sync: A characteristic of sound that is apparently synchronized with onscreen actions of secondary importance. This technique is often used for the linking of stock sound footage to mobs, parades, battles, or other large-scale scenes where the viewer cannot possibly check whether each sound is actually synchronized to an onscreen image. Already employed in the early Fox Movietone News, this technique facilitates the use of *generic sound* and *sound loops*. It is heavily used by television news to accompany background action in still photographs.

sound advance: The practice of introducing a sound before the image with which it is associated. The sound advance is especially characteristic of (1) silent film accompaniment, where musicians are encouraged to anticipate the nature of the coming scene; (2) suspense films, where music or effects connoting danger are often heard just before we cut to the monster (or other menace); (3) live network television, where audience applause or theme music is regularly used to introduce a celebrity; (4) recent adventure films, where the sound advance has become a standard aural punctuation device, equivalent to a wipe. The term *sound lag* might be used to designate situations where a certain amount of time lapses after a first shot has disappeared and before the sound associated with a second shot is introduced.

sound balance: The all-important balance between various sound sources. While Hollywood regularly dips music and all *semi-sync* sounds to assure the intelligibility of dialogue, or arranges for a lull in the dialogue whenever a narratively important effect is to take place, Godard and Altman often allow separate sound sources to compete for our attention.

sound envelope: Hetero 6

sound hermeneutic: Cinema sound typically asks the question: "Where [does this sound come from]?" Visually identifying the source of the sound, the image usually responds: "Here!" The sound hermeneutic is the full question and answer process, as followed by the film spectator/auditor.

sound loop: A continuous loop of recorded sound, usually containing some variety of *generic sound,* designed to provide background sound throughout a scene, often in a *semi-sync* manner.

sound scale: The apparent size attributed to characters and objects by the characteristics of the sounds they make. For example, Fritz Lang's first American film, *Fury,* regularly chooses a sound scale corresponding to the image scale, whereas most Hollywood films pay attention to *scale matching* only in specially selected situations.

soundscape: The characteristic types of sound commonly heard in a given period or location. For example, the late nineteenth-century American soundscape was largely limited to unamplified, live sounds, while the soundscape of the mid-twenties included radio, electrically recorded disks, and public address, as well as live music, theater, and an increasing number of unmuffled motors. In much of the world, today's soundscape is characterized by competition among multiple amplified sounds, along with attempts (like the Walkman and acoustic panels) to restore individual aural autonomy in sound micro-atmospheres. Rural, maritime, and Third World soundscapes of course offer their own particularities, as do early morning and late evening soundscapes.

spatial signature: The testimony provided by every sound as to the spatial circumstances of its production. In order to recognize a given sound's spatial signature we must be sensitive to multiple aspects of the sound's physical nature, including its ratio of direct to indirect sound, its frequency range (as compared to culturally conditioned expectations), and its volume (with respect to perceived distance). Spatial signature can of course be manipulated by postproduction techniques such as gating, equalizing, filtering, or adding reverb.

sustain: Hetero 5

textual speech: Chion 2
theatrical speech: Chion 2
timbre: Hetero 1
vibration: Hetero 3
voice-over: Dark Corners 3

Notes

1. The Material Heterogeneity of Recorded Sound

1. Bordwell 1990. Not surprisingly, technical manuals aimed at the production of sound rather than at aesthetic analysis of sound present a far broader terminology. The best and most complete of these manuals is by Stanley R. Alten.

2. As a general rule, sound waves will be reflected by (that is, bounce off) obstacles having dimensions greater than the wavelength of the sound. Since audible sounds have wavelengths varying from about one and one-half inches (the C above the piano, 8372 Hz) to 70 feet (the C below the piano, 16 Hz), with the fundamentals of most sounds having wavelengths between one and eight feet, most acoustic situations will produce a combination of reflected and refracted (that is, bent) sound.

2. Sound Space

1. "Reproducing Sound from Separate Film," *JSMPE* 16 (Feb. 1931), p. 152. Just three months later a patent taken out by W. Bouwa, for "Apparatus and Method for Localization of Sound on Screen," was reported on in *JSMPE* 16.5 (May 1931), 643–44.

2. On the particular outlook of sound technicians during this period, see Altman 1992.

3. It is difficult, however, to reconcile Maxfield's total mastery over everything related to reverberation with an obvious oversight in his 1938 reprinting of the microphone placement chart from the 1931 article (p. 73). Whereas before 1931 only omnidirectional microphones were available in Hollywood, by 1938 the ribbon bidirectional mike and the cardioid mike were widely used, especially where dialogue had to be recorded with lenses of large focal length, such as those charted in Maxfield's graph. Now, it is generally recognized that the cardioid (directional) microphone collects far less reflected sound than an omnidirectional mike at the same distance, thus permitting placement of the cardioid mike at 1.7 times the distance appropriate for an omnidirectional mike. Is Maxfield's blind spot perhaps a sign of fidelity to the parent Bell/WE/ERPI complex? Whereas Olson's directional mikes were developed for RCA in the early thirties, Western Electric did not have a successful directional

mike until Marshall and Harry's 1939 offering ("A Cardioid Directional Microphone," *JSMPE* 33 [Sept. 1939], 260). One wonders if Maxfield would have repeated exactly the same chart had his own company had a successful directional mike on the market.

4. The tyranny of the continuous sound track is regularly reflected in early evaluations of sound film technique. Writing in *Variety* on June 25, 1930, Albert S. Howson points out that: "With surprising rapidity, rules governing the length of camera shots grew up, rules incidentally which do not hold good at all today. For example, if an artist began to sing in close-up it was thought inadvisable to cut into a long shot, because, at that time, the volume of sound remained the same and the thought was that it would be unnatural to have a figure suddenly diminish in size, yet continue to sing in the same volume of voice. It is interesting to note that this is frequently done today and that audiences adapt themselves readily to it." The practice of synching more than one camera to a single sound source, similar to current television studio mixing, was facilitated by a German invention permitting the synchronization of several motion picture cameras with a single sound recording device, thus assuring constant mismatches between sound scale and image scale. See "Report of the Progress Committee," *JSMPE* 13 (May 1929), 74. In 1934, RCA's Autophone 16mm sound camera was designed to give the same sound level no matter which of three lenses was being used. Note that, in spite of their electronic sophistication, current camcorders provide no automatic method of matching sound level to image scale.

5. On MGM's early development of the microphone boom, see Richardson. The importance of the microphone boom in freeing the image has been insufficiently recognized. While scholars regularly stress the development of cranes, camera booms, dollies, etc., as instrumental in mobilizing the camera, they often fail to recognize that none of these innovations in camera mobility could claim any success without parallel innovations in microphone mobility.

6. On this point see especially the work of Dreher, Hunt and Maxfield, cited above; in addition, see Mueller and Altman 1986a.

7. It is interesting to note that the sound for Hawks' 1938 film, *Bringing Up Baby*, which reveals almost no scale-matching, was engineered by none other than John L. Cass, the outspoken early thirties proponent of the unified body approach, with ears at a fixed distance from eyes. In the early golf course scene, for example, Kathryn Hepburn's voice retains the same volume level whether she is shot in medium shot through a windshield or in close-up with no intervening windshield. The subsequent bar scene offers the same medium close-up sound quality no matter what the image scale.

8. Note that the examples from *Union Pacific* and *Only Angels Have Wings* are chosen more or less at random to exemplify the standard practice of the late thirties. While cutting during dialogue and other markers of obliviousness to scale-matching of course existed in the late twenties and early thirties, these techniques constitute no more than a small proportion of the extremely diverse sound solutions devised by early sound technicians; only later would the number of potentially acceptable solutions be reduced, and the rejection of scale-matching become generalized (with the standard exception of point-of-audition sound, discussed later in the article).

9. DeForest, 72. A *Variety* sidebar, on July 25, 1928, suggests that talking shorts, as compared to vaudeville, guaranteed everyone a front row seat (p. 4).

10. Dreher 1931, 756ff. The most important technical study on the relationship between

intelligibility and naturalness was conducted by Harvey Fletcher (1929) of Bell Labs; see especially pp. 281ff.

11. On the topic of theatrical sound reinforcement and the theater's progressive conformity to the new code of reality/intelligibility represented by sound cinema, see Burris-Meyer.

12. In theater, the late twenties and thirties were a period of intense experimentation with new standards of comprehensibility. In 1928, Eugene O'Neill gave voice to his characters' innermost thoughts in *Strange Interlude*. The previous year saw the formation of the most influential directors' group of its time, the Cartel (Jouvet, Baty, Dullin, and Pitoëff). For an analysis of the Cartel's concern to stress the text above all else, see Jomaron.

13. For examples of this confusion, see Doane 1980a, 54–55; Doane 1980b, 45–46; Bordwell 1985a, 302, and Neale, 97.

14. Maxfield 1931 and Maxfield 1938. Note how seldom point-of-audition sound occurs in the early years of sound cinema. The "My Gal Sal" number of *The Jazz Singer*, for example, places Yudelson in the bar attached to the music hall where young Jakie is singing. Instead of taking this perfect opportunity to bridge the two spaces by having Yudelson clearly hear and recognize Jakie's voice, Director Alan Crosland awkwardly brings Yudelson within eyesight of Jakie. Transitions like this one, handled visually in 1927, will regularly be handled aurally a decade later, with the help of point-of-audition sound.

15. On this important jurisdictional episode, see Altman 1991b.

16. On microphone development during this period, and its relation to representational codes, see Altman 1985b and 1986a.

3. Reading, Writing, and Representing Sound

1. Levin makes some provocative connections to the notion of "aura" developed in Benjamin. Unfortunately, by appeals to nearness, co-presence, etc. as essential attributes of sound, Levin appears to be "mourning a loss with respect to 'live' music" despite his explicit objections to the contrary.

2. Levin, 57–58. The phrase is not Levin's but is a fair characterization of his position.

3. PP. 24–32. See, especially, his comments on the social dimensions of sound's "objecthood."

4. No doubt the "transparency" of the original/copy relationship accounts for the efficacy of sound recording's ideological effects. However, ideological analysis is not the necessary basis of a comprehensive theory of sound representation, but one of its essential components.

5. Altman's "The Material Heterogeneity of Recorded Sound" is an important point of reference. Very often it is precisely those characteristics of a sound which indicate that we are not getting the "best" perspective on it which are most salient for us, since they indicate, among other things, whether the sound is directed toward us, whether the source is advancing toward or retreating from us, etc.

6. Transformations wrought by the "original" environment might be identical to those wrought by recording, and therefore, neither "technology"—concert hall or radio— is inherently more "transformative." The primary difference is the means of *commodification* employed.

7. Cited in Levin 1984, 67. In fact, even the commodification of sound accomplished

by recording is not accomplished by recording popular music, since in its very structure it is already "pre-consumed" or simply structured for mass consumption. See Adorno 1982, 270–318.

8. In fact, Tom Levin has just published an excellent piece on Adorno's early gramophone essays (1991). There he explicitly retreats from the claims I criticize here, and advances an argument which I believe confirms my own, even employing the same vocabulary (inscription, iterability, citation, etc.) I advance in the latter half of this essay, although neither of us met until each had long since written these essays. I have benefited a great deal from some brief conversations with Tom Levin on this subject, and thank him.

9. This approach seems validated by Raymond Williams' arguments about the importance of art as *practice* rather than object, and his analysis of TV as a cultural form rather than as a technology. Cf. Williams 1980, 1974.

10. Heidegger's much-discussed example of the hammer in *Being and Time* seems to support my argument. A hammer, so the argument goes, is only a hammer through its use, i.e., in view of hammering. Indeed, the hammer "itself" is said to "withdraw" in its use. As such, tools are always already inserted in a pragmatic context which fundamentally defines them. See, for example, Heidegger 1962, 95–105, and *passim*.

11. Foti, 65. Foti does a commendable job sorting out the positions of these three thinkers on the nature of the representational image. I am heavily indebted to her interpretation.

12. André Gaudreault's work on film narration provides an interesting parallel. In particular, his division of "monstration" into "scenic monstration" and "filmic monstration" indicates a sensitivity to the extent to which it is in the field of the pro-filmic (or "pro-phonographic") that much of the work of narration is accomplished.

13. It might be argued that, ultimately, "voices" (be they Jolson's, Lahr's or Mischa Elman's violin) were the only sounds that Hollywood had an inherent *need* to reproduce accurately in synchronization. Although the theoretical discourse promoted the importance of recording music (an emphasis derived from the Vitaphone's "disc" format?), almost every "problem" with the apparatuses involved either synchrony or dialogue—rarely, if ever, inaccurate rendering of instrumental timbre.

14. Although in the Vitaphone shorts (e.g., the *Tannhäuser* overture) the moving violin bow, the cymbal crash and various other visible manifestations of sync replace the moving lips, it is not difficult to see the analogy between these types of sounds and speech.

15. Recorded musical accompaniment for films such as *Don Juan* and *Old San Francisco* was important to the extent that it further standardized the commodity, but the added cost to producers could not have been an effective inducement to convert to sound. The musical and sound effects accompaniment typical of both films was not necessarily any better synchronized than that provided by a gifted theater orchestra, so novelty was minimal. Warners stood to profit most through the presentation of vaudeville and concert acts which were salable precisely by providing their signature sounds in a manner which left no doubt that the persons depicted on the screen were producing those sounds. Concerns with sound source were prominent in Bell Labs' Public Address research as well. See, e.g., Downey.

16. This is similar to Altman's claim about the relation between technology and technique, but is perhaps broader in application. See Altman, 1984.

17. Aside, that is, from certain forms of (narrative driven) ethnic accent. The importance of these deviances from the King's, or rather Bell Labs', English is their ability to provide motivations for certain forms of melodramatic narrative. Warners' *Old San Francisco, Noah's Ark,* and *The Jazz Singer* all attest to this use of accent (the first only in intertitles). Moreover, such accents rarely if ever impede dialogue intelligibility, while they often provide important character information and plot complication.

18. See Altman's discussion of "for-me-ness" in Altman 1985b and 1986a.

19. Interestingly, the tendency to think of sound representations as records of perception duplicates the early tendency to treat the individual shots of, say, a chase film, as autonomous wholes whose unity is provided by point of view rather than a higher-level narrative unity. See Gunning, Musser, and Gaudreault.

20. For example, Hunt, 481–2. It also makes clear that very "normal" kinds of sound recording paid no heed to the credo which claimed that the "eyes and ears" of the recording apparatuses had to be linked like those in a real body. It further indicates that at least a portion of the technicians involved in research around problems in sound film were aware that Hollywood was primarily in the business of selling narratives, not optical and acoustic effigies of real experience. For a good example of a technician grappling with the pair intelligibility/naturalness see Dreher, 1931.

21. Bartholemew, 25–33. The investigators seem fully aware that their standards are, if not conventional, at least agreed upon by groups of "professionals."

22. The attitude that it is *we* who are inadequate to and must conform to the demands of the technology is a fairly widespread idea in this period. See, for example, Banning, who exhorts us to reform our speaking habits to the demands of the telephone.

23. A notable exception are those sound effects requiring a strong dose of spatial acoustics in order to be generically recognizable. Hence we often get sound/image scale mismatches which do not disturb us in the least because the rendering of the sound stresses its "name" rather than its actuality.

24. Fletcher 1929, 280–285. This remarkable work stood as the standard of acoustic research for at least two decades, and merits a study of its own.

25. In other words, the meaning of any writing is radically dependent upon context, and therefore cannot be understood as self-defining, or as defined by any *particular* discursive situation. This form of iterability is constitutive of speech as well, which I would argue is just as "inscribed" in particular contexts as is writing.

4. "She Sang Live, But the Microphone Was Turned Off"

1. I am indebted to John Peters, Scott Curtis, Edward Branigan, and Rick Altman for their comments on earlier versions of this essay.

2. Of course, the proliferation of VCRs and the practice of time-shift recording have changed this situation so that pseudo-live TV programming increasingly might be thought of as that which is "to be recorded."

3. The textual practice of sampling in contemporary popular music similarly problematizes the unity of the event posited by the *fully recorded* (position IV). By foregrounding different moments, spaces and registers of production (different instances of origin), sampling questions the entire notion of original and originality (hence the frequent copyright disputes). More than simply a (post)modernist gesture that foregrounds textual production and the act of representing, sampling's multiple

260 / Sound Theory/Sound Practice

instances of production are constituent of a particular kind of textuality and commodity, and hence the positing of a specific kind of subjectivity. Here, the relationship between the auditor and the text's posited event involves the recognition of a plurality of origins-events.

Introduction: Sound History

1. Thanks to my colleague, Lauren Rabinovitz, for bringing this intriguing example to my attention.

2. "Radio Talking Pictures," *American Cinematographer*, April 1, 1922: 24. Note that the Rothacker experiment is far from an isolated instance. A German medical lecture broadcast by radio and synchronized with a projector is reported by the London Times for February 25, 1927, as well as by *Motion Pictures Today* (March 26, 1927; 6); and *Transactions of the Society of Motion Picture Engineers* 11, No. 29 (July 1927; 24). Two years later, *Variety* reported (May 29, 1929; 2B) that Pathé's sound newsreel crew resorted to a radio hookup with New York to record the Kentucky Derby during a Churchill Downs downpour (in sync with location cameras!).

3. Jean-Louis Comolli has made a similar point apropos of technical categories such as the "close-up" (Comolli 1985).

4. This term is based on the notion of "reading formations," as defined in Bennett.

5. For contemporary testimony on this problem see S. D. Humphrey and M. Finley, *A System of Photography, Containing an Explicit Detail of the Whole Process of Daguerrotype* (Canandaigua, N.Y.: Ontario Messenger, 1849), 6–7; and Antoine Claudet, "Researches on the Theory of the Principal Phaenomena of Photography in the Daguerreotype Process," *London, Edinburgh, and Dublin Philosophical Magazine and Journal of Science* (November, 1849), 10–11; both in *The Daguerrotype Process: Three Treatises, 1840–49*, ed. Robert A. Sobieszek (New York: Arno, 1973). On the general history of lens development, see Rudolf Kingslake's authoritative *A History of the Photographic Lens* (Boston: Academic Press, 1989).

6. This approach to history writing will receive fuller definition and appropriate exemplification in another publication: Rick Altman, *Writing Sound History;* volume one of *Hollywood Sound Systems* (forthcoming).

6. Historical and Theoretical Issues in the Coming of Recorded Sound to the Cinema

1. This is to speak only of *historical* understanding. One may argue that contemporary thinking does represent a *theoretical* advance on Bazin; the problem is to make it help us better understand film history.

2. Not only was so-called "silent" cinema almost never silent; it was also only rarely without color of some sort. Black and white seems to have become standard for the early talkies for two unrelated reasons: because it took some time to correct problems of interference between color and sound processes (except with disk systems); and as an economy measure, because the great expense of the conversion to recorded sound made the additional costs of color seem rarely justified.

3. Though it would be an exaggeration to claim a radical difference between this argument and Bazin's, since he defined "realism," precisely, as mechanization.

4. The most obvious limitation of the book, for the study of film sound, is how little attention it devotes to the crucial matter of how (and why) the conventions of the sound track evolved. And evolve they did, very quickly. Matters like the relative

volume and reverberation levels of music, dialogue, and effects, or the varying acoustic perspectives of different microphone positions and their relation to camera distance, were resolved in less than three years, though not without some (now often quite funny) false starts. Arguably the best way to begin study of this crucial area is not with the early "100% talkies," but with part-talkies like *Noah's Ark* (Curtiz/ Warners, 1929).

5. Using a list of almost 30,000 films produced between 1915 and 1960, the authors used a random-number table and the relative happenstance of print availability to arrive at a sample of one hundred titles, roughly thirty percent of which is "silent."

6. Of the three great cinema art movements of the 1920s, Expressionism seems the least oppositional to classical Hollywood style. Its demise in Germany was largely related to politics, though the coincidence of new technology and new political context is—here as elsewhere—striking.

7. Translating America: The Hollywood Multilinguals 1929–1933

1. The incapacity of the model to allow for "contradiction" or alternative modes of development is also an important point in Barry King's review of Bordwell, Staiger and Thompson's *Classical Hollywood Cinema*, but applies, *mutatis mutandis,* to all theoretical constructs drawing on the concept of "basic film apparatus," as Rick Altman points out (Altman 1984).

2. Gomery, 84. In this article Gomery's aim is to adjust or even counter, as too simplistic, claims made by Robert Sklar and Thomas Guback regarding the emancipatory role of language for the European film industries in the early thirties. Gomery is arguing that the impact of cartelization, as well as adversary economic factors— various modes of state interventions in the form of quotas, and the impact of the Depression on the US film industry—need to be given their proper role along with the issue of language difference. When it becomes necessary to address directly one form of interface between economy and language, in this case dubbing, Gomery misaligns them in a symptomatic fashion, however. While the fundamental language problem emerges because of the audiences' "adverse reaction to (dubbing)" (83), leading in turn to the FLV experiment, it is eliminated when "dubbing greatly improved and became less expensive" (84). Shifting the agency of development from reception to production, that is, from the terrain of aesthetics/ideology to that of economy, allows him then to proceed with a scenario where issues of national film industries remain defined in terms of the logic of capital. On the limits of this model of explanation see especially Edward Branigan, "Color and Cinema: Problems in the Writing of History" (in Nichols 1985).

3. Three notable exceptions are: de Uzabel, which includes a chapter on the impact of the Spanish- and Portugese-language versions on the Latin American market; the more recent Vincendeau, overlapping to some extent (especially in its account of the procedures involved in the production of FLVs) with the area covered here; and Chittick, considering the use in FLVs of a single star, Buster Keaton.

4. For a case study of the historical link between the earliest responses to the problem of American sound films and current aesthetic policies, see for instance Nowell-Smith, "Italy *Sotto Voce.*"

5. To my knowledge the only article in English addressing among other things the problem of linguistic heterogeneity in relation to cinema is Ella Shohat's and Robert Stam's "Hollywood After Babylon: Language, Power, Difference."

6. Thompson, 164; *Variety* 16 May 1928, 45.

7. Tom Hoier, "An American Actor Answers to Mr. Atkinson," *Variety* July 15, 1925, 2; "Ashton Stevens Answers Atkinson of England," *Variety* July 8, 1925, 3; "The English—Indeed!," *Variety* July 8, 1925, 16.

8. More explicitly class-conscious versions of a similar anxiety were registered in Britain around the spectacle of Ford workers arriving at the factory in their own Model T's (Costigliola, especially chapter 5).

9. B. P. Schulberg, "American Film Producer on Atkinson," *Variety,* August 5, 1925, 22.

10. For instance, Harald Josse's meticulously documented history of the development of sound film in Germany mentions, in a discussion of Tri-Ergon's first public experimental screening, that while the program was announced only to include well-known opera arias, a jazz band and the American duo "The Dodge Sisters" were added on request of the theatre management (Josse, 235–36). For an evocative study of how jazz and modern dance are the carriers of "cosmopolitanism" in the service of American interests, see Bragaglia.

11. Hence, for instance, MGM's worry that it couldn't find a sufficient number of Spanish-speaking Chinese extras ("celestiales hispanoparlantes") for a Spanish version of the railway drama *Wu-Li-Chang* (in *Sound Waves* 4/11, Spanish edition, October 1930, 36).

12. Formulations of a general and vaguely aesthetic opposition to lip-syncing appear, for instance, in the editorials of a semi-professional publication like *Sound Waves*. In January 1930 Geoffrey Shurlock, Paramount's foreign production supervisor (and in that respect perhaps particularly favorably inclined toward the FLVs) simply states: "It has been irrefutably proven that foreign-language dialog cannot be 'dubbed' into a picture made in another tongue" (10).

13. An option earlier vigorously denied by the Hays office. In *Variety* of October 24, 1928 Paul Kohner of Universal mentioned for the first time the possibility of FLV operations abroad, and was immediately criticized by AMPAS, which had throughout discouraged the idea of moving American productions onto foreign territory (6). More detailed accounts of the actual operations of the Joinville studio can be gathered primarily from autobiographies covering the period. See for instance Adolphson, Andrieu, Pagnol and Witta-Montrobert, as well as more general surveys by Andrew and Vincendeau.

14. With the shift to sound, companies began to rehearse for substantial lengths of time—up to ten days before shooting (*Variety,* November 14, 1928, 4). While this was no doubt primarily a way of minimizing problems in dealing with the new technologies, the routine may also have developed as a result of wholesale purchases of theatre repertory companies by several film majors.

15. Remakes, by contrast, tend to be clearly separable (in time/space of production) interpretations of the same synopsis. For an intricate analysis of the implications of such separation, see the comparison of the French (1959) and the American (1983) versions of *Á bout de souffle* by Pamela Falkenberg.

16. This essay addresses only the American, that is, the most radical variant of the FLVs. The procedure itself existed also, however, on a smaller scale (usually bilaterally) between various European countries (in a few instances, as in the case of UFA, producing an English-speaking version for the American market). There are thus, most importantly, Franco-German, as well as German-Italian and Franco-Italian versions (as well as a few British-French-German versions), German-Czech

versions, etc. While these "bilinguals" could be considered, from an institutional point of view, as a precedent for the later, quite common co-productions (with their *ad hoc*—rather than serial—assembly, financing, distribution), like FLVs proper they generated two or more non-identical texts from the same *découpage*, tailoring them for two or more particular national/linguistic audiences.

17. The other versions were *Une Femme a Menti* (French, dir. Charles de Rochefort, 1930); *Seine Freundin Annette* (German, dir. Felix Basch, 1930); *Perché No?* (Italian, dir. Amleto Palermi, 1930) and *Dona Mentiras* (Spanish, dir. Adelqui Millar, 1930).

18. One way of formalizing these impressions might be with the help of the concept of "involuntary" or "unintentional" signs, which Martin Esslin borrows from Umberto Eco. In this category fall both signals perceived by the spectator while not intended as such (generated for instance by miscasting a character), and signals intended to signify precisely "unintentional" reactions (blushing, minute body movements etc.— types of responses on the borderline between biology and cultural conventions) whose function is to create the effect of spontaneity. A shot-by-shot comparison of the American and the foreign-language version should permit an understanding of variations in the interaction of the predetermined *découpage* and what there is left of the individual performance.

19. In both versions there is, by contrast, one foreign character, a heavily accented maid with one speaking line. The same signifier is thus "mythologized" (in Barthes' sense) in two different structures—Colbert's as thickening the character (the code of the real), the maid's as establishing a class hierarchy (the cultural code)—and it is the latter, the code of common knowledge, that gives the text away as American (foreignness being aligned with lower class—a formation completely alien to the ethnically homogeneous Sweden, where a maid would most likely be a peasant woman speaking perhaps with a regional but distinctly not a "non-Swedish" accent).

20. In this context it is possible to be reminded of Brecht's theories of character construction in the epic theatre, where an actor's relationship to the role is to be determined by exterior circumstances rather than by an imitation of introspective psychology: "The idea is that the spectator should be put in a position where he can make comparisons about everything that influences the way in which human beings behave" (from *Brecht on Theatre*, quoted in Salomon, 363). The point is, of course, that while in the FLVs the commodified nature of Hollywood cinema appears in its most extreme form, the recognition of this fact (i.e. the didactic working through of the contradictions at hand) is not part of the pleasure conventionally expected from the classical cinema. It might, however, be worth registering that it was in connection with a film made in both a German and a (very successful) French version—namely G.W. Pabst's *Threepenny Opera*—that Brecht took up most extensively the problem of origin and appropriation in cinematic discourse. His argument intended to show the contradictory status of authorship in commercial filmmaking is summarized in his "Der Dreigroschenprozess: ein soziologisches Experiment."

21. On the technology and history of this optical trick process see for instance Brownlow, 323 and 575; Pasinetti, 192; Salt (1983), 234, and Thompson, 162.

22. Had the institutional structure of the Hollywood studios been subject to change, the FLVs might have been a first step toward an increasingly decentralized type of multinational film industry. In May 1929, visiting Warsaw, Adolph Zukor seems to have promised that FLV's were simply a first step in a new phase, the final goal of which would be 100% Polish films based on Polish literature and folklore (quoted in Halberda, 22–25).

23. Thompson quotes a 1930 Department of Commerce document dividing the potential European film export territories into three groups: those that could be supplied with an FLV in their own language (English, French, German, Spanish); those that would not accept a "major" FLV from the first group but constituted too small a market to warrant a FLV in their own language (for instance the Scandinavian countries, Poland, Hungary, Czechoslovakia); and those that would accept an FLV with subtitles in their "native" language (for instance the German version in the Baltic states or Finland) (in Thompson, 160). The division is worth considering for its curious mix of the issues of function versus status of a foreign language: while for instance in Czechoslovakia, Poland or Hungary the German versions could have been released as far as comprehension is concerned (given the substantial numbers of German speakers in both countries), it was clear that in the wake of the Austro-Hungarian Empire's disintegration German was not acceptable to the political and cultural establishment of the countries (see also note 25 below).

24. C. J. North and N. D. Golden, for instance, judge subtitles to be "out so far as dialog films are concerned, but still may be employed on 'musicals' where a minimum of dialog is used" (757).

25. It was for instance the very fact of *hearing* the much-resented German that caused havoc to the point of street demonstrations and physical destruction of the interiors of several movie theatres in Prague in fall of 1930. According to some sources, the nationalist fervor, far from entirely spontaneous, was discreetly sponsored by American firms hoping to edge out the German competition. Instead, distributors chose (given the shortage of domestic films) either FLVs, silent versions with Czech intertitles, or French versions with Czech subtitles (Brož and Frída, 14–16).

26. As Nowell–Smith points out, this across-the-board decision had a paradoxical impact on the Italian sound film in general: due to the substantial investments made in sound dubbing equipment, the practice of postsynchronization effectively contaminated domestic filmmaking to the point where the original sound track itself today has an acoustic quality that is exactly like the dubbed "substitute" sound track of foreign films.

27. This is particularly interesting in light of the fact that Mussolini (along with Will Hays and G. B. Shaw) was among the very first public personalities to appear in the new medium, actively pursuing the possibilities of using William Fox's Movietone system for propaganda purposes (efforts furthermore linked to the need to reach the very large Italian immigrant community in the USA). The ideology of totalitarianism and the technology of totalization pair off here in an exemplary fashion.

28. Most often, the pretext for this debate was provided by the activities at Joinville or other directly industry-related matters (in the numerous commentaries, for instance, on the vagaries of the French language abroad—in the USA as well as in the French colonies—published in the magazines *Cinémonde* and *Ciné-Miroir*), but pure fiction (for instance Paul Morand's 1934 xenophobic novel from the world of French cinema, *France la Douce),* and "serious" cultural essays (for instance René Jeanne's two long essays in the *Revue des Deux Mondes*) also explicitly postulate the link between loss of national identity and the sound film. Indeed, the point of departure of Ginette Vincendeau's article (see note 3 above) is the very intensity of the resentment against the multilinguals on the part of the high-art critics, a resentment cast in terms of national culture; she, in turn, is interested in the multilinguals primarily as an instance of *popular* cinema.

29. In *Variety* an MGM spokesman declared that the studio would nonetheless look for

"lesser stage talent who could use the job," in order to proceed with the dubbing needed to amortize the American product abroad ([July 28, 1931], 11).

30. On the broad outlines of this legislation see Léglise, 263–65. It is also in the course of these negotiations between France and the USA that the foundation was established for the proportional mix of "versions originales" (i.e. subtitled foreign films) and dubbed foreign films which has so fundamentally shaped the subsequent development of French film culture.

31. Here Doane is drawing extensively on Pascal Bonitzer's essay "Les silences de la voix," *Cahiers du Cinéma* (1975) 256, especially his point that the example of voice-off is indicative, on the one hand, of the epistemological power of the disembodied voice in cinema, and on the other, of the capacity of the narrative cinema to capitalize on the marginal anxiety generated by this disembodiment.

32. Another model might be pursued with the help of ideas suggested in Edward Branigan's "Sound and Epistemology in Film." While his aim, too, is to revise the status of sound in the overall understanding of the filmic experience, Branigan suggests that two different (and in effect "contradictory") cognitive processes may be involved in ascribing a sound to its source: the "top-down" model of expectations and the "bottom-up" model of perceptual processes. One implication is that it might finally be impossible to isolate *sound* as one of the fundamental dimensions of the filmic experience; instead much more narrow limits would have to be set to the object of investigation. Clearly, the notion of unity as it is presented by a psychoanalytically informed film theory would be abandoned here; a dubbed or a subtitled film would simply not be in the same category as a "version originale" at all. In that case the question would be: what *kind* of object is a "foreign" film? An advantage to this approach is that it skirts the invariably *normative* dimension that accompanies any explanation founded on the concept of "unity" (putting more emphasis on the conventionalized character of reception).

33. Hence the permanent alliance of certain American actors with their dubbers. For a few years exclusive voice contracts were drawn for instance for Joan Crawford's and Marie Dressler's French "alter-voices" Isabelle Kloncovsky and Paula Marsa (*Variety* [October 4, 1932], 11).

34. By the mid-thirties Hollywood's exports (that is, Hollywood cinema's international attraction) stabilized—if not up to the pre-sound 80–95% of several European markets, at least back to substantial profits. Thomas Guback and Robert Sklar attribute the partial loss in the early thirties to competition from domestic producers and to the new importance of national language cinemas—points which Gomery thinks must be seen in context of the fall of the US dollar and the Depression (Gomery, 93).

35. The subtlest discussion of the meaning a rising American star may have had for a European audience at approximately this moment is Thomas Elsaesser's "Lulu and the Meter Man: Louise Brooks, Pabst and *Pandora's Box*," *Screen* 24, No. 4–5 (1983). This example—drawn from, and carefully elaborated within, one particular silent German film—illuminates all the better the idiom in which Americanness, femininity and modernity could have been articulated as "cinema itself" in the context of one European high culture. A more general (and in that respect less interesting) formulation of the difference between silent and sound film stars by Gilles Gourdon divides the former group into three categories: (1) actors who efface themselves with respect to their character so completely that only the role remains visible; (2) actors who vampirize their character and force it to take on their own mythical persona;

(3) actors who identify with their character but nonetheless manage to impress it partially with their own persona. The silent stars vanishing with the onset of sound would here belong to the second group, "their mannered acting excluding in effect communication for the benefit of a sort of sovereignty that refers to itself and gratifies itself in a kind of narcissistic fascination" (Gourdon, 26–27). What emerges from both discussions is that the quality embodied in a new star is something like "an epitome of expressive neutrality"; and that the paradoxical nature of such a figure is exactly what makes it both multipliable and reproducible. If we ask, finally, what makes the same figure/star equidistant to both its "domestic" (American) and "foreign" spectator, the question should bring us back to the issue of emergent "nationalization" of the USA touched upon at the beginning of this paper.

8.   1950s Magnetic Sound: The Frozen Revolution

1.   For a discussion of the concept of participation, see Belton 1990.

2.   Sound editors, accustomed to editing by reading the modulation on optical tracks, initially resisted magnetic tracks because it was impossible to "see" sound on them. See Stewart, 58; also Elisabeth Weis's interviews with Rudi Fehr and Ed Scheid, 1975. Loren Ryder soon developed a "modulation scribe," which traced a varying amplitude line onto the magnetic film, enabling editors to read its modulation visually (Ryder, 529).

   Scheid reports to Weis that magnetic tape facilitated the recording of sound effects to match action on screen; previously, library sound effects footage had to be cut to match the action; with magnetic film, the effects could be recorded, after filming, to the image as it was screened in a re-recording studio.

3.   William Lafferty reports that "full-coated 35-mm magnetic film cost $20 to $30 per thousand feet less than the cost of a thousand feet of processed sound negative and accompanying print, the savings compounded by the magnetic medium's reusability" and that "a study by Loren Ryder indicated . . . that for every half-hour of sound recording for 35-mm film, magnetic recording saved over 82% of the cost of the optical negative-positive process with no loss in sound quality" (Lafferty, 184).

4.   Letter, dated January 7, 1958, Selznick folder, Box 111, Sponable Collection, Columbia University Libraries.

5.   Memo from Zanuck to All Producers, Directors, Writers, Editors, dated December 24, 1954, Box 10, Philip Dunne Collection, USC Archives of Performing Arts.

6.   In a memo to Skouras, Herbert Bragg of the research and development unit wrote that "it is clearly a difficult problem to make good use of the fourth track in such a way as to enhance the picture and, at the same time, produce a picture which will be compelling in those theatres having only three tracks, and still again, in those theatres using only optical sound. The very fact that we release pictures in several types of sound versions seems to me to preclude the possibility of putting anything on the fourth track which is absolutely essential to an understanding of the picture." Memo, dated April 6, 1955, "Skouras" or "Sound" file, Box 112, Sponable Collection.

7.   A 12kc signal controlled the fourth track, turning it on only when needed in order to reduce system noise. Activation of the fourth track introduced an audible new sound "presence" in the theater, thus signalling attentive spectators to the track's impending operation. This tended to draw unwanted attention to the technology, making it "visible."

8. This practice actually dates back to 1953, when Fox began to pan and travel mono tracks in order to dub foreign language releases of magnetic stereo films; it was also used in several instances on dialogue in the original, English-language versions. See letter, dated June 10, 1953, from Earl Sponable to Carl Faulkner and letter, dated July 21, 1953, from N. Katkoff to Spyros Skouras, "Dubbing" file, Box 94, Sponable Collection, Columbia University Libraries.

9. The SMPTE's "Progress Committee Report for 1956" noted that the number of 4-track stereo release prints declined in 1956 in comparison to the number available in 1955 *JSMPTE* 66.5 (May 1957), 246. The 35mm stereo output of studios other than Fox dropped markedly in 1957 to a total of seven—five at M-G-M and two at Warner Bros. See "Progress Committee Report for 1957," *JSMPTE* 67.5 (May 1958), 295.

10. Letter from Theo Hoffman to Spyros Skouras, dated April 6, 1957, Box 114, Sponable Collection, Columbia University Libraries.

11. For Comolli, for example, primitive depth of field did not evolve directly into the deep focus of William Wyler in the late 1930s and of Orsen Welles in the early 1940s but took a detour through the shift from orthochromatic to panchromatic film stock, which sacrificed the depth of images available on the former for the more realistic range of tones and "colors" on the latter (Comolli 1986, 437).

12. See "Edison's Vitascope," *The New York Dramatic Mirror* 35, No. 904 (April 25, 1896): 20; and "The Cinématographe at Keith's," *The New York Dramatic Mirror* 36, No. 914 (July 4, 1896): 17. Cited in Pratt, 13–14.

13. The familiar phrase is actually a condensation of a description of the Cinématographe which appeared in *La Poste* on December 30, 1895: "C'est la vie même, c'est le mouvement pris sur le vif." See Sadoul, 119.

14. *Filma,* No. 260 (9/11/29), cited in Neale, 96.

15. Program booklet for *This Is Cinerama,* circa 1952.

16. "The CinemaScope Demonstration," *Harrison's Reports* 35, No. 12 (March 21, 1953).

17. Herbert Bragg, Speech on Stereophonic Sound, Twentieth Century-Fox Press Conference, Hotel Plaza (New York City), March 30, 1954. Publicity file, Box 106, Sponable Collection.

18. Approximately 30 surround speakers were installed in the Roxy for the premiere of *The Robe* (though no mention is made of ceiling speakers). See letter from Earl Sponable to Harry Enequist, dated November 20, 1953, "AGA" file, Box 86, Sponable Collection.

19. Memo from Zanuck to Sid Rogell, Carl Faulkner, Sol Halprin, Alfred Newman, All Producers, All Producers-Directors, dated January 8, 1955, Box 10, Philip Dunne Collection, USC Archives of Performing Arts.

20. *Ibid.*

21. Willem Bouwmeester and John Harvey of the International Cinerama Society, in conversation with the author, May 12, 1991.

22. Cinerama Program Booklet.

23. Zanuck memo on *How to Marry a Millionaire* sent to Nunnally Johnson, Jean Negulesco, Sid Rogell, Sol Halprin, Earl Sponable, dated March 25, 1953, Zanuck file, Box 116, Sponable Collection.

24. Zanuck reported that in *Battle Cry* "a character on the screen would be talking to someone off the screen and the off-stage reply would *definitely* be off stage. This gave a real sense of audience participation and . . . the effect is excellent." See Zanuck memo to Sid Rogell et. al., dated January 8, 1955, Philip Dunne Collection, USC.

25. "Progress Committee Report," *JSMPTE* 64.5 (May 1955), 233.

26. Memo from Ryder to Earl Sponable, dated June 16, 1953, Box 119, Paramount folder, Sponable Collection, Columbia University Libraries.

27. Bob Gitt, UCLA film archivist, in conversation, January 8, 1989.

28. Limited experiments with FM/AM radio broadcasts of music in stereo, as well as high-end home stereo tape players, also tended to identify the stereo format with music for pre-1953 audiences.

29. Al Lewis, interview with the author, October 20, 1990.

30. Certain studios, such as Columbia, never even used the fourth track, according to the SMPTE Progress Report Committee, *JSMPTE* 64.5 (May 1955), 233.

9.   Women's Voices in Third World Cinema

1. In an article in *The New York Times,* Flora Lewis writes that "the idea of a 'third world' . . . was generated at the 1955 Bandung conference" and "reinforced at the 1961 non-aligned summit conference in Belgrade." The term's original "purpose was to reject the polarization of the world into blocs led by the U.S. and the Soviet Union, to map a third way, and to spur decolonization" ("Words and Work," *The New York Times,* January 18, 1985, p. 27).

2. Adding "within which as a woman . . . I am created and trying to create" (Rich, 1986, 212).

3. Martin and Mohanty note that the "claim to a lack of identity or positionality" is a colonialist gesture of the West's, "based on privilege, on a refusal to accept responsibility for one's implication in actual historical or social relations, on a denial that positionalities exist or that they matter, the denial of one's own personal history and the claim to a total separation from it" (208). The result of this gesture, according to Martin, Mohanty and Minnie Pratt, is "cultural impersonation," taking on " 'the identity of the Other in order to avoid not only guilt but pain and self-hatred' " (Pratt, 207).

4. If "a place on the map is a locatable place in history," Trinh is all over the map, moving from Vietnam to Paris, Berkeley to Dakar, Senegal, framed as her current project "India/China" suggests by the unique colonial conjunction of the place known as French Indo-China, otherwise known as Vietnam. Her refusal to be restricted to an "insider" position as the West's authority on Asia by making films originally about Africa is something she discusses in her 1988 article.

5. While it is important to remember that this is a fictionalized recreation of reality (an enactment of a documentary), the accents are not "acted." They attest to the *speaker's* "otherness" or distance from the language she speaks, and by one remove, to the *character's* distance/absence from the world of the speaker (the U.S.) and the world of the film. This accent is one that links Trinh herself, through her voice-over narration, to the actresses/characters in the film.

6. In Peckham, 35. For Peckham, "translation is a truer image of the interpenetration of textualities that occur in an individual" (35).

7. It has also been pointed out that the film does not directly address contemporary *Vietnamese* political issues either, including the invasion of Cambodia, the boat people, and their exploitation by pirates. The latter may indeed be alluded to by the slow motion, grainy black-and-white footage of people in boats that recurs throughout the film and is especially privileged by being placed near the beginning and the end. The ambiguous beauty of these images situates them in the realm of poetry (where they are undeniably powerful) but at the same time limits their ability to serve as references to specific political events.

8. This argument takes Rick Altman's concept of "ventriloquism" (synchronization's illusion that the image produces the sound) a step further (1980c). To quote Edward Branigan, in this film synchronization itself forms the foundation for "a staging of a documentary about *voices and bodies which are absent*" (my emphasis). At once we move into the realm of Metz's "imaginary signifier" where the essential cinematic illusion of presence signifies a profound absence. I would argue that Trinh rewrites this absence as a *political* absence—of the exile, of those left behind, and of the exclusion from historical consciousness of women's experience of both exile and abandonment. I am also indebted to Kaja Silverman for her provocative reading of the film's presentation of the body, raised in discussion at the Sound Symposium, Iowa City, April 1990.

10. The Sound of the Early Warner Brothers Cartoon

1. I would like to thank Rick Altman, Jennifer Barker, and Steve Wurtzler for their valuable comments on an earlier draft of this essay, and I would also like to extend my appreciation to Leith Adams of the Warner Bros. Archive at USC.

2. Warner Bros. Music Legal Files, Box No. 1110, Warner Bros. Archives, USC School of Cinema-Television, Los Angeles, CA.

3. This refers to the process of acquiring permission to use copyrighted material.

4. Memo from the Warner Bros. Music Legal Files, Box No. 1109.

5. This method is certainly not limited to animation. Ernst Lubitsch did the same thing for the wedding march at the beginning of *The Love Parade* (1929).

6. Charles Wolfe discusses the issue of vocal performance in the Vitaphone shorts at length in "On the Track of the Vitaphone Short."

7. Thanks to Bob Gitt of the UCLA Archives for this information.

11. Imaging the Sound(s) of Shakespeare

1. Techniques not discussed here, but which could preserve the sense of "centripetal" space, might include limiting sound-off during a shot but allowing sound bridges between shots, de-emphasizing non-diegetic and subjective sound, and using only sync sound.

2. Even though Henry is turned from us in this scene, the sound of his voice does not of necessity have to be any less direct than were he facing the camera. A different mike placement could lead to an entirely different effect. Also, recall that reverb and other sound qualities can be simulated, altered, or removed in postproduction. In this scene and others like it, Oliver, by design, matches a spatial proportion on the sound track to a visual space.

3. It should be noted that in writing this essay I listened to an unrestored version of *Macbeth*. UCLA Film Archives and The Folger Shakespeare Library, Washington, D.C., have recently released a restored version of the film. This "restoration"

smooths over many of the "bad" sound qualities I discuss here. (There are also other variations. The unrestored version I listened to is somewhat shorter. However, the unrestored version is not simply cut down; in the restored version, a voice-over by Lady Macbeth which *is* included in the unrestored version, is heard over a shot *not* included in the unrestored version.) In general, the restoration transforms the often jarring sounds I heard in the unrestored version to closer approximations of standard Hollywood sound. This is quite an interesting commentary on our definitions of "good" sound. Further research into the "restoration" of sound seems vital to the study of film sound theory.

4. This essay is obviously not meant to be an exhaustive exploration of forms of theatrical adaptation, nor of sound strategies for adaptations. It discusses two basic approaches which preserve, in different ways, certain traces of Shakespearean theatre, or theatrical text, on film. Interested readers are encouraged to explore other approaches which preserve different aspects of theatre on film.

13. And Then There Was Sound

1. In a foreground-background sound system, as described by Rick Altman, one voice or sound plane predominates, while other sounds blend together into a generic audible fabric that may have specific meaning, but does not command our primary attention. This type of sound can be likened to a musical composition in which the primary melodic line of a single instrument's voice is supported by orchestral chordal structures. Deep space sound can be likened to contrapuntal, polyphonic composition, in which many voices follow individual paths perceivable as such, even while their relationships to other voices create collective chordal structures that color the whole.

Works Cited

The following list is limited to works cited within this volume. When Claudia Gorbman prepared her extremely useful bibliographies for *Cinema/Sound* (Altman 1980a) and *Film Sound: Theory and Practice* (Weis and Belton 1985), the notion of film sound was clearly circumscribed, limited to classical film sound theory and articles on film sound technology. In recent years the bibliography relating to film sound has grown tremendously, not because so much has been written on film sound, but because scholars have begun to discover how much is relevant to film sound. My own working bibliography on sound now totals nearly one hundred pages, far too much to reproduce here. For additional bibliography, readers are directed to the Gorbman bibliographies mentioned above, to the special sound issue of *Screen* (25.3 [May–June 1984]), to a forthcoming special issue of *Wide Angle,* and to journals which carry a heavy proportion of articles on sound, like the *Journal of the Society of Motion Picture [and Television] Engineers* (hereafter *JSMP[T]E*) and the *Journal of the Acoustical Society of America* (hereafter *JASA*).

Adolphson, Edvin. *Edvin Adolphson berättar om sitt liv med fru Thalia. fru Filmia och andra fruar* (Stockholm: Bonniers, 1972).

Adorno, Theodor.
1941   "On Popular Music," in *Studies in Philosophy and Social Sciences* 9.1 (April), 17–49.
1945   "A Social Critique of Radio Music," in *Kenyon Review* 7.2; 208–217.
1982   "On the Fetish Character in Music and the Regression in Listening," in *The Essential Frankfurt School Reader,* ed. Andrew Arato and Eike Gebhardt (New York: Continuum, 1982), 270–318.

Agee, James. "Henry V," in Mast 1974, 333–336.

Allen, Robert C. and Douglas Gomery. *Film History: Theory and Practice* (New York: Alfred A. Knopf, 1985).

Alten, Stanley, *Audio in Media* (Belmont, California: Wadsworth Publishing Company, 1990; 3rd ed.).

Altman, Rick (Charles F.).
1977   "Psychoanalysis and Cinema: The Imaginary Discourse," in *Quarterly Review of Film Studies* 2, 257–72; reprinted in Nichols 1985, 517–531.

1980a   ed., *Cinema/Sound,* special issue of *Yale French Studies* 60.

1980b   "Introduction to *Cinema/Sound,*" in Altman 1980a, 3–15; reprinted (as "The Evolution of Sound Technology") in Weis and Belton, 44–53.

1980c   "Moving Lips: Cinema as Ventriloquism," in Altman 1980a, 67–79.

1984   "Toward a Theory of the History of Representational Technologies," in *Iris* 2.2, 111–125.

1985a   "The Evolution of Sound Technology" in Weis and Belton 1985, 44–53.

1985b   "The Technology of the Voice," part 1, in *Iris* 3.1, 3–20.

1986a   "The Technology of the Voice," part 2, in *Iris* 4.1, 107–119.

1986b   "Television/Sound," in *Studies in Entertainment: Critical Approaches to Mass Culture,* ed. Tania Modleski (Bloomington: Indiana University Press), 39–54; reprinted in *Television: A Critical View,* ed. Horace Newcomb (New York: Oxford University Press, 1987, 4th edition).

1987   *The American Film Musical* (Bloomington: Indiana University Press).

1988   "Pour une histoire hétérogène du parlant: La technologie du son chez Bell pendant les années vingt," in *Du Muet au parlant* (Perpignan: Cahiers de la Cinémathèque), 46–50.

1989   "Technologie et représentation: l'espace sonore," in *Histoire du cinéma. Nouvelles approches,* ed. Jacques Aumont, André Gaudreault, Michel Marie (Paris: Publications de la Sorbonne), 121–130.

1990   Response to Marilyn Somville, "Sound 'Bad': Vocal Gesture in Verdi's *Macbeth,*" Sound Theory/Sound Practice Symposium, University of Iowa, April 14, 1990.

1991a   "24-Track Narrative? Robert Altman's *Nashville,*" *Cinéma(s)* 1.3, 102–125.

1991b   "Le son contre l'image ou la bataille des techniciens," forthcoming in *Hollywood, 1927–41,* ed. Alain Masson (Paris: Editions Autrement), 74–86.

Andrew, Dudley, "Sound in France: The Origins of a Native School," *Yale French Studies* 60 (1980), 98–103.

Atkinson, G.A.

1925a   "American Films Menace Decent British Homes," *Variety* (July 1, 1925), 1, 3.

1925b   "Filmdom's Social Outcast," *Variety* (August 5, 1925), pp 1, 2.

Balazs, Bela. *Theory of the Film: Character and Growth of a New Art* (New York: Dover, 1970).

Bandy, Mary Lea. ed. *The Dawn of Sound* (New York: Museum of Modern Art, 1989).

Banning, William. "Better Speech," *Bell Telephone Quarterly* 9.2 (April 1930), 75–82.

Barr, Charles. "Cinemascope: Before and After," in Mast 1974.

Barrier, Mike. "An Interview with Carl Stalling," *Funnyworld* (Spring 1971), 21–27.

Bartholomew, Wilmer T. "Physical Definition of 'Good Voice-Quality' in the Male Voice," in *JASA* 6.1 (July 1934), 25–33.

Baudry, Jean-Louis.

1974   "Ideological Effects of the Basic Cinematographic Apparatus," in *Film Quarterly* 27.2 (1974–75), 39–47.

1980   "The Apparatus," in *Apparatus,* ed. Theresa Hak Kyung Cha (New York: Tanam, 1980).

Bazin, André.

1967a   *What is Cinema?* I, trans. Hugh Gray (Berkeley: University of California Press).

1967b   *What is Cinema?* II, trans. Hugh Gray (Berkeley: University of California Press).

1974   "Othello," in *Film Theory and Criticism,* ed. Gerald Mast and Marshall Cohen (New York: Oxford University Press), 337–339.

1978   *Orson Welles: A Critical View,* trans. Jonathan Rosenbaum (New York: Harper and Row).

Belton, John.
    1985   "CinemaScope: The Economics of Technology," in *The Velvet Light Trap* 21 (Summer 1985).
    1987   "Bazin Is Dead! Long Live Bazin," in *Wide Angle,* 9.4.
    1988   "The Development of CinemaScope by Twentieth Century-Fox," in *JSMPTE* 97.9 (September), 718–19.
    1990   "Glorious Technicolor, Breathtaking CinemaScope, and Stereophonic Sound," in *Hollywood in the Age of Television,* ed. Tino Balio (Boston: Unwin Hyman).

Benjamin, Walter. "The Work of Art in the Age of Mechanical Reproduction," in *Illuminations,* trans. Harry Zohn (New York: Shocken Books, 1969), 217–252.

Bennett, Tony. "Texts, Readers, Reading Formations," in *Bulletin of the Midwest MLA* 16.1 (Spring 1983), 3–17.

Benson, Thomas and Carolyn Anderson. "The Rhetorical Structure of Frederick Wiseman's *Model,*" in *Journal of Film and Video* 36 (1984), 30–40.

Berg, A. Scott. *Goldwyn: A Biography.* (New York: Knopf, 1989).

Bhabha, Homi K. "The Other Question: Difference, Discrimination, and the Discourse of Colonialism," in *Screen* 24:6 (1983), 18–36.

Blake, Larry, "Mixing Dolby Stereo Film Sound," in *Recording Engineer/Producer* 12.1 (February 1981).

Blake, William. "Auguries of Innocence," in *William Blake: Selected Poetry and Prose,* ed. David Punter (New York: Routledge, 1988).

Bonitzer, Pascal. "Les silences de la voix," *Cahiers du cinéma* 256 (1975).

Bordwell, David.
    1985a   (with Janet Staiger and Kristin Thompson) *The Classical Hollywood Cinema: Film Style and Mode of Production to 1960* (New York: Columbia University Press).
    1985b   *Narration in the Fiction Film* (Madison: University of Wisconsin Press).
    1990   (with Kristin Thompson) *Film Art: An Introduction,* 3rd ed. (New York: Alfred A. Knopf).

Bragaglia, A. G. *Jazz Band* (Milano: Edizioni Corbaccio, 1929).

Branigan, Edward.
    1979   "Color and Cinema: Problems in the Writing of History," in Nichols 1985, 121–143.
    1989   "Sound and Epistemology in Film," in *The Journal of Aesthetics and Art Criticism* 47.4 (Fall), 311–324.

Brecht, Bertolt. "Der Dreigroschenprozess: ein soziologisches Experiment," reprinted in *Photo: Casparius* (Berlin: Stiftung Deutsche Kinemathek, 1978), 391–431.

Brownlow, Kevin. *The Parade's Gone By* (Berkeley: University of California, 1968).

Broz, Jaroslav and Myrtil Frida. *Historie československého filmu v obrazech (1930–1945)* (Prague: Orbis, 1966).

Burris-Meyer, Harold. "Sound in the Theater," in *JASA* 11 (Jan. 1940), 346–351.

Buscombe, Edward. "Sound and Color," in Nichols 1985, 83–92.

Cameron, Evan William, ed. *Sound and the Cinema: The Coming of Sound to American Film* (Pleasantville, N.Y.: Redgrave, 1980).

Carroll, Noel. *Mystifying Movies: Fad and Fallacies of Contemporary Film Theory* (New York: Columbia University Press, 1988).

Carringer, Robert L. *The Making of Citizen Kane* (Berkeley: University of California Press, 1985).

Carringer, Robert. *The Jazz Singer* (Madison, Wisc.: University of Wisconsin Press, 1979).

Cass, John L. "The Illusion of Sound and Picture," in *JSMPE* 14 (March 1930), 323–326.

Cavell, Stanley. *The World Viewed* (Cambridge: Harvard University Press, 1979).

Cherry, Colin. *On Human Communication* (London: Wiley, 1957).

Chirat, Raymond. *Catalogue des films français de long métrage: films sonores de fiction 1929–1939* (Brussels: Cinémathèque Royale de Belgique, 1975).

Chittick, Melissa. "Foreign Language Versions and their Relationship to Buster Keaton," unpublished paper, University of California at Santa Barbara, June 1987.

Chion, Michel.
   1982   *La Voix au cinéma* (Paris: Cahiers du Cinéma/Editions de l'Etoile).
   1985   *Le son au cinéma* (Paris: Cahiers du Cinéma/Editions de l'Etoile).
   1988   *La Toile trouée* (Paris: Cahiers du Cinéma/Editions de l'Etoile).

Comolli, Jean-Louis.
   1980   "Discussion," in De Lauretis 1980a, 57.
   1985   "Technique and Ideology: Camera, Perspective, Depth of Field," part 1, trans. Diana Matias, in Nichols 1985.
   1986   "Technique and Ideology: Camera, Perspective, Depth of Field," parts 3 and 4, trans. Diana Matias (with revisions by Marcia Butzel and Philip Rosen), in *Narrative, Apparatus, Ideology,* ed. Philip Rosen (New York: Columbia University Press).

Connor, Steve. "The Flag on the Road: Bruce Springsteen and the Live," in *New Formations* 3 (Winter 1987), 129–137.

Costigliola, Frank. *Uneasy Alliance: American Relations with Europe. 1918–1939* (Ithaca: Cornell University Press, 1984).

Crowther, Bosley. "Sound and (or) Fury: Stereophonic System is Debated in Hollywood," in *The New York Times* (Jan. 31, 1954), section 2, p. 1.

Dahl, Ingolf. "Notes on Cartoon Music," in *Film Music Notes* 8.5 (1949).

DeForest, Lee. "Recent Developments in 'The Phonofilm,' " in *JSMPE* 27 (Jan. 1927), 64–76.

de Lauretis, Teresa.
   1980a   ed. (with Stephen Heath), *The Cinematic Apparatus* (New York: St. Martin's Press).
   1980b   "Through the Looking Glass," in De Lauretis 1980a, 187–202.
   1986   ed., *Feminist Studies/Critical Studies* (Bloomington: Indiana University Press).

1988   "Displacing Hegemonic Discourses: Reflections on Feminist Theory in the 1980s," in *Inscriptions* 3/4.

de Rochefort, Charles. *Secrets des Vedettes: le film de souvenirs de Charles de Rochefort,* ed. Pierre Andrieu (Paris: Société Parisienne d'Edition, 1943).

de Uzabel, Gaizka S. *The High Noon of American Films in Latin America* (Ann Arbor: UMI Research Press, 1982).

Derrida, Jacques.
1982   "Signature Event Context," in *Margins of Philosophy,* trans. Alan Bass (Chicago: University of Chicago Press).
1989   *Introduction to Edmund Husserl's Origin of Geometry* (Lincoln: University of Nebraska Press).

Doane, Mary Ann.
1980a   "Ideology and the Practice of Sound Editing and Mixing," in De Lauretis 1980a, 47–56; reprinted in Weis and Belton 1985, 54–62.
1980b   "The Voice in Cinema: The Articulation of Body and Space," in Altman 1980a, 33–50; reprinted in Weis and Belton 1985, 162–76.

Downey, T. A. "Public Address Systems," in *Bell Laboratories Record* 3.2 (1926), 50–56.

Dreher, Carl.
1929a   "This Matter of Volume Control," in *Motion Picture Projectionist* 2 (Feb.), 11+.
1929b   "Stage Technique in the Talkies," in *American Cinematographer* 10.9 (Dec.) 2+; reprinted from *Radio News.*
1931   "Recording, Re-recording, and Editing of Sound," in *JSMPE* 16.6 (June), 756–765.

Ehrenburg, Ilya G. *Fabrika snov: khronika nashego vremeni* (Berlin: Petropolis, 1931).

Eisenstein, Sergei. "A Statement on the Sound-Film," co-signed by V.I. Pudovkin and G.V. Alexandrov, 1928, trans. Jay Leyda, in *Film Form: Essays in Film Theory* (New York: Harcourt, Brace, & World, 1949), 257–260.

Ellis, John. *Visible Fictions: Cinema, Television, Video* (Boston: Routledge & Kegan Paul, 1982).

Elsaesser, Thomas. "Lulu and the Meter Man: Louise Brooks, Pabst and *Pandora's Box,*" *Screen* 24.4/5 (1983).

Ennis, Bert. "Sophie Goes Talkie: The Last of the Red-Hot Mamas Falls for the Films," in *Moving Picture Classic* 29.3 (May 1929), 43.

Esslin, Martin. *The Field of Drama: How the Signs of Drama Create Meaning on Stage and Screen* (New York: Methuen, 1986).

Falkenberg, Pamela. "Hollywood and the Art Cinema as a Bipolar Modeling System: *A bout de souffle* and *Breathless,*" in *Wide Angle* 7.3 (1986), 44–53.

Fletcher, Harvey.
1929   *Speech and Hearing* (New York: Van Nostrand, 1929).
1953   "Stereophonic Recording and Reproducing System," in *JSMPTE* 61.3 (September).

Fornatale, Peter and Joshua E. Mills. *Radio in the Television Age* (Woodstock: The Overlook Press, 1980), 121–123.

Foti, Veronique M. "Representation and the Image: Between Heidegger, Derrida, Plato," in *Man and World,* 18 (1985), 65.

Framework 36 (1989), special issue on "Third Scenario: Theory and Politics of Location."

Franklin, Harold B. "A Year in Sound," in *JSMPE* 14 (March 1930), 302–308.

Frayne, John G. and Halley Wolfe. *Elements of Sound Recording* (New York: John Wiley, 1949).

Freud, Sigmund. *Civilization and its Discontents,* ed. James Strachey (New York: W. W. Norton, 1961).

Gardette, L. "Conducting the Nickelodeon Program," in *The Nickelodeon* (March 1909), 79–80.

Gaudreault, André. "The Infringement of Copyright Laws and its Effects (1900–1906)," in *Framework* 29 (1985), 2–14.

Geduld, Harry. *The Birth of the Talkies: From Edison to Jolson* (Bloomington: Indiana University Press, 1975).

Gilbert, Craig. "Reflections on *An American Family,*" in *Studies in Visual Communication* 8.1 (Winter 1982), 24–54.

Gomery, J. Douglas. "Economic Struggle and Hollywood Imperialism: Europe Converts to Sound," in Altman 1980a, 80–93.

Goodwin, Andrew. "Sample and Hold: Pop Music in the Digital Age of Reproduction," in *Critical Quarterly* 30:3 (1988), 34–49.

Gorbman, Claudia. *Unheard Melodies: Narrative Film Music* (Bloomington: Indiana University Press, 1988).

Gordon, Deborah. ed. *Inscriptions* 3/4 (1988).

Gourdon, Gilles. "Les Masques du silence," in *Cinématographe* 47 (May 1979), 26–27.

Grignon, Lorin D. "Experiments in Stereophonic Sound," in *JSMPTE* 61.3 (September 1953).

Gunning, Tom. "Non-Continuity, Continuity, Dis-Continuity: A Theory of Genres in Early Film," in *Iris* 2.1 (1984), 101–112.

Handzo, Stephen. "A Narrative Glossary of Film Sound Technology," in Weis and Belton 1985, 383–426.

Heidegger, Martin.
1962   *Being in Time,* trans. Edward Robinson and John Macquarrie (New York: Harper and Row).
1971   "A Dialog on Language," in *On the Way to Language,* trans. Peter D. Hertz (San Francisco: Harper and Row).

Hincha, Richard. "Selling CinemaScope: 1953–1956," in *The Velvet Light Trap* 21 (Summer 1985), 44–53.

Hindman, James and Victoria Costell. eds. *The Independent Documentary: The Implications of Diversity: A Conference Report* (Washington, D.C.: American Film Institute, 1983).

Hodges, Ralph. "Sound for the Cinema," in *db magazine* (March 1980), 31.

Hoier, Tom. "An American Actor's Answer to Mr. Atkinson," in *Variety* (July 15, 1925), 2.

Hopkins, H. F.
 1930a   "Acoustical Characteristics of Movie Screens," in *Bell Laboratories Record*
          8.11 (July), 531–534.
 1930b   "Considerations in the Design and Testing of Motion Picture Screens for
          Sound Picture Work," in *JSMPE* 15.3 (September), 320–331.

Hopper, F. L. "The Measurement of Reverberation Time and its Application to Acoustic
 Problems in Sound Pictures," in *JASA* 2.4 (April 1931), 499–505.

Hunt, Franklin L. "Sound Pictures: Fundamental Principles and Some Factors Which
 Affect their Quality," in *JASA* 2.4 (April 1931), 476–484.

Hymes, Dell. "Models of the Interaction of Language and Social Life," in *Directions of
 Sociolinguistics,* ed. John J. Gumperz and Dell Hymes (New York: Holt, Rinehart and
 Winston, 1972), 35–71.

Izod, John. *Hollywood and the Box Office, 1895–1986* (New York: Columbia University
 Press, 1988).

Jeanne, René.
 1930   "L'invasion cinématographique américaine," in *Revue des deux mondes* (Feb-
          ruary 15), 857–884.
 1931   "La France et le film parlant," in *Revue des deux mondes* (June 1), 536–554.

Jomaron, Jacqueline. "Metteurs en scène du Cartel et texte théâtral," in *Revue d'histoire
 littéraire de la France* 77 (November/December 1977), 900–915.

Jones, D. B. "The Canadian Film Board Unit B," in *New Challenges for Documentary,*
 ed. Alan Rosenthal (Berkeley: University of California Press, 1988), 133–147.

Josse, Harald. *Die Entstehung des Tonfilms: Beitrag zu einer faktenorientierten Medien-
 geschichtsschreibung* (Freiburg: Verlag Karl Alber, 1984).

Kaplan, E. Ann. "The Place of Women in Fritz Lang's *The Blue Gardenia,*" in *Women
 in Film Noir,* ed. E. Ann Kaplan (London: BFI Publishing, 1980).

Kerr, Paul ed. *The Hollywood Cinema: A Reader* (London: BFI, 1986).

King, Barry.
 1986   "Stardom as Occupation," in Kerr.
 1987   *"The Classical Hollywood Cinema:* A Review," in *Screen* 27.6, 74–90.

Knudsen, Vern O. "The Hearing of Speech in Auditoriums," in *JASA* 1.1 (October 1929),
 56–82.

Koszarski, Richard. "On the Record: Seeing and Hearing the Vitaphone," in Bandy, 15–
 21.

Kozloff, Sara. *Invisible Storytellers: Voice-Over Narration in American Fiction Film*
 (Berkeley: University of California Press, 1988).

Kracauer, Siegfried.
 1960   *Theory of Film: The Redemption of Physical Reality* (New York: Oxford
          University Press).
 1987   "Cult of Distraction: On Berlin's Picture Palaces," trans. Tom Levin," in
          New German Critique 40 (Winter 1987).

Kreuger, Miles. *The Movie Musical: From Vitaphone to 42nd Street* (New York: Dover,
 1975).

Kroesen, J. C. "New Light on 'Talkies,' " in *American Cinematographer* 9.4 (July 1928),
 8+.

Lafferty, William. "The Early Development of Magnetic Sound Recording in Broadting and Motion Pictures, 1928–1950," Ph.D. Dissertation, Northwestern University, 1981, 170–219.

Lastra, Jim. "Auditing the Books: Reading, Writing, and Representing Sound," Sound Theory/Sound Practice Conference, University of Iowa, April 14, 1990.

Lawrence, Amy. "The Pleasures of Echo: The Listener and the Voice," in *Journal of Film and Video* 40.4 (1988), 3–14.

Léglise, Paul. *Histoire de la politique du cinéma français: le cinéma et la IIIe République* (Paris: Pierre Lherminier), 1969).

Levin, Thomas Y.
1984   "The Acoustic Dimension: Notes on Film Sound," in *Screen* 25.3 (May–June), 55–68.
1991   "For the Record: Adorno on Music in the Age of Its Technological Reproducibility," in *October* 55 (Winter), 23–47.

Lewin, George. "Dubbing and its Relation to Sound Picture Production," in *JSMPE* 16.1 (January 1931), 30–48.

MacDougall, David. "Beyond Observational Cinema," in *Principles of Visual Anthropology,* ed. Paul Hockings (The Hague: Mouton, 1975), 109–124.

MacNair, Walter A. "Optimum Reverberation Time for Auditoriums," in *Bell System Technical Journal* 9.2 (1930), 390ff.

Maltin, Leonard. *Of Mice and Magic: A History of American Animated Cartoons,* revised edition (New York: New American Library, 1987).

Mamber, Stephen. *Cinéma Vérité in America: Studies in Uncontrolled Documentary* (Cambridge: MIT Press, 1974).

Marcorelles, Louis. *Living Cinema: New Directions in Contemporary Filmmaking* (London: George Allen & Unwin, 1973).

Marie, Michel. "Direct," in *Anthropology-Reality-Cinema: The Films of Jean Rouch,* ed. Mick Eaton (London: BFI, 1979), 35–39.

Martin, Biddy and Chandra Mohanty. "Feminist Politics: What's Home Got to Do With It?" in De Lauretis 1986, 191–212.

Mast, Gerald.
1974   ed. (with Marshall Cohen), *Film Theory and Criticism* (New York: Oxford University Press, 1974).
1977   *Film/Cinema/Movie: A Theory of Experience* (New York: Harper and Row).

Maxfield, Joseph P.
1929   "The Artistic Possibilities of Acoustical Control," in *American Cinematographer* 10.8 (November), 4+.
1930a   "Acoustic Control of Recording for Talking Motion Pictures," in *JSMPE* 14.1 (January), 85–95.
1930b   "Technic of Recording Control for Sound Pictures," in *American Cinematographer* 11.1 (May), 11+; reprinted from *Academy Technical Digest: Fundamentals of Sound Recording and Reproduction for Motion Pictures* (Hollywood: Academy of Motion Picture Arts and Sciences, 1929–30), 193–208.
1931   "Some Physical Factors Affecting the Illusion in Sound Motion Pictures," in *JASA* 3.1 (July), 69–80.
1938   (with A. W. Colledge and R. T. Friebus), "Pick-up for Sound Motion Pictures (Including Stereophonic)," in *JSMPE* (June), 666–679.

Metz, Christian. "Aural Objects," in Altman 1980a.

Miller, Wesley C. "The Illusion of Reality in 'Sound Pictures,' " in *AcademyTechnical Digest: Fundamentals of Sound Recording and Reproduction for Motion Pictures* (Hollywood: Academy of Motion Picture Arts and Sciences, 1929–30), 101–108.

Mohanty, Chandra Talpade.
    1984   "Under Western Eyes: Feminist Scholarship and Colonial Discourses," in *boundary 2* 12:3/13:1 (Spring/Fall), 333–358.
    1987   "Feminist Encounters: Locating the Politics of Experience," in *Coypright* 1 (Fall), 30–44.

Moi, Toril. ed. *The Kristeva Reader* (New York: Columbia University Press, 1986).

Morand, Paul. *France la douce* (Paris: Gallimard, 1934).

Morgan, Robin, ed. *Sisterhood is Global: The International Women's Movement Anthology* (New York: Anchor Press/Doubleday, 1984).

Mueller, W. A. "A Device for Automatically Controlling Balance Between Recorded Sounds," in *JSMPE* 25.1 (July 1935), 79–86.

Mullin, John T. "Creating the Craft of Tape Recording," *High Fidelity Magazine* (April 1976).

Musser, Charles. "The Travel Genre: Moving Towards Narrative," in *Iris* 2.1 (1984), 47–60.

Neale, Steve. *Cinema and Technology: Image, Sound, Color* (Bloomington: Indiana University Press, 1985).

Nichols, Bill.
    1983   "The Voice of Documentary," in *Film Quarterly* 36.3 (Spring), 17–30.
    1985   ed., *Movies and Methods*, II (Berkeley: University of California Press, 1985).

North, C. J. and N. D. Golden. "Meeting Sound Film Competition Abroad," in *JSMPE* 15.6 (December 1930), 757.

Nowell-Smith, Geoffrey. "Italy *Sotto Voce*," in *Sight and Sound* 37.3 (Summer 1968), 145–147.

O'Connell, P. J. "Robert Drew and the Development of Cinéma-Vérité in America," unpublished Ph.D. dissertation, Penn State University, Department of Speech Communication.

Offenhauser, W. H. and J. J. Israel. "Some Production Aspects of Binaural Recording for Sound Motion Pictures," in *JSMPE* 32 (February 1939), 139–155.

Ong, Aihwa. "Colonialism and Modernity: Feminist Representation of Women in Non-Western Societies," in Gordon.

Pagnol, Marcel. *Confidences: memoires* (Paris: Julliard d'Edition, 1943).

Passinetti, Francesco. ed. *Filmlexicon: piccola enciclopedia cinematografica* (Milano: Filmeuropa, 1948).

Peck, A. P. "Giving a Voice to Motion Pictures," in *Scientific American* 136 (June 1927), 378–379.

Peckham, Linda. "*Surname Viet, Given Name Nam:* Spreading Rumors and Ex/Changing Histories," in *Frame/work* 2:3 (1989), 31–35.

Peirce, Charles S. *The Philosophical Writings of Peirce*, ed. Justus Buchler (New York: Dover, 1955).

Penley, Constance and Andrew Ross. "Interview with Trinh T. Minh-ha," in *Camera Obscura* 13/14 (1985), 86–111.

Pereboom, Pieter. "Early Sound, Radio and Codes of Realism," paper delivered at SCS Conference, Montreal, May 1987.

Physioc, Lewis W. "Technique of the Talkies," in *American Cinematographer* 9.5 (August 1928), 24–25.

Prall, Robert. "Studio Gambles 10 Millions in Bid to Woo TV," in New York *World Telegram & The Sun* (September 14, 1953), 21.

Pratt, George. *Spellbound in Darkness*, I (Rochester: University of Rochester, 1966).

Pratt, Minnie Bruce. "Identity: Skin Blood Heart," in *Yours in Struggle: Three Feminist Perspectives on Anti-Semitism and Racism* (Brooklyn, New York: Long Haul Press, 1984).

Prendergast, Roy M. *A Neglected Art: A Critical Study of Music in Films* (New York: New York University Press, 1977).

Rabiger, Michael. *Directing the Documentary* (Boston: Focal Press, 1987).

Rainey, P. L. "Some Technical Aspects of the Vitaphone," in *JSMPE* 11 (July 1927), 294–317.

Raymond, Alan and Susan Raymond. *"An American Family,"* in *American Cinematographer* 54 (May 1973), 590–91+.

Reagon, Bernice Johnson. "Coalition Politics: Turning the Century," in *Home Girls: A Black Feminist Anthology,* ed. Barbara Smith (New York: Kitchen Table, Women of Color Press, 1983), 356–368.

Renov, Michael. "Raw Deal: The Woman in the Text," in *Wide Angle* 6.2 (1984).

Rich, Adrienne. *Blood, Bread, and Poetry: Selected Prose 1979–1985* (New York: W. W. Norton, 1986).

Richardson, Elmer C. "A Microphone Boom," in *JSMPE* 15 (July 1930), 41–45.

Ruoff, Jeffrey K.
1988   " 'Nothing in our films is ever not in sync': The MIT Film Section," Paper presented at the Society for Cinema Studies and University Film and Video Association in Bozeman, MT.
1989a   "Interview with Jacqueline Donnet," unpublished.
1989b   "Interview with David Hanser," unpublished.
1990   "Interview with Lance Loud," unpublished.

Russell, Ruth. "Voice is Given to Shadows of Silver Screen," in Chicago *Tribune* (September 16, 1926).

Ryder, Loren L. "Magnetic Sound Recording in the Motion Picture and Television Industries," in *JSMPTE* 85.7 (July 1976).

Sadoul, Georges. *Louis Lumière* (Paris: Editions Seghers, 1964).

Salomon, Maynard. ed. *Marxism and Art* (Detroit: Wayne State University Press, 1979).

Salt, Barry.
1983   *Film Style and Technology: History and Analysis* (London: Starword).
1985   "Film Style and Technology in the Thirties: Sound," in Weis and Belton, 37–43.

Sanjek, Russell. *American Popular Music and its Business: The First Four Hundred Years,* 3 vols. (New York: Oxford University Press, 1988).

Schulberg, B. P. "American Film Producer on Atkinson," in *Variety* (August 5, 1925), 22.

Shohat, Ella and Robert Stam. "Hollywood After Babylon: Language, Power, Difference," in *Screen* 26.3/4, 35–58.

Shurlock, Geoffrey. "Versions," in *American Cinematographer* 11.9 (1931), 10.

Silverman, Kaja. *The Acoustic Mirror: The Female Voice in Psychoanalysis and Cinema* (Bloomington: Indiana University Press, 1988).

Silverstone, Roger. *Framing Science: The Making of a BBC Documentary* (London: BFI, 1985).

Singer, Mark. "Predilections," in *The New Yorker* (February 6, 1989).

Spargo, John S. "Jolson's Songs Help *The Jazz Singer* at New York Premiere," in *Exhibitor's Herald* (October 15, 1927).

Stam, Robert and Louise Spence. "Colonialism, Racism and Representation: An Introduction," in Nichols 1985, 632–49.

Steinberg, J. C. "Effects of Distortion Upon the Recognition of Speech Sounds," in *JASA* 2.4 (October 1930), 132.

Stewart, James G. "The Evolution of Cinematic Sound: A Personal Report," in Cameron.

Tarkovsky, Andrei. *Sculpting in Time: Reflections on the Cinema,* trans. Kitty Hunter-Blair (Austin: University of Texas Press, 1989).

Théberge, Paul. "The 'Sound' of Music: Technological Rationalization and the Production of Popular Music," in *New Formations* 8 (Summer 1989), 99–111.

Thompson, Kristin. *Exporting Entertainment: America in the World Film Market, 1907–1934* (London: British Film Institute, 1985).

Thu Van, Mai. *Viet Nam, un peuple, des voix* (Paris: Pierre Horay, 1983).

Trinh, Minh-ha.
   1988   "Not You/Like You: Post-Colonial Women and the Interlocking Questions of Identity and Difference," in *Inscriptions* 3/4.
   1989   *Woman Native Other: Writing postcoloniality and feminism* (Bloomington: Indiana University Press).
   1990   "Documentary Is/Not a Name," in *October* 52 (Spring).

Vincendeau, Ginette. "Hollywood Babel," in *Screen* 29.3 (Spring 1988).

Walker, Alexander. *The Shattered Silents: How the Talkies Came to Stay* (New York: W. Morrow & Co., 1979).

Weaver, William R. "Chicago Tests Vitaphone, Approves Eastern Verdict," in *Exhibitors' Herald* 27.2 (September 25, 1926), 29.

Weis, Elisabeth and John Belton. ed. *Film Sound: Theory and Practice* (New York: Columbia University Press, 1985).

Wilcox, H. M. "Data for Projectionists on Operation of Vitaphone," in *Exhibitors Herald,* Better Theatres supplement (July 9, 1927), 11–12.

Williams, Alan.
   1980   "Is Sound Recording Like a Language?" In Altman 1980a.
   1981   "The Musical Film and Recorded Popular Music," in Rick Altman, ed., *Genre: The Musical* (London: Routledge & Kegan Paul, 1981, pp. 147–158).

Williams, Raymond.
   1974   *Television: Technology and Cultural Form* (New York: Shocken).
   1980   *Problems in Materialism and Culture: Selected Essays* (London: New Left Books).

Witta-Montrobert, Jeanne. *La Lanterne Magique: memoires d'une scripte* (Paris: Calmann-Lévy, 1980).

Wolf, S. K. "The Western Electric Reproducing System," in *Recording Sound for Motion Pictures,* ed. Lester Cowan (New York: McGraw-Hill, 1931), 286–303.

Wolfe, Charles.
   1989   "On the Track of the Vitaphone Short," in Bandy, 35–41.
   1990   "Vitaphone Shorts and *The Jazz Singer,*" in *Wide Angle* 12.3 (July), 58–78.

Zheutlin, Barbara. "The Politics of Documentary: A Symposium," in *New Challenges for Documentary,* ed. Alan Rosenthal (Berkeley: University of California Press, 1988), 227–44.

Index

Ad libs, 107–108
Adorno, Theodor, 38, 69, 71–72
Agee, James, 211
Alien (1979), 108
Allen, Robert, 219
Altman, Rick
  foreign language versions (FLVs), 152
  Hollywood sound practice debate, 97
  image/sound hierarchy in musicals, 200
  new realisms, 79
  point-of-audition sound, 76
  privileging of sound production, 78–79
  original sound events, 68, 83
  relativization of speech, 110
  sound conventions in classical Hollywood cinema, 217
  sound hermeneutic, 236
  sound recordings as staged representations, 73
  spatial signature, 77
  textual practices of American television, 91
  ventriloquism concept, 269
  Vitaphone technology, 197–98
  Welles' use of sound in *Macbeth*, 212
Altman, Robert, 110, 252
An American Family (1973), 219–20, 225, 226, 227–28, 229–34

An American Family: The Louds Ten Years Later (1983), 229
The American Film Musical (Altman), 13
Anahatan (1953), 108
Anderson, Carolyn, 222
Animation, 44, 174. *See also* Cartoons
Anti-Semitism, 150–51
Anzieu, Didier, 38
Applause (1929), 51
Approximate subject positioning, 99
Arnheim, Rudolf, 37
Atkinson, G. A., 140–41
Attack, 18
Auditory perspective, 49
Auteurs, 176
Authenticity, 79

Balázs, Béla, 37
Barr, Charles, 159
The Battle of San Pietro (1945), 230
Bazin, André, 43, 126–27, 158–59, 204–205, 209, 210
Bell Laboratories, 120–21
Bennett, Tony, 42
Benson, Thomas, 222
Bergman, Ingmar, 108, 243
Blackwell (1929), 109
Blake, William, 238

sound scale and early sound techni-
cians, 49, 50–51, 54, 55, 56
Maysles brothers, 219
Media shifts, 175
Mediation, 11–12
Medium, 17
Melodrama, 133–35
Melody, 21
Merrie Melodies, 194–96
Metz, Christian, 68–69
MGM studios, 143, 147
Mickey-mousing, 201–202
Microphones, 24–26, 53, 197–98, 224–
25, 255–56
Milli Vanilli, 87–88
Mirror (1974), 235, 248
Mohanty, Chandra Talpade, 182–84
Monstration, 258
Morris, Errol, 223
Moving Picture World, 116
Multidiscursivity, 9–10
Multilinguals. *See* Foreign language ver-
sions
Multiplicity, 4–5
Music. *See also* Jazz
cartoons, 193–96
cinema as illustrated, 114–15
contemporary popular, 92–95
documentaries, 226–29
instability, 11
nondiegetic, 100–102
sampling and popular, 259–60
silent films, 175
sound terminology, 15–16
as topic for film criticism, 173–74
Musicals, 193
Mussolini, Benito, 264
Mutt and Jeff Talking Pictures, 117

Name, sounds, 19–20
Narrative, 19–23, 24, 196
Nashville (1975), 110
National Film Board of Canada, 218–19
Nominalist fallacy, 40–42
Nostalgia (1983), 235–36, 238, 240,
244–45, 246–47

Obenhaus, Marc, 228
Offenhauser, W. H., 55
Offscreen dialogue, 163, 268
Olivier, Laurence, 206–10, 211, 214
Only Angels Have Wings (1939), 56–57,
60
Ontological fallacy, 37–39
Opera, 116–17
Optical sound, 155–56
Original sound, 66–86
Othello, 205
Otterson, J., 150
Our Town, 230–31
Overtones, 17

Parallel sound, 243–46
Paramount Studios, 143–44, 147, 149,
150–51
The Pasciaks of Chicago (1976), 228
Pathé Frères, 117
Peckham, Linda, 185, 188, 189
Peirce, C. S., 202
Performance, 8–9
Perspective, sound, 96–99
Phonography, 120–21
Photography, 114
Photoplay, 125
Photophone process, 128
Physioc, Lewis W., 49
Pidgin, Charles F., 117–18
Pincus, Ed, 219, 222
Pitch, 15–16
Point-of-audition sound, 60–61, 63–64,
76–77, 251, 257
Polanski, Roman, 214–15
Pomeroy, Roy, 142
Powers, Harry J., Jr., 118
Practice, sound, 96–102
Pressure changes, 17
Production, sound, 79
Proliferation, speech, 107–108

Quotas, import, 140

Rabiger, Michael, 223
Radio, 118–20, 155
Rainer, Yvonne, 180–81

List of Contributors

RICK ALTMAN is Professor of French and Communication Studies at the University of Iowa.

JOHN BELTON teaches cinema in the English Department at Rutgers University.

MICHEL CHION has written many volumes on film sound from his Paris headquarters.

SCOTT CURTIS is a graduate student in film studies at the University of Iowa.

NATAŠA ĎUROVIČOVÁ shuttles between the University of Iowa and the University of California at Santa Barbara, teaching cinema at both ends.

MARY PAT KLIMEK is a former graduate student in film studies at the University of Iowa.

JAMES LASTRA has just accepted a job teaching film in the Department of English at the University of Chicago.

AMY LAWRENCE teaches cinema at Dartmouth College.

JEFF RUOFF is a filmmaker and graduate student in film studies at the University of Iowa.

ANDREA TRUPPIN is a filmmaker and graduate student in film studies at the University of Iowa.

ALAN WILLIAMS teaches cinema in the French Department at Rutgers University.

STEVE WURTZLER is a graduate student in film studies at the University of Iowa.